A HISTORICAL GUIDE TO
James Fenimore Cooper

D1526033

A
Historical Guide
to James Fenimore Cooper

EDITED BY
LELAND S. PERSON

1/10

OXFORD
UNIVERSITY PRESS

2007

OXFORD
UNIVERSITY PRESS

Oxford University Press, Inc., publishes works that further
Oxford University's objective of excellence
in research, scholarship, and education.

Oxford   New York

Auckland   Cape Town   Dar es Salaam   Hong Kong   Karachi
Kuala Lumpur   Madrid   Melbourne   Mexico City   Nairobi
New Delhi   Shanghai   Taipei   Toronto

With offices in

Argentina   Austria   Brazil   Chile   Czech Republic   France   Greece
Guatemala   Hungary   Italy   Japan   Poland   Portugal   Singapore
South Korea   Switzerland   Thailand   Turkey   Ukraine   Vietnam

Copyright © 2007 by Oxford University Press, Inc.

Published by Oxford University Press, Inc.
198 Madison Avenue, New York, New York 10016

www.oup.com

Oxford is a registered trademark of Oxford University Press

Library of Congress Cataloging-in-Publication Data
A historical guide to James Fenimore Cooper / edited by Leland S. Person.
p. cm.
Includes bibliographical references and index.
ISBN 978-0-19-517312-3; 978-0-19-517313-0 (pbk.)
1. Cooper, James Fenimore, 1789–1851—Criticism
and interpretation.
2. Literature and history—United States—History—19th century.
I. Person, Leland S.
PS1438H57   2006
813′.2—dc22   2006018336

1 3 5 7 9 8 6 4 2

Printed in the United States of America
on acid-free paper

Contents

A HISTORICAL GUIDE TO
James Fenimore Cooper

Introduction

Fenimore Cooper's Literary Achievements

Leland S. Person

America owes almost as much to Cooper as to Franklin and Washington: for if these great men created the Union, by skill in legislation and force of arms, it was Cooper, the unassuming storyteller, who broadcast the news of it across the seas by the interest of his tales and the fidelity of his patriotic feelings.

George Sand (1856)[1]

When I think of remarkable phenomena in American literary history, I think first of the nearly 1,800 poems discovered after Emily Dickinson's death in a bureau in her Amherst, Massachusetts, home. I also think of William Faulkner's creation of Yoknapatawpha County in Mississippi and of the many interconnected works set in that fictional space. But then I think of the five novels James Fenimore Cooper wrote about the improbably named frontier hero, Natty Bumppo. The Leatherstocking Tales feature episodes in Natty's life, beginning with his young manhood (in *The Deerslayer*) and ending with his death (in *The Prairie*). Cooper fans know, of course, that Cooper didn't write

3

the series in chronological order. He introduced Natty in *The Pioneers* (published in 1823 but set in 1793) when the hero was already in his seventies. He then backtracked in *The Last of the Mohicans* (1826) to depict Natty in the prime of his life in 1857, during the French and Indian Wars, before following out the logic he had established at the end of *The Pioneers*, when Natty leaves Templeton for the West, by having Natty die climactically at the end of *The Prairie* (1827). Roughly a decade and a half later, hoping to breathe some new life into a writing career that was foundering, Cooper resurrected Natty in *The Pathfinder* (1840; also set during the French and Indian Wars), an interesting hybrid novel that is both frontier romance and sea tale. Most surprising, a year later Cooper took his hero back even further in time in *The Deerslayer* (1841), which, like *The Pioneers*, is set at Lake Otsego (called Lake Glimmerglass) but at a much earlier moment (1740), before any settlement has occurred. Cooper's tacking back and forth in time as well as his use of Lake Otsego and Cooperstown (fictionalized as Templeton) in both *The Pioneers* and *The Deerslayer* have fascinated literary scholars for years.

The Deerslayer was the first novel I had to read as a freshman in high school, but I suspect that very few high school students today know anything about Cooper or his writing. His reputation and the presence of his novels even on college reading lists have waned in recent years—the victim of laudable efforts to expand the nineteenth-century American literary canon to include more works by women and African American and Native American writers. If college instructors want an early frontier novel, instead of one of the Leatherstocking Tales they are likely to assign Lydia Maria Child's *Hobomok* (1824) or Catharine Maria Sedgwick's *Hope Leslie* (1827), novels by women that also seem, in their depiction of interracial marriage between Indian men and white women, more contemporary than novels, such as *The Last of the Mohicans*, in which interracial marriage is proscribed. Cooper also did not write with college-level anthologies in mind. That is, he did not write tales or short stories, and his novels tend to be lengthy. When his writing finds a place in anthologies, therefore, it is represented by excerpts from one or more novels: the slaughter of the pigeons from *The Pioneers* (in the Norton Anthology and, along with the wasteful seine-fishing scene, also in the Heath Anthology). Such partial representation is unfortunate, as many of Cooper's novels have a grand sweep to their plots, and their inauguration of so many key characters and situations for the American literary canon deserves an important place in any history of American literature.

Perhaps Cooper is still trying to recover from the savaging he endured at the hands of Mark Twain (né Samuel Clemens), whose notorious "Fenimore Cooper's Literary Offenses" (*North American Review*, July 1895) was designed to discount Cooper's fiction in favor of the brand of realism that Clemens was promoting and writing. With his tongue smugly tucked in his cheek, Clemens famously accused Cooper, "in the restricted space of two-thirds of a page," of scoring "114 offenses against literary art out of a possible 115. It breaks the record" (Dekker and McWilliams 277). Although Clemens referred to several Cooper novels, he reserved most of his venom for *The Deerslayer*, which he climactically labeled "not a work of art in any sense" but a "literary *delirium tremens*": "It has no invention; it has no order, system, sequence, or result; it has no lifelikeness, no thrill, no stir, no seeming of reality; its characters are confusedly drawn, and by their acts and words they prove that they are not the sort of people the author claims that they are; its humor is pathetic; its pathos is funny; its conversations are—oh! indescribable; its love-scenes odious; its English a crime against the language" (286–287). Of course, a case has been made that Clemens was covering his tracks in that essay—covering up his own debts to Cooper in *The Adventures of Tom Sawyer* and *Adventures of Huckleberry Finn*.[2] But it is pointless to try to refute Mark Twain's case against Cooper. As the title of this introductory chapter suggests, I prefer to focus on Cooper's considerable achievements.[3]

Because critical and scholarly interest in Cooper tends to be reserved overwhelmingly for the five Leatherstocking Tales, many readers will be surprised to learn how prolific and versatile an author Cooper was. Coming late to novel writing (he was thirty-one when his first novel, *Precaution* [1820], appeared), he averaged a novel a year for the rest of his life, writing thirty-two in all. By the time he had published just his fourth book (*The*

Pilot, which joined *Precaution*, *The Spy* [1821], and *The Pioneers*
when it appeared in 1824), Cooper had experimented with four
genres, two of which he had invented. *Precaution* is a sentimental
romance, *The Spy* a Revolutionary War narrative, *The Pioneers*
represents the first long frontier romance in our literature, and
The Pilot the first sea novel. It is in the latter two genres that
Cooper felt most comfortable. Besides the five Leatherstocking
Tales, he wrote six other frontier novels: *The Wept of Wish-ton-
Wish* (1829), *Wyandotté; or, The Hutted Knoll* (1843), a trilogy—
Satanstoe; or, The Littlepage Manuscripts (1845), *The Chainbearer; or,
The Littlepage Manuscripts* (1845), *The Redskins; or, Indian and Injun*
(1846)—and *The Oak Openings; or, The Bee-Hunter* (1848).

Our conception of Cooper as our earliest and best frontier
fiction writer, however, eclipses his achievement in sea fiction.
Writing in 1840, Honoré de Balzac offered the opinion that
Cooper was equally adept at "painting the sea and seamen" and
at "idealizing the magnificent landscapes of America" (Dekker
and McWilliams 196). An anonymous critic for the *New-York
Mirror*, reviewing *The Pilot* shortly after its publication, would
claim that "Cooper is, body and spirit, a sailor. The ocean is truly
his element—the deck his home. He confers reality on all his
descriptions. We hear the roar of the waves—the splash of the
oars—the hoarse language of the seamen. We see the waters—
the ships—the manning of the yards—the heaving of the lead—
the very cordage of the vessels. Every movement—from that of
the tracking of the frigate to the launching of the whaleboat, is
visible to our eyes, and we actually take part in the proceedings
and conversations of the crew" (Dekker and McWilliams 74–75).
Cooper wrote as many sea novels (eleven) as frontier novels, in
fact. He followed *The Pilot* with *The Red Rover* (1828) and *The
Water-Witch; or, The Skimmer of the Seas* (1830) before experimenting with other genres (coincident with his seven-year tour of Europe). After he returned to the sea novel in 1838 with *Homeward
Bound; or, The Chase*, he went on to write seven more sea narratives in the final decade of his career: *Mercedes of Castile; or, The
Voyage to Cathay* (1840), *The Two Admirals* (1842), *The Wing-and-
Wing; or, Le Feu-Follet* (1842), *Afloat and Ashore; or, The Adventures of*

Miles Wallingford (1844), a sequel, *Miles Wallingford* (1844), *Jack Tier; or, The Florida Reef* (1848), and *The Sea Lions; or, The Lost Sealers* (1849).⁴

Critical emphases change over time, and although I think that Cooper's fiction has repaid analysis for every critical generation, sometimes a writer's work gets too closely identified with a particular type of criticism and thereafter seems limited in its significance. Cooper's writing—the Leatherstocking Tales at least— certainly became a hallmark for American myth criticism, which was so prominent in the post–World War II decades and so instrumental in liberating American literature and American studies from their colonization by English literature. Ironically in that regard, the British writer D. H. Lawrence inaugurated the mythic approach to the novel by claiming in 1923 that the reverse chronological order of the series enacted the "true myth of America," a movement "backwards, from old age to golden youth."⁵ For R. W. B. Lewis, Natty Bumppo, along with Chingachgook, epitomized the American Adam, "timeless and sturdily innocent, their world all the more fresh, free, and uncluttered."⁶ Henry Nash Smith called Leatherstocking "by far the most important symbol of the national experience of adventure across the continent."⁷ Roy Harvey Pearce also saw the Leatherstocking Tales as enacting a key American myth: "Progressing thus towards high civilization, American society sweeps over Leatherstocking, the man of the forest mythically perfected. For even such perfection as his must disappear, since it is in the end not civilized perfection."⁸ Leslie Fiedler emphasized the similarities of the five novels (as well as their similarity to such books as *Robinson Crusoe, Ivanhoe,* and *Treasure Island*), collapsing them into "the central myth of our culture"—an adolescent fantasy: "All involve adventure and isolation plus an escape at one point or another, or a flight from society to an island, a woods, the underworld, a mountain fastness—some place at least where mothers do not come."⁹ Fiedler did not necessarily mean to disparage Cooper's writing by noting its appeal to adolescents; myth criticism took many of its cues from Sigmund Freud and Carl Jung and assumed a romantic bias in which the child was father to the man and dreams the unconscious registers of conscious truths. An early reviewer of *The Last of the Mohicans* observed that readers

> are carried onward, as through the visions of a long and fever-
> ish dream. The excitement cannot be controlled or lulled, by
> which we are borne through danger, and sudden deliverance;
> while, like some persecuting dæmon of slumber, the fiendlike
> image of a revengeful spirit scowls every where, and haunts
> the powerless fancy, from the moment when the malignant
> eyes first glared in the wilderness, with the unutterable mean-
> ing of hatred, upon those in whom we are interested, until
> they are extinguished for ever in the dreadful catastrophe.
> (Dekker and McWilliams 90)

Although the myth that such criticism considered Cooper to epitomize now seems limited—male-centered, racist, and imperialistic—a writer who can appeal so deeply to a reader's fears does not appeal simply to the adolescent within the man, except in the sense that all adults are prone to returns of the repressed. Cooper let his imagination run, and he carries us with him, even into places where we might not consciously want to go.

That is just one of the reasons, it seems to me, to keep reading Cooper and to expand our list of those novels that deserve to be read and studied. Cooper had a brilliant, scenic imagination—what I am tempted to call a cinematic imagination. Balzac asserted that "never did typographed language approach so closely to painting" as in Cooper's fiction (Dekker and McWilliams 197). As early as W. H. Gardiner's lengthy 1822 review of *The Spy*, critics have praised Cooper for his ability to write action scenes. As Gardiner would assert:

> Wherever there is something to be done, he sets about doing
> it with his whole soul; the reader's attention is chained to the
> event; every other interest is absorbed in the deed, which is ex-
> hibited with a boldness of outline and vividness of coloring,
> proportioned to its importance in itself, or in its results. The
> flight, the hot pursuit, the charge, the victory, pass before you
> with the rapidity, and the distinctness too, of forked lightning
> which plays in the summer cloud; and the reader, not less than
> the writer, is irresistibly borne on by the subject.[10]

Even a quick survey of Cooper's fiction reveals a remarkable number of scenes whose basic structures and elements we take for granted and seem deeply embedded as a kind of deep structure in our imaginations.

The Pioneers is, among other things, our first environmental novel, anticipating Henry David Thoreau's *Walden* in many respects. Besides the obvious conservationism that Natty Bumppo espouses in his many conversations with Judge Marmaduke Temple and Sheriff Richard Jones, *The Pioneers* uncannily examines both the psychology and the ethics of ecological being—the individual subjectivity that originates, mirrorlike, in relation to the natural world. Cooper was way ahead of his time in his remarkable sensitivity to place and to the idea of situated identity. One of the most beautiful scenes he ever wrote occurs in chapter 24 of *The Pioneers*, in nearly the exact center of the novel (which has forty-nine chapters), when Natty Bumppo and Chingachgook paddle across the lake to take Elizabeth Temple, Louisa Grant, and Oliver Effingham on a late-night fishing trip. Intriguingly, Cooper renders the scene from Elizabeth's point of view, placing his "camera" with her and Louisa as they watch the canoe materialize from across the lake. Cooper had a brilliant eye.

Through the obscurity, which prevailed most, immediately under the eastern mountain, a small and uncertain light was plainly to be seen, though, as it was occasionally lost to the eye, it seemed struggling for existence. They observed it to move, and sensibly to lower, as if carried down the descent of the bank to the shore. Here, in a very short time, its flame gradually expanded, and grew brighter, until it became of the size of a man's head, when it continued to shine, a steady ball of fire.[11]

The effect is magical and obviously symbolic—a visionary experience to be centered in Natty's imagination (head), which will illuminate the natural world for Elizabeth, who will of course inherit this land.

When we recall that this scene occurs right after the gross scene of waste in chapter 23, in which the townsmen drag the lake for thousands of fish, many of which will simply rot upon the bank, we recognize Cooper's environmental purpose. Even the judge acknowledges the "wasteful extravagance" of seine fishing and fears, prophetically, that the fish, "like all other treasures of the wilderness," are already beginning to disappear (*Pioneers* 260). Natty of course spears a single salmon trout at the climax of the scene that follows, illustrating the principle of taking only what he needs from the natural world. But the more important lesson, I think, is psychological. Cooper stages this scene very carefully over several pages. To Elizabeth it seems that the canoe glides over the water "by magic." She sees thousands of fish beneath the surface, "for the light of their torch laid bare the mysteries of the lake, as plainly as if the limpid sheet of the Otsego was but another atmosphere" (268). We hear the echo of this vision in Thoreau's observation that "the clear portion of the air above [the pond] being shallow and darkened by clouds, the water, full of light and reflections, becomes a lower heaven."[12] Like Thoreau peering through the first ice on Walden Pond (*Walden*, 246–247), Natty bends his body forward, "straining his vision, as if desirous of penetrating the water, that surrounded their boundary of light." As Natty's light "penetrated to the bottom," rendering the lake transparent, Elizabeth "saw a fish of unusual size, floating above small pieces of logs and sticks" (*Pioneers* 269). Natty plays the hunter in this scene, but this is a sacred hunt more than a simple one—a visionary quest for knowledge and understanding and one in a long line of visionary moments in nineteenth-century American literature in which individuals seek to render the natural world transparent so that they may enjoy an unmediated imaginative relationship with its mysteries. Natty kills the huge fish, bringing Elizabeth out of her trance, "created by this scene, and by gazing in that unusual manner at the bottom of the lake," while Chingachgook blesses the "catch" with the single word "Good" (270). But the main objective exceeds the obvious object lesson in conservation. Cooper seemed to recognize that conservation needed to be rooted in appreciation, in a subject-object relationship between human and natural being that at least approached a subject-subject relationship. As Natty's light penetrates to the lake's bottom, presenting Elizabeth a gift of vision of the huge lake trout, Cooper notes that the "curiosity excited by this unusual exposure of the secrets of the lake, seemed to be mutual between the heiress of the land and the lord of these waters, for the 'salmon-trout' soon announced his interest, by raising his head and body, for a few degrees above a horizontal line, and then dropping them again into a horizontal position" (269).

As I said, this scene represents one of the most beautiful and beautifully staged scenes that Cooper ever wrote—an example of his cinematic vision. This is a quiet, lyrical scene, and slow-paced. At the other end of the cinematic spectrum, consider the extended chase scene in chapter 20 of *The Last of the Mohicans* in which one canoe pursues another across Lake George. Natty directs the lead canoe down one side of an island, while the chasing canoe must take the opposite side. Like a modern-day movie director, Cooper cuts between the two canoes, creating suspense, and even gives us bird's-eye views of the two boats together on the lake.

Natty's death scene at the end of *The Prairie* has been duplicated so many times that reading Cooper's 1827 version may now seem hackneyed:

The trapper had remained nearly motionless for an hour. His eyes, alone, had occasionally opened and shut. When opened his gaze seemed fastened on the clouds which hung around the western horizon, reflecting the bright colours and giving form and loveliness to the glorious tints of an American sunset. The hour—the calm beauty of the season—the occasion all conspired to fill the spectators with solemn awe. Suddenly, while musing on the remarkable position in which he was placed [Duncan] Middleton felt the hand which he held, grasp his own, with incredible power, and the old man, supported on either side by his friends, rose upright to his feet. For a moment, he looked about him, as if to invite all in presence to listen, (the lingering remnant of human frailty) and then, with a fine military elevation of the head, and with a voice that might be heard in every part of that numerous assembly he pronounced the word—
"Here!"[13]

Here, too, we can imagine the scene on film. We have seen it many times: the music rising as Natty slowly stands up, the camera moving in to his face (as the spectators do) for the climactic "Here!" and then backing away rapidly to catch the whole scene, as Natty dies off into the sunset.

As sublime as this climactic scene is, there is no scene in the Leatherstocking Tales that resonates as powerfully with readers reared on western movies as the scene in *The Deerslayer* in which Natty kills his first Indian. If we hadn't seen so many gunfights in westerns, we would be more impressed at how many modern conventions Cooper anticipated. He carefully stages the scene on a point of land jutting out into Lake Glimmerglass. He isolates his two characters. He takes us into the mind of his hero, who resists the temptation to shoot the Indian who has just leapt from the bushes. "No—no—that may be red-skin warfare, but it's not a christian's gifts. Let the miscreant charge, and then we'll take it out like men."[14] Natty fires his rifle only when the Indian pulls his own trigger: "Both parties discharged their pieces at the same instant" (*Deerslayer* 121). Natty's shot, of course, is truer—and fatal—but just before the Indian dies, he bestows on Natty the name he will have for the rest of the series: Hawkeye. It is an amazing scene for the carefully orchestrated structure it possesses—a deep structure, ritualistic in its symbolic meaning although largely unaware of another layer of symbolism in which Natty's right to kill the Indian on his own ground, so to speak, might be contested.[15]

Cooper's marginalization during the past twenty years, a period when connections between literature and history have been emphasized, is all the more surprising because his writing so actively engages historical and cultural issues. For example, Cooper wrote during a time when the very concept of the United States as a geographical entity changed radically. Only eleven states had ratified the Constitution when Cooper was born in 1789, and U.S. territory extended only as far as the Mississippi River. By the time he died in 1851, California had joined the union as the thirty-first state, and the United States and its territories looked the same as the continental United States does today (except for the Gadsden Purchase territory, acquired from

Mexico in 1853). The United States bought the Louisiana Purchase territory from France in 1803, and Thomas Jefferson sponsored the remarkable exploratory journey of the Corps of Discovery, led by Meriwether Lewis and William Clark, just a year later, inspiring Cooper to set *The Prairie* in the new western territory. Cooper's main subject, even in his frontier novels, was American society and its values; his novels consistently feature debates about political and social issues. Francis Parkman argued in an 1852 retrospective that the Leatherstocking Tales was Cooper's supreme creation, because his "life conveys in some sort an epitome of American history, during one of its most busy and decisive periods" (Dekker and McWilliams 253). And as this introduction's epigraph from George Sand suggests, Cooper's writing actively reflected the hard work of early American democracy and its conflicts. He wrote the first three Leatherstocking novels, for example, in the run-up to the Indian Removal Act of 1830, and he published the final books in the series shortly after the terrible Trail of Tears in 1838–1839. Dana Nelson's essay for this volume exemplifies the value of examining the many important intersections between the Leatherstocking novels and American social issues, the way that "groupings of male and female characters across lines of class, habitude, and race provide readers a series of contrasts that foreground the problems of creating new identities that can support and sustain the democratic aims of the early United States." Rather than emphasizing the asocial or mythic dimensions of Cooper's frontier novels, Nelson explores "some of the questions he raises about women and men, as well as questions he opens up about the possibility of relationship across race, gender, and class differences."

Cooper's novels of the Revolutionary War, historical reconsiderations of revolution and political, as well as social, experimentation during the antebellum period, offer rich data fields for interpreting and reinterpreting the American experiment. In his essay for this volume, John P. McWilliams focuses on the three Revolutionary War novels, as well as on *The Pioneers* (in which the war figures prominently as background), to offer a new perspective on some of Cooper's female characters. Cooper's depiction of women has been sharply criticized, but McWilliams not only finds much to appreciate in characters such as Frances Wharton (*The Spy*), Katherine Plowden (*The Pilot*), and Agnes Danforth (*Lionel Lincoln*), but he puts the Revolutionary War novels into conversation with two American predecessors, Susanna Rowson's *Charlotte Temple* (1791) and Hannah Foster's *The Coquette* (1797).

Cooper's politics, to be sure, are relatively conservative, although as Gerald Kennedy notes in his essay in this volume, he also felt "disdain for royalty." According to McWilliams's assessment, Cooper was Democratic (rather than Whig) in his politics, but he "steadfastly denied any connection with the Democratic party of New York," preferring to stay free of party labels and party orthodoxy.[16] Republican in his leanings, he worried about too much democracy and the threat of mob rule. He admired Andrew Jackson, although with his patrician background he found Jackson's "lack of Gentlemanly breeding" off-putting (McWilliams, *Political Justice*, 192). In *The American Democrat* (1838), an uncharacteristically brief exercise in political theorizing, Cooper laid out his views on various issues. He embraced democracy. He claimed, only half facetiously, in the introduction that the "writer believes himself to be as good a democrat as there is in America," but he would immediately qualify that assertion by adding that "his democracy is not of the impracticable school."[17] By that he means that "he is not a believer in the scheme of raising men very far above their natural propensities" (70). He thus accepted as "natural" many of the inequalities (based, for example, on gender, race, education, property ownership) that most Americans have spent at least the past century and a half fighting against. In advocating such a limited notion of democracy, Cooper was of course ratifying those principles written originally into and those rights excluded from the U.S. Constitution. He was branding himself, in our terms, a conservative rather than a liberal, content with conserving a status quo that he identified, tellingly, with nature.

He accepted the notion that women's interests are identical with "those of their male relatives," for example, and so can be represented effectively by men, and he did not "doubt that society is greatly the gainer, by thus excluding one half its members, and the half that is best adapted to give a tone to its domestic happiness, from the strife of parties, and the fierce struggles of political controversies" (*American Democrat* 106). We have learned to call this idea the doctrine of "separate spheres." Only seven years after Cooper wrote those words, Margaret Fuller would refute this patronizing idea in *Woman in the Nineteenth Century* (1845).[18] Cooper noted that the "principal advantage of a democracy, is a general elevation in the character of the people" (121), but he distrusted the "masses" of men, and he believed that the "tendencies of democracies is, in all things, to mediocrity, since the tastes, knowledge and principles of the majority form the tribunal of appeal" (129). And the "mass of no community," he claimed, "is qualified to decide the most correctly on any thing, which, in its nature, is above its reach" (129–130). Indeed, it seems axiomatic for him to argue that "there can be no question that the educated and affluent classes of a country, are more capable of coming to wise and intelligent decisions in affairs of state, than the mass of a population" (113). Cooper enters a debate about equality and equal rights that continues to this day—a debate over equality of rights and opportunity and equality of condition. He argues that "there is no natural equality" (136) even though "one man is as good as another in rights" (137). He trusts that people will naturally reach their appropriate levels: "By possessing the same rights to exercise their respective faculties, the active and frugal become more wealthy than the idle and dissolute; the wise and gifted more trusted than the silly and ignorant; the polished and refined more respected and sought, than the rude and vulgar" (137). If this sounds naïve, Cooper acknowledges what he calls the "legitimate advantages of birth," as well as the "natural" tendency that "men of the same habits, the same degree of cultivation and refinement, the same opinions" will "associate together" (139). Like many other aristocrats, Cooper believed that natural or merited superiority conferred certain responsibilities on those who rose in the ranks. "The social duties of a gentleman are of a high order. The class to which he belongs is the natural repository of the manners, tastes, tone, and, to a certain extent, of the principles of a country" (147). Because gentility is identified with England and associated with birth,

Cooper wishes to differentiate between a "democratic gentle-man" and an "aristocratical gentlemen" (153). He defines a natu-ral aristocracy, a social meritocracy: "In a democracy, men are just as free to aim at the highest attainable places in society, as to obtain the largest fortunes; and it would be clearly unworthy of all noble sentiment to say, that the groveling competition for money shall alone be free, while that which enlists all the liberal acquirements and elevated sentiments of the race, is denied the democrat" (153).

Cooper's views on slavery were hardly enlightened, although he acknowledged that, in its consequences, it was an "impolitic and vicious institution" (*American Democrat* 220). But he could also observe that it is "quite possible to be an excellent christian and a slave holder, and the relations of master and slave, may be a means of exhibiting some of the mildest graces of the character, as may those of king and subject, or principal and dependent" (221). Reflecting commonly held racist or racialist beliefs, he could conclude that "slavery may actually benefit a man, there being little doubt that the African is, in nearly all respects, better off in servitude in this country, than when living in a state of bar-barism at home" (221). The Coopers owned slaves, and Cooper's views on slavery and abolition make him even more conservative than Nathaniel Hawthorne, whose support for Franklin Pierce and for the gradualist view that slavery would cease to be eco-nomically viable and would decline and disappear "naturally" over time, have continued to be criticized. Cooper in fact explic-itly promoted the gradualist view even as he anticipated the in-evitably of civil war, without recognizing that war would repre-sent the cataclysmic means of ending slavery: "The time must come when American slavery shall cease, and when that day shall arrive, (unless early and effectual means are devised to obviate it,) two races will exist in the same region, whose feelings will be embittered by inextinguishable hatred, and who carry on their faces, the respective stamps of their factions. The struggle that will follow, will necessarily be a war of extermination" (222). But Cooper did not advocate the abolition of slavery, believing that such an amendment to the Constitution would have no chance of success and would only irritate southern slaveholders (223).

Just when we think we have pigeon-holed Cooper as a reactionary, however, he surprises us. In his essay for this volume Gerald Kennedy not only makes a strong case for the importance of the travel narratives and novels Cooper wrote during his extended stay in Europe (1826–1833), but also credits Cooper with remarkably astute perceptions about American politics in the transnational context that his temporarily expatriate status afforded him. Kennedy emphasizes Cooper's "insights into national identity and his determination to write against the American nation in order to reform it." While writing about Switzerland, for example, Cooper finds ways at the same time to write about America. Kennedy's main interest, an important contribution to perspectives on Cooper's writing, involves the author's investigation of national identity and its origins: "Whereas Americans imagine themselves a nation largely because they share common democratic ideals, the Swiss sense of nationhood is more profoundly rooted in geography and landscape." Kennedy's most provocative point, however, involves Cooper's criticism of America—his view, for example, that Americans do not enjoy as much freedom as they profess because their neighbors and the power of public opinion operate as a moral police force, or, in an invidious comparison to the French, that Americans worship money as "the very base of all distinction." The temptation to let the majority rule on every public policy question and, regardless of the Bill of Rights, to run roughshod over minority rights has always weighed heavily in the scales of American justice. Cooper's fear of majoritarian tyranny pervades his social novels and, as Kennedy notes, his European narratives.

Cooper has been fairly criticized for his easy division of Indian tribes into "good Indians" and "bad Indians." His treatment of white characters shows a similar tendency to put black hats on villains such as Richard Jones and Hiram Doolittle (*The Pioneers*), Christopher "Kit" Dillon (*The Pilot*), and Tom Hutter and Harry March (*The Deerslayer*). In Hutter and March, Cooper carefully documented the racism and rationalizations of Indian hating. Even many of Cooper's "bad" Indians, however, are complex characters who espouse complex views of Indian-white relations. Magua and especially Tamenund in *The Last of the Mohicans* are angry and eloquent spokesmen for Indian rights. In the essay she has contributed to this collection, Barbara Mann offers a new perspective on Cooper's characterization of native peoples, as she argues that Natty Bumppo himself is at least half Indian and that Cooper's representation of natives was far more sympathetic and enlightened than his detractors in both the nineteenth and twentieth centuries allowed. In fact, she argues that criticism of Cooper's Indians originated with those, such as Lewis Cass, who had vested interests in promoting removal and extermination policies. Accused in effect of being a traitor to his race, Cooper should actually be considered, in Mann's view, one of the good guys on the subject of native peoples and Indian-white relations.

Cooper wrote so much that the essays in this historical guide cannot possibly cover all of his fiction and nonfiction. Because the five Leatherstocking Tales still attract the most attention from readers, this volume makes an effort to place those novels in their historical and political context. Barbara Mann discusses Cooper's Indian tales (including *The Wept of Wish-ton-Wish*) in the context of nineteenth-century debates over Indian rights and character. Dana Nelson also focuses primarily on the Leatherstocking Tales. In addition to providing some guidance to the Tales and to ways that those five novels might be situated in their historical and cultural context, we have made an effort to expand the Cooper canon at least a little. John McWilliams, as already noted, focuses on the lesser-known but still important Revolutionary War novels that Cooper wrote early in his career. Gerald Kennedy places Cooper's European travel writings into a context informed by current interests in postcolonial and globalist issues.

In the space remaining, I would like to suggest the value of attending to two other novels, *Home as Found* (1838) and *The Ways of the Hour* (1850). The novels occupy crucial places in Cooper's career. *The Ways of the Hour* represents his last published novel and so offers his last word, so to speak, on American society and American issues. *Home as Found*, published in the same year as its prequel, *Homeward Bound*, and *The American Democrat*, reflects Cooper's reengagement with America after the eight years he and his family spent in Europe. The novel also occupies a pivotal

place in relation to the Leatherstocking novels. Not only is Natty
Bumppo mentioned several times in the novel, which features
the descendants of Oliver and Elizabeth Effingham (of *The Pioneers*), but the novel represents a logical bridge between *The Pioneers* and *The Deerslayer* in its depiction of the Otsego landscape
and helps to explain the decision Cooper made to move Natty
Bumppo progressively backward in time in the last two novels
of the series. Put another way, *The Deerslayer* makes even more
sense when read not just after *The Pioneers*, but after *Home as
Found*.[19]

As the Effinghams return to Templeton, their entrance into
the town retraces the same "ancient route" that Elizabeth Temple had followed at the beginning of *The Pioneers*, and they enter
the forest at the "precise spot" where Judge Temple had shot
Oliver Effingham in the earlier novel.[20] As the Effinghams follow
a path that offers "proofs of the ravages man had committed
in that noble forest" in recent times, they proceed toward what
Eve hopes will be "some spot hallowed by a deed of Natty
Bumppo's" (124). Immediately receiving her wish, Eve first views
Lake Otsego from the "Vision," the mountain-top from which
Judge Temple had first seen the lake. As Cooper carefully explains, "This was the Templeton of 'The Pioneers,' and as the
progress of society during half a century is connected with the
circumstance, we shall give the reader a more accurate notion of
its present state than can be obtained from incidental allusions"
(126). As he contemplates the Otsego valley from this special vantage point, Edward Effingham approaches Natty's poetic reverence for nature, expressed so eloquently in the earlier novel.
"This is truly a place," he recognizes, "where one might fancy re-
pose and content were to be found for the evening of a troubled
life" (130). Long since dead (in *The Prairie*), Natty presides over
the lake in spirit; for, as Eve conducts her family and guests on
a tour of the lake, she points out the site of Leatherstocking's
original cabin (burned in *The Pioneers* by Natty himself) and eulo-
gizes his character: "There, near the small house that is erected
over a spring of delicious water, stood the hut of Natty Bumppo,
once known throughout all these mountains as a renowned
hunter; a man who had the simplicity of a woodsman, the hero-

ism of a savage, the faith of a Christian, and the feelings of a poet. A better than he, after his fashion, seldom lived" (196). In Eve's various efforts to become reacquainted with Natty's habitat, in her father's reiteration of his "visions," Cooper reintroduces the Effinghams to the happier past of the earlier novel, in contrast to the "ravages" they encounter in the present. It becomes clear, therefore, that the index to moral value in *Home as Found*, as in *The Pioneers*, is man's relationship to the land. Some characters, such as Natty and Chingachgook, revere the integrity of nature, whereas others, such as Richard Jones and Aristabulus Bragg, exploit natural resources for personal gain. Continually at pains to emphasize his characters' attitudes toward the natural world, Cooper suggests that contemporary Templeton has been overrun by transients who feel no attachment to the land, "birds of passage" (165) who threaten to "destroy whatever there is of poetry or of local attachment in any region where they resort" (166). The distinction Cooper makes is not simply aesthetic. As in *The Pioneers*, he emphasizes a more intimate, ethical, imaginative relationship to the land. "I fear this glorious scene is marred by the envy, rapacity, uncharitableness, and all the other evil passions of man!" observes Mr. Effingham. "Perhaps it were better as it was so lately, when it lay in the solitude and peace of the wilderness, the resort of birds and beasts." When Eve rejoins that birds and beasts also prey on each other, her father agrees, but adds, "I never gaze on one of these scenes of holy calm, without wishing that the great tabernacle of nature might be tenanted only by those who have a feeling for its perfection" (131). In echoing Natty Bumppo's statement in *The Pioneers* that none can know the wonders of nature but those who "rove it for a man's life," Cooper suggests a key question in *Home as Found*: whether Natty Bumppo's influence, operating through the Effinghams, can reverse the ravages wrought by the town's present citizens, who seem more the heirs of Richard Jones's exploitive vision of nature than of Natty's conservative or ecological vision.

Now in its "second growth" (*Home as Found* 201), the wilderness in *Home as Found* has continued in the state of decline described in *The Pioneers*. The spring near which Natty built his hut in *The Pioneers* has been renamed the "Fairy Spring" by some "flight of poetry that, like so many of our feelings, must have been imported" (197), and it thus has lost any specific association with Leatherstocking. In fact, the only indigenous relic the Effinghams discover is a "Silent Pine," which "now stood in solitary glory, a memorial of what the mountains which were yet so rich in vegetation had really been in their days of nature and pride" (202). Despite its symbolic value for contemporary culture, the pine evokes the tightly enclosed and protected oasis of Lake Glimmerglass, which Cooper would recreate in *The Deerslayer*. It speaks, Eve says, "of the fierce storms that have whistled round its tops" and "of all that has passed on the Otsego, when this limpid lake lay like a gem embedded in the forest" (202). Imaginatively, then, the pine, like the Leatherstocking, is a relic of the past, "an American antiquity" (202). "Alas!" sighs John Effingham, "the days of the 'Leather-Stockings' have passed away. He preceded me in life, and I see few remains of his character in a region where speculation is more rife than moralizing" (197).

Although the Effinghams seem determined to "hold a little communion with the spirit of the Leather-Stocking" (*Home as Found* 203), Natty's hallowed memory no longer functions as part of the community's collective imaginative life. Though the Effinghams, more than anyone else, retain a degree of reverence for the past and for Natty's spirit, like Cooper they find themselves increasingly alienated from the present landscape and reduced to mourning for an earlier time. Such a time, of course, would have to predate even that of *The Pioneers*, because in that novel Natty himself was already mourning the passing of the wilderness he saw when he first arrived at Lake Otsego. Thus, although *Home as Found* records the failure of its characters' effort to invoke the spirit of Leatherstocking as a shaping force in the American present, the novel also lays the foundation for Natty's metamorphosis in *The Deerslayer* into a mythic and idealized figure and for the imaginative rejuvenation of Lake Otsego as Lake Glimmerglass.

The nostalgic and erstwhile mythic dimensions of *Home as Found* occupy a relatively small, albeit central, place in the novel. In the rest of the narrative Cooper focuses on the manners and mores of an impressive variety of characters and character types, and, notoriously, he fictionalizes the legal squabble in which he became embroiled with the people of Cooperstown. In *The Ways of the Hour* he also emphasizes manners and legal issues, although the latter dimension of the novel looms much larger. Even the Leatherstocking Tales, of course, include an unusual range of characters, as well as at least one romantic love story. Several love plots, with conventional twists and turns, drive *The Ways of the Hour* along even as the main suspense centers in the lengthy murder trial that initially seems to make little progress. If Cooper had had the foresight to title the novel *The Lady-Killer*, I daresay the novel would be better known today. As it is, the novel is too long and includes too many conversations designed to voice his conservative complaints about the deteriorating condition of American society. Its Federalist politics, especially its open distrust of "the people" and its near obsessive worry about tyranny by the majority, make it seem reactionary in its sympathies. Despite his prejudices, Cooper understood current political debates, and he presents them coherently in many conversations. As the title suggests, the novel is embedded in its cultural moment and in ongoing political debates about the balance of powers, voting rights, women's rights, and slavery.

Published in the same year as *The Scarlet Letter*, *The Ways of the Hour* deserves to be discussed alongside Hawthorne's novel as male-authored, proto-feminist fiction. Like Hester Prynne, Mary Monson (alias of Mildred Millington) finds herself at odds with the community—accused of crimes (a double murder, robbery, and arson) and reviled by the townspeople as she refuses to provide information about the circumstances of the crimes. A strong woman, married unhappily to an older man, a foreigner who married her for her wealth, Mary will not tell her story even to her attorney. Contemporaneously set, unlike *The Scarlet Letter*, of course, *The Ways of the Hour* engages in a spirited debate about the Married Women's Property Act of 1848. That important legislation, enacted in the same year as the first women's rights convention in Seneca Falls, New York, gave women the right to retain ownership of all property held at the time of marriage, as well as the right to own property acquired after marriage. The law comes into play in *The Ways of the Hour* because it enables the heroine to retain control of her considerable fortune and eventually to buy her way out of her unhappy marriage.

Throughout much of the novel, Cooper uses the lawyer, Thomas Dunscombe, to voice conservative opinions about important cultural and political issues. Dunscombe is not opposed to slavery, for example, believing in Providence as he does and having "little doubt that African slavery is an important feature in God's Laws."[21] He thinks that abolishing slavery in the District of Columbia "would be unjust towards the slave-holders" (124). And he opposes the provisions of the Married Women's Property Act. By the end of the novel Dunscombe has proved ineffectual, however, and Mildred Millington has taken control of her own legal case. Women emerge to speak for themselves and their own political interests. Counseling her young friend, Anna Updyke, Mildred advises her not to marry, because matrimony is "unsuited to ladies" (313). When Anna asks her how long she has held this opinion, Mildred replies, "Just as long as I have been made to feel how it crushes a woman's independence, and how completely it gives her a master, and how very, very humiliating and depressing is the bondage it inflicts" (314). These are strong views, and they contrast with the gradualist, providential views that Hester Prynne expresses to the women who seek her counsel after she returns from England at the very end of *The Scarlet Letter*, when she assures them of "her firm belief, that, at some brighter period, when the world should have grown ripe for it, in Heaven's own time, a new truth would be revealed, in order to establish the whole relation between man and woman on a surer ground of mutual happiness."[22] Even though Cooper overdoes the conversations in many of his novels, especially in the frontier romances, he had a good ear for the controversies of his day, and he consistently showed his interest in debating them in his fiction. Considering that a primary goal of this historical guide is to situate Cooper in the cultural context in which he wrote and was read, that feature of his writing constitutes one of his most important achievements.

However mixed his recollection of reading Cooper early in his life, Herman Melville happily contributed a letter to the Cooper memorial in 1852. "Whatever possible things in Mr. Cooper may have seemed to have in some degree provoked the occasional treatment he received," Melville wrote, "it is certain that he possessed not the slightest weaknesses but those which are only noticeable as the almost infallible indices of pervading greatness. He was a great, robust-souled man, all whose merits are not even, yet fully appreciated. But a grateful posterity will take the best care of Fenimore Cooper" (Dekker and McWilliams 244). This historical guide, published more than a century and a half after Cooper's death, represents a small effort, I am happy to say, to "take the best care of Fenimore Cooper."

NOTES

1. George Sand, "Fenimore Cooper," in *Fenimore Cooper: The Critical Heritage*, ed. George Dekker and John P. McWilliams (London: Routledge and Kegan Paul, 1973), 266.

2. See Sacvan Bercovitch, "Huckleberry Bumppo: A Comparison of *Tom Sawyer* and *The Pioneers*," *Mark Twain Journal* 14 (1968): 1–4, and my own essay, "The Leatherstocking Tradition in American Fiction; or, The Sources of *Tom Sawyer*; A Descriptive Essay," in *James Fenimore Cooper: His Country and His Art*, ed. George A. Test (Oneonta: State University of New York Press, 1987), 67–77.

3. Cooper's reputation among his peers was mixed long before Mark Twain indicted him for various literary offenses. In reviewing a new edition of *The Red Rover*, Melville recalled, "Long ago, & far inland, we read it in our uncritical days, & enjoyed it as much as thousands of the rising generation will when supplied with such an entertaining volume" (Hershel Parker, *Herman Melville: A Biography*, *Vol. 1: 1819–1851* [Baltimore: Johns Hopkins University Press, 1996], 110). Melville's comment suggests of course that he would not be so gullible at the present moment, that he had outgrown Cooper's writing and surpassed it in his own work. Edgar Allan Poe would go on, in terms that anticipate Mark Twain's, to disparage Cooper's *Wyandotté*. Anticipating the distinction Melville would make between writers, Poe listed Cooper's fiction at the head of the "more popular division"—"read with pleasure but without admiration"—whereas he listed Charles Brockden Brown, John Neal, William Gilmore Simms, and Nathaniel Hawthorne in the other division of

"not so popular" but more skillful writers (Dekker and McWilliams 208).

4. After *The Spy: A Tale of the Neutral Ground* (1821), Cooper returned to the Revolutionary War in both *The Pilot* (1824) and *Lionel Lincoln; or The Leaguer of Boston* (1825). While he toured Europe from 1826 to 1833, he wrote several European novels: *The Bravo* (1831), *The Heidenmauer; or, The Benedictines* (1832), and *The Headsman; or, The Abbaye des Vignerons* (1833). He wrote one of the first American novels of manners with *Home as Found* (1838) and experimented with several other genres. *The Monikins* (1835) is a satire in the tradition of Swift's *Gulliver's Travels* in featuring an Antarctic world of educated monkeys. *The Crater; or, Vulcan's Peak: A Tale of the Pacific* (1847) is a utopian/dystopian novel about a Pacific island. And *The Ways of the Hour* (1850), about which I shall have more to say below, is a murder mystery.

5. D. H. Lawrence, *Studies in Classic American Literature* (New York: Viking, 1961), 54.

6. R. W. B. Lewis, *The American Adam: Innocence, Tragedy, and Tradition in the Nineteenth Century* (Chicago: University of Chicago Press, 1955), 103.

7. Henry Nash Smith, *Virgin Land: The American West as Symbol and Myth* (Cambridge, MA: Harvard University Press, 1970), 61.

8. Roy Harvey Pearce, *Savagism and Civilization: A Study of the Indian and the American Mind* (Baltimore: Johns Hopkins University Press, 1965), 204.

9. Leslie Fiedler, *Love and Death in the American Novel*, rev. ed. (New York: Dell, 1966), 182, 181.

10. Dekker and McWilliams 63. Originally published in the *North American Review* 15 (July 1822): 250–282.

11. James Fenimore Cooper, *The Pioneers, or the Sources of the Susquehanna; A Descriptive Tale*, ed. James Franklin Beard, Lance Schachterle, and Kenneth M. Andersen Jr. (Albany: State University of New York Press, 1980), 263.

12. Henry David Thoreau, *Walden; or, Life in the Woods*, ed. J. Lyndon Shanley (Princeton, NJ: Princeton University Press, 1973), 86.

13. James Fenimore Cooper, *The Prairie: A Tale*, ed. James Paul Elliott (Albany: State University of New York Press, 1985), 385.

14. James Fenimore Cooper, *The Deerslayer; or, The First Warpath,*

ed. James Franklin Beard, Lance Schachterle, Kent Ljungquist, and James Kilby (Albany: State University of New York Press, 1987), 117.

15. Passage of the Indian Removal Act occurred just a decade before Cooper wrote *The Deerslayer*, and the abominable Trail of Tears occurred only two years before the novel appeared. For an extensive examination of *The Deerslayer* within this historical context, see Philip Fisher, *Hard Facts: Setting and Form in the American Novel* (New York: Oxford University Press, 1985), 23–88.

16. John P. McWilliams Jr., *Political Justice in a Republic: James Fenimore Cooper's America* (Berkeley: University of California Press, 1972), 193.

17. James Fenimore Cooper, *The American Democrat* (New York: Penguin, 1989), 70.

18. Tacitly supporting the reformist idea that women's interests should be represented by women, Fuller makes fun of the opposing argument that, because "men are privately influenced by women," they cannot "fail of representing their interests." See *Woman in the Nineteenth Century*, ed. Larry J. Reynolds (New York: Norton, 1998), 18–19.

19. For a more extensive account of *Home as Found* in relation to the Leatherstocking series and to the other novels in the Otsego trilogy (*The Pioneers* and *The Deerslayer*), see my "Home as Found and the Leatherstocking Series," *ESQ: A Journal of the American Renaissance* 27 (1981): 170–180.

20. James Fenimore Cooper, *Home as Found* (New York: Capricorn, 1961), 122, 124.

21. James Fenimore Cooper, *The Ways of the Hour* (Phoenix Mill, UK: Alan Sutton, 1996), 125.

22. *"The Scarlet Letter" and Other Writings*, ed. Leland S. Person (New York: Norton, 2005), 166.

James Fenimore Cooper, 1789–1851

A Brief Biography

Wayne Franklin

On September 15, 1789, a New Jersey couple ushered a new son into their crowded quarters in the old Quaker city of Burlington. Wheelwright William Cooper had been an energetic but impoverished nineteen-year-old when, on the eve of the American Revolution in 1774, he convinced Elizabeth Fenimore, three years his senior, to run off and marry him. In the topsy-turvy conditions produced by the war, such a man was not to be kept down. As fighting raged on in the Delaware Valley and elsewhere, he threw up a store on a piece of vacant land outside Burlington and soon coaxed into existence there a hamlet of a dozen or so buildings that he called "Coopertown." His ambition whetted by this experience, he began looking farther afield. With a Burlington partner in 1785, he wrested control of forty thousand frontier acres in New York from the heirs and creditors of the colorful trader and Indian agent George Croghan. Soon he was on the spot, selling lots and farms and establishing his own foothold. By October 1790, a little more than a year after his son James's birth, William Cooper packed up his family's belongings and, over his hearth-loving wife's protests, drove the lot of them through a miserable, muddy fall landscape to this other eponymous raw village, this one to be called "Cooperstown." There his fortune would be made.[1]

Resting at the foot of a pristine blue-green lake, Cooperstown grew quickly at first, then slowed and settled into the state of rural beauty and peace where it still exists today. For its modest size and somewhat obscure location, it is one of the more famous American villages. But it was not William Cooper, despite his eventual wealth and his swaggering political career as a judge and congressman, who made it so. Cooperstown was put on the map by the literary art of his youngest son, James Cooper (he added the "Fenimore" in 1826 as a tribute to his mother), in the flood of novels, travel books, histories, and polemical works he authored between 1820 and 1851.[2]

James Cooper's first great theme was the frontier world where he had grown up. His father viewed the process of settlement with naïve self-satisfaction, boasting of his role in "reclaiming" great quantities of land from, as he put it, "the waste of the Creation."[3] The novelist had a more nuanced understanding: he saw, first of all, that the triumph of a new order entailed the defeat of older ones. European settlement in this sense *unsettled* the ancient Indian economy that had long organized the New World. "Savages," most white leaders and writers still called the Indians. Cooper taught a wiser lesson. He personally knew some of the "last" of New York's native inhabitants, especially the Oneidas and the Mohegan and Stockbridge families they had invited to join them in the area just to the northwest of Cooperstown.[4] Although no native inhabitants had permanently resided on the shores of Lake Otsego, he located them there in his fiction to drive home his larger moral point: viewing the frontier from both sides, and therefore imagining possession and dispossession as linked truths, he made loss a salient theme in all his frontier books. He portrayed Native Americans receding as soldiers, scouts, and backwoodsmen invaded their lands; in turn, he showed his deerskin-clad white hunters fading away before newer foes, the axmen and agriculturalists; even his sturdy pioneers, mostly oblivious to the ruination they caused, would be supplanted in his later books by newspapermen and lawyers, town merchants, and tourists. Moreover, beyond the pathos these cycles of change evoked, Cooper saw all human history as dirtying the deep green face of nature. His best works entomb the memory of a continent stretching in silence under the arch of heaven, with people small or distant—inconsequential actors in a world better left to itself. Among his several Otsego books, from *The Pioneers* (1823) and *Home as Found* (1838) to *Wyandotté* (1843), the most poignant is thus *The Deerslayer* (1841), in which the old hunter Natty Bumppo (or "Leatherstocking") is reborn to green youth himself and set loose in the forest and on the lake, from which most signs of later human history have been erased by Cooper's imagination. This was to be a backward glance that most of Cooper's frontier romances managed, including all five Leatherstocking Tales (*The Last of the Mohicans* [1826], *The Prairie* [1827], and *The Pathfinder* [1840], *Pioneers* and *Deerslayer*); *The Wept of Wish-ton-Wish* (1829); *The Oak-Openings* (1848); the Littlepage series (*Satanstoe* [1845], *The Chainbearer* [1845], and *The Redskins* [1846]); and *Wyandotté*.

Cooper sailed and rowed Lake Otsego and ran its embowering woods, so it was natural for much of his feeling and his fiction to center there or in similar landscapes elsewhere. In fact, however, he spent few of his first forty-five years in Otsego. Perhaps that is one reason for the poignancy of his frontier vision. He began his education in the village grammar school, but on two occasions interrupted it to pass a year with his mother and an older brother in exile in her native Burlington, where the boys, fresh from their forest playground, were first tutored in Latin. Mrs. Cooper, who always found New Jersey more agreeable than her husband's rough border village, forced the congressman to buy her a house in Burlington in 1798 and went back there with the boys a third time, threatening never to return them to Otsego. Her defiance called forth that of the boys, however, and in the heated contest of wills James and Samuel won. The newly bought house was quickly put up for sale, they dragged their mother triumphantly back to Cooperstown, and they went no more to school in New Jersey. She in turn rarely left the large new mansion her husband built for her on a slight rise above the New York lake.

That mansion was barely finished when, in 1801, eleven-year-old James Cooper left Otsego again, carried off in a farmer's wagon to Albany. There he was deposited on the doorstep of the local Episcopal rector, a Cambridge scholar and royalist, to be taught a good deal about British character—along with more Latin, enough to ready him for college. Soon he went on to New Haven for nearly three years of fun and fighting interrupted by sporadic study, all of it terminated when he was expelled by Yale's president, Rev. Timothy Dwight, for setting off a gunpowder charge in the door lock of another student. After a brief return in 1805–1806 to the family home and a new tutor (who later recalled, perhaps anachronistically, that fiction provided his pupil's only intellectual excitement), he rebelled and ran off to join the revolutionary expedition that had been recruited in New York by Venezuelan patriot Francisco de Miranda. Soon, disillusioned with that impulsive goal and short of cash, Cooper came back to his father's house and won permission to go before the mast in a merchant ship to Europe. At the time, this was an oddly humble berth for a congressman's son, but William Cooper agreed that if James liked (and survived) the experiment, he might try for an officer's warrant in the U.S. Navy. Here was a career suited to an active young man enamored of gunpowder.

As an ordinary seaman on the merchant vessel *Stirling*, Cooper saw a great deal of the world on that year-long adventure, from the Thames estuary and the sights of London to the Bay of Biscay, Gibraltar, and the warm, exotic south coast of Spain. He also got his fill of history. The ill-fated British admiral, Lord Nelson, recently had beaten back the French naval threat at Trafalgar, past which Cooper's ship passed. But Napoleon was still wreaking havoc on the Continent and the seas were thick with English patrols and venturesome pirates. The spectacle remained vivid in Cooper's mind to the end of his life. Yet it was politics rather than the war itself that most deeply affected him. Of wholly English ancestry, he had been raised by his Federalist father as a thoroughgoing Anglophile. What he saw of English policies and attitudes in 1806–1807, however, turned him against the motherland and made him instead a decided nationalist. British warships chased pirates away from the *Stirling*, but they also routinely stopped and boarded American vessels with impunity, kidnapping the best seamen of whatever nationality—Swedish, American, English, it didn't matter—and forcing them to serve in the Royal Navy. Cooper himself saw several such men seized. Even his Maine captain was grabbed while in London, to be rescued only when Cooper rushed ashore with the man's papers to prove that down-easter John Johnston was, of course, no subject of the king. On another occasion, the seventeen-year-old sailor risked his own skin by intervening (unsuccessfully this time) between a fellow crewman and a British boarding party. His anger at such encounters matured into a profound distaste for England and the English during his two longish visits in London and its environs. The seeming arrogance of the English toward Americans, an implicit rejection of what the Revolution had proved, rankled in Cooper's mind and helped shape his politics and his art for the rest of his life. In this sense, he was a perfectly postcolonial writer.

Later in his life, Cooper reminisced about his merchant seaman days in *Ned Myers* (1843), an as-told-to sketch of the life of one of his unfortunate shipmates. He also based a portion of his four-volume nautical novel, *Afloat and Ashore* (1843–1844), on his experiences on the Atlantic and the Mediterranean in 1806–1807. But he did not just write *about* his nautical experience: he wrote *out of* it, creating and developing a new literary form, the sea novel, in a dozen books stretching from *The Pilot* (1824), *The Red Rover* (1828), and *The Water-Witch* (1830), to *The Two Admirals* (1842), *The Wing-and-Wing* (1842), *Jack Tier* (1848), and *The Sea Lions* (1849). Like his other great creation, the frontier tale, the sea novel was to be one of his most suggestive gifts to other writers, including such masters of the form as Herman Melville and Joseph Conrad, two other famous sailor-authors who fully praised him.

Cooper's European voyage confirmed his naval ambitions. Joining the navy would allow him to return to deep water, where, he hoped, he might protect American rights from British violence. Turning eighteen the very day his ship entered the capes of the Delaware and headed upriver to Philadelphia, he paid another brief inland visit to Cooperstown, then with his father's help secured his midshipman's warrant in January 1808.

Cooper's naval career began well but soon became a series of frustrating disappointments. His first posting was in New York waters, where he was assigned to the bomb ketch *Vesuvius*, a vessel in such poor condition that she was laid up for repairs from the start of the year until, in July, Cooper was reassigned to a largely symbolic mission: helping to oversee the construction of the nation's first war vessel on the Great Lakes. Only once, toward the end of his Lake Ontario service in July 1809, did the midshipman manage to spend much time on the water—fresh water at that—when he and his friend and commander, Melancthon T. Woolsey, fought their way against fierce headwinds all the way to Niagara in a launch, a run recreated in his Ontario romance, *The Pathfinder*.

So eager for real nautical life was Cooper that he now threatened to take a furlough from the service and go off on another merchant voyage. But he could find no suitable berth and, convinced he should give the navy a final try, he took up a new assignment in New York City. His hopes for stirring adventure aboard the sloop of war *Wasp*, commanded by the battle-tested hero James Lawrence, soon evaporated. Like the *Vesuvius*, this vessel was in such bad shape that she was laid up for repairs off the Brooklyn navy yard for the next several months. Worse yet, Cooper himself was stationed on land as a recruiting officer. Naval recruiting was a disagreeable business in 1810: officers would rent cheap quarters at a waterside tavern, encourage the landlord to liquor up desperate seamen, set a band playing patriotic ditties, and then move in for the inevitable consequence of too much drink, too little cash, and a murky sense of duty. Cooper later swore that he tried to run things on a higher level, but given the usual practices of that era, "higher" was a decidedly relative term. By late March, when the *Wasp* at last was seaworthy, he happily bid his recruiting rendezvous good-bye and rushed aboard for a quick run to Boston. That brief experience, Cooper's only salt-sea voyage during two and a half years of navy life, was also his farewell to a venture that had fulfilled none of his ambitions. Once back in New York in the spring of 1810, he took a furlough and never really looked back.[5]

Other things were pulling him away. His wealthy father had died the previous December, apparently ensuring James's financial independence. Cooper would not need any career, certainly not the unsatisfying one offered by the navy. Furthermore, the heir to a sixth part of Judge Cooper's large estate had very good personal reasons for staying ashore. He recently had met and wanted to marry Susan DeLancey, a pretty young member of a distinguished family that had sided with Britain during the Revolution, but she would not agree unless he promised to abandon his military dreams. When he married her on New Year's Day 1811, Cooper no doubt imagined a life of well-heeled bliss with Susan and their children (eventually they had seven, five of whom survived to adulthood) near her family at their Westchester County, New York, estate or among the Coopers of Cooperstown.

The newlyweds spent their first two and a half years in Westchester before relocating, in July 1813, to a parcel of land overlooking Otsego Lake, where they lived in a modest new frame dwelling while work slowly progressed on their large stone mansion. Cooper raised sheep and dabbled in local affairs, helping to organize county Bible and agricultural societies. All seemed relatively peaceful and prosperous. But appearances were deceptive. From 1809 to 1819, Cooper's older brothers in sequence served as executors of their father's estate. There was a good deal of debt on the books, some of it long neglected, and most of the estate's assets were in real estate (including a preponderance of wild or minimally developed land on the Canadian border) rather than in cash or other, more secure investments. When land prices began to fall along the northern New York frontier during the War of 1812, and continued low after peace returned early in 1815, a crisis began to gather for the family at large. As their wealth evaporated, and the older Cooper sons coincidentally died (all four of them were gone by 1819, none having reached the age of forty), James was left to preside alone over the collapse of the wheelwright William Cooper's grand design. His old illusion of an easy future was dying fast.

Precipitating the end was a series of court suits brought by the son of a long-dead creditor, Thomas Bridgen. The elder Cooper had been a partner of Bridgen's father in the 1790s in a doomed attempt to sell parcels in a tract, originally set aside for New York veterans, where land titles proved hopelessly confused. William Cooper took in virtually nothing from the venture but remained legally obligated to pay Bridgen some $4,500 for the sales. Although the principal was cut in half over the next few years, interest on the unpaid balance kept accruing, until by 1818 young Thomas Bridgen was due more than $11,000. In better times, the Coopers could have paid him off handily. But 1819, ushering in a financial panic that sent land prices lower still, was not among those better times. When the last of his older brothers died in October of that year, James Cooper inherited the somber duty of trying to settle with the Bridgens even though he had few assets with which to do so.

Ultimately, the Bridgen claim ate up most of the remaining assets of the Cooper family, including the grand home, Otsego Hall, begun by William Cooper in 1798 as part of his scheme to welcome his homesick wife back from Burlington. Modeled on the mansion of Stephen Van Rensselaer, the "patron" or lord of the enormous Dutch manor of Rensselaerwyck near Albany, and valued at $15,000 in William Cooper's will, the Cooper mansion brought a mere $1,650 at auction in 1821. The family's favorite picnic grounds, Three Mile Point on the lake above Cooperstown, fetched just $30. Soon the forced sales turned toward other family holdings. Four thousand acres in Broome County, near Binghamton, New York, netted $1,600, a tenth of its value in the Cooper will; another twenty-five thousand acres located in St. Lawrence County, near the Canadian border and worth $50,000 on paper, realized a tenth of that amount. For a year, all over the state, the Cooper family bled money.[6]

These legal troubles arose at a time when James Cooper himself was also finding money hard to come by. Having borrowed heavily for years on the expectation of a rich inheritance, he was caught short as the estate's assets evaporated. As early as the spring of 1817, Cooper and his wife closed up their farmhouse on the lake, abandoned the still unfinished stone mansion, and returned to live a more frugal existence in Westchester, first with her family but then in an inexpensive new house hastily erected on land given them as a help by Susan's father. On a speculation, Cooper set up a cousin in a general store in St. Lawrence County that same year, using borrowed funds for the purpose; he and Susan also began disposing of any salable lands then in their hands; and they continued to borrow money, sometimes at usurious interest rates, in the hope that they might ride out the bad times and regroup afterward.

Cooper undertook two other financial speculations in this period. In 1819, he formed another partnership, bought a merchant ship, fitted her out as a whaler, and sent her in three successive years to the rich whaling grounds of the South Atlantic. The expensive investment paid reasonably good returns each time. It also stocked Cooper's memory with images he would draw on in his nautical tales from *The Pilot* to *The Sea Lions*. But it offered no permanent solution to his financial ills. Fortunately, it did not have to. Following his family's return to Westchester, Cooper began spending a good deal of time in Manhattan. It was there, for instance, that he found his future whaler early in 1819 and then saw to her repair and refitting before his partner took her out Long Island Sound to the whaling port of Sag Harbor that July and saw her on her way. While lingering in the city, Cooper renewed old acquaintances and made new ones. He socialized with the politicians, lawyers, wits, editors, and businessmen who constituted the city's intelligentsia and who in their spare time were authoring the literary works for which the city was becoming well-known in the United States at large. Buying a membership in the circulating library of bookseller Andrew T. Goodrich, Cooper avidly read American books and British imports, whiling away his free hours but all the time planting the seeds of a new, secret ambition.

Early in 1820, with his whaler still in the South Atlantic, Cooper abandoned the city for an extended stay in Westchester. Among his oldest acquaintances in New York was former mayor and republican DeWitt Clinton, now serving in Albany as state governor. Clinton rewarded Cooper's friendship with a series of appointments to the officer corps of the Westchester militia starting in 1819. In return, when Clinton stood for reelection the following spring, Cooper energetically ran the governor's campaign in Westchester. With his candidate's victory in April, Cooper would have ended his exile from the city except for a sudden event: the unexpected death of his mother-in-law, Elizabeth DeLancey, from typhoid fever. Susan Cooper took the loss hard, and her husband, striving to lighten her thoughts, spent much time reading aloud to her from recent books, mostly imported English novels he no doubt had borrowed from Andrew Goodrich's collection. On one particular occasion, Cooper took a dislike to the book he was reading and flung it down, boasting, "I could write you a better book than that myself!"[7] The claim was outrageous coming from Cooper, who was notoriously uncomfortable even holding a pen in his hand, let alone inscribing page after page of script. But for some time he appears to have been contemplating the stunning financial success of one British novelist in particular, Walter Scott, whose phenomenal earnings from his historical romances since 1814 were widely reported in the American press. If Cooper could somehow look into his own heart and mind and write, he, too, might find the means to reverse his losses and secure his future and that of Susan and their children. Frontier stores and whale ships caused endless effort, consumed large quantities of scarce resources, called Cooper away from home with insistence, and offered no certain returns. Writing, if he could manage to do it at all, was something he could accomplish at home—something that, comparatively, would cost very little. In contemporary New York society, furthermore, it was a perfectly acceptable vocation, or at least avocation, for a gentleman.

Cooper did not feel comfortable blurting out these wild thoughts to his wife in May 1820. Hence his somewhat staged disgust with the British tale. When Susan, at first incredulous, encouraged him to make good on his boast, however, Cooper immediately began what he called a "moral tale" and wrote enough of it to think that he should, indeed, attempt a full-length novel.[8] Discarding the first attempt, he plunged into the second with such energy that within three weeks he had written thirty-three chapters. With his wife's continuing support, he decided that he would try to publish it. Soon he was making arrangements with bookseller Goodrich to see it through the press.

Precaution (1820), as the book was called, owed a good deal to English writers such as Amelia Opie and Jane Austen. It centered on the marital anxieties of three genteel families sequestered in the English countryside in the last years of the Napoleonic era, a topic about which Cooper of course knew very little. Barely had he finished the book before he began a second, much more ambitious novel. This one, *The Spy* (1821), was stimulated by a convergence of sources and purposes. Cooper had long been intrigued by the drifting lore of the American Revolution, in part because this defining national event had happened just before his birth, and in part because so few of his largely pacifist relatives had taken any active part in it. We know that Judge Cooper's brother, who *had* fought in the war, shared revolutionary anecdotes with his young namesake, anecdotes that remained fresh in Cooper's memory decades afterward. We also know that other veterans who settled in the Cooperstown vicinity, among them one of the schoolmasters under whom young Cooper first studied, had similarly riveting tales to pass on.

Some narratives of the war were the boastful tales of the victors. But Cooper also was exposed to (and particularly attracted to) the darker aspects of what had been, after all, a civil war as well as a successful Revolution against British authority. While at Yale, he became especially close to a young professor, Benjamin Silliman, whose father, General Gold Selleck Silliman of the Connecticut militia, had suffered profoundly at the hands of the new state government he had heroically helped establish. In Westchester, Cooper's neighbors recalled for him the ravages visited on that area, where American and British armies continually skirmished and irregular forces on both sides harried the local residents throughout the war. From the statesman John Jay, a close friend of Judge Cooper, the budding novelist knew details of the spies who had operated in that region, often at great risk of exposure and death. Even closer to home, Cooper knew well that his wife's family, the loyalist DeLanceys, had fallen from a position of great power in New York as the colonial regime collapsed.

All of these sources contributed to Cooper's decision to site his second novel in the difficult historical terrain, the "neutral ground," just outside his Westchester window. The kind of tale he would tell was determined, clearly enough, by his wish to emulate Walter Scott, whose masterful novels of the Scottish borderlands, beginning with *Waverley* (1814), had established a new literary mode. But Cooper, criticized by some of his New York friends for setting *Precaution* in Britain, would not repeat that mistake. Now he was writing a decidedly *American* novel, a story of espionage and personal sacrifice centered on the ideological issues that had come to define American political and cultural identity—and, indeed, Cooper himself as a self-conscious "Americanist"—in the country's postcolonial period.

The book, the first successful American historical novel, went through three editions in its first few months. Its public acceptance convinced Cooper that he not only could contribute to current debates about national culture but also could make a living from literature. Because his financial situation was worsening throughout the period when he wrote the book (in fact, he renewed his commitment to the interrupted project precisely when his father's Cooperstown mansion was put up for auction in the fall of 1821), the second insight was crucial. What had begun as a staged boast in May 1820 had become a career by the start of 1822.

Cooper already knew what his third book would concern. Based on his own experience on the Otsego frontier, it defined for a nation furiously expanding to the West the deeper meanings of its pioneer experience. To later generations familiar with the western as a literary and cinematic form, Cooper's innovations may be less apparent than they were at the time. He was the novelist who first christened the settlers "pioneers"; this was no cliché, but a fresh borrowing from the military lexicon, a borrowing that suggested a good deal about the militancy, even violence, of nation building. Moreover, in the debauched but at last reinvigorated figure of Chingachgook, Natty Bumppo's Mohican companion, Cooper for the first time gave a Native American character a complex literary expression, showing both the devastation visited on Chingachgook by white society and his inherent nobility. Cooper performed a similar transformation on the white frontiersman himself. Long viewed as an ignorant, self-indulgent refugee from civilization, the backwoodsman was transformed by Cooper into a stoic hero notable for his self-control—as well a political symbol well suited to a country on the verge of the Jacksonian revolution. (Cooper, following De-Witt Clinton's lead, was to be a strong supporter of Andrew Jackson because of Jackson's championing of the ordinary American. When Jackson's first run for the presidency, in 1824, resulted in an electoral tie, Cooper traveled to Washington to observe firsthand the resulting runoff in the House of Representatives.)

In addition to these other important accomplishments, *The Pioneers* painted alluring pictures of the typical scenes of border life: sleighing at Christmas, a turkey shoot, the mindless slaughter of seemingly endless (but eventually exterminated) flocks of passenger pigeons, night fishing under torchlight on the lake, maple sugaring, a roaring forest fire set by the villagers who chase down Natty Bumppo—"kearless fellows," as Leatherstocking scornfully describes them, "who thought to catch a practys'd hunter in the woods after dark."[9] Such word-pictures captivated readers and inspired painters, who from this point on in Cooper's career found his art a rich inspiration for their own.

For these reasons and others, Cooper's third novel was a huge success, selling 3,500 copies the first morning in New York. The sales were particularly gratifying because, although Cooper now was issuing his books through a larger New York firm, Wiley & Halsted, who acted more as his publishers than just his agents, he still retained ownership of his works. Like Cooper's frontier store and his whale ship—and real estate, his family's source of wealth and woe alike—authorship was a speculation aimed at profit. Although that attitude had its deleterious side, Cooper's constant pursuit of profit in fact helped establish literature as a viable commercial venture in the United States. He not only tried out new forms and formulas that would prove appealing (and profitable) for his contemporaries and followers, but he also established models for managing a literary career, thereby demonstrating that writing could be a profession rather than just an avocation. For a democratic culture in which the market was already becoming the test of success, this was a complex and fertile innovation.

More success followed when Cooper, well into his most innovative period, published a fourth novel in as many years. *The Pilot* was a direct, defiant challenge to Walter Scott, whose *The Pirate* (1822), in Cooper's view, showed its British author to be only superficially acquainted with the sailor's life on the open ocean. Readers who may have been mystified by the maritime argot Cooper deployed in his book could find ample reward in its romantic conception of the sea and the book's historical aspects; it was a second Revolutionary War novel, focused on the career of the mysterious John Paul Jones. Such a mixture of modes was to become an increasingly important aspect of Cooper's fiction. In his fifth book, *Lionel Lincoln* (1825), he thus joined Revolutionary War events (including the Battle of Bunker Hill, so vividly recreated that historian George Bancroft would praise it as a tour de force) with a first attempt at Gothic themes, madness and midnight obscurity being important in the book, along with the motif of concealed identity. But *Lionel Lincoln*, despite its impressive aspects, was not a success, forcing Cooper to abandon his ambitious plan for a series of "Legends of the Thirteen Republics" that it was announced as initiating.

The book was Cooper's (and his readers') first letdown, but it was soon forgotten in the huge popular and financial success that greeted Cooper's next book, *The Last of the Mohicans*. Inarguably his most widely read novel, it has never been out of print since and has been translated and retranslated into many languages. That its title has entered popular culture as a catch phrase is another instance of how deeply Cooper's invention has penetrated the popular mind. But the sixth book, a classic instance of the flight-and-pursuit formula in popular fiction, is also something more. For one thing, even as it succeeded in introducing the idea of wilderness adventure to readers, activating the American forest as a domain of seemingly unique spatial and natural conditions, it also began Cooper's lifelong experiment in adumbrating the life of his most extraordinary inventions, Natty Bumppo and

Chingachgook. Hints hidden away in the old hunter's monologues in *The Pioneers* provided the basic framework for Cooper's elaboration of the man's heroic participation with his Mohican allies in "the Old French War," when America was not a nation but a collection of colonies happily subdued under the protective shield of Britain. As a prequel to *The Pioneers*, the second Leatherstocking tale was aesthetically as well as financially profitable. It did not repeat the formulas of the first book but fleshed out their background, revealing the genuine skills of the old hunter who served as Elizabeth Temple's quasi-humorous knight in the 1823 novel. In Uncas, the tragic Mohegan hero, it also solidified the "good Indian" as a signal figure in Cooper's fictional universe.

With *The Last of the Mohicans*, Cooper once more changed his business partners: Carey & Lea became his nominal publishers, although again he retained ownership of his works, merely licensing them to that Philadelphia firm for set periods of time. Soon he also licensed Carey & Lea to reissue his earlier novels, an arrangement that ensured the continuing availability of most of them from 1827 on. It was a time to consolidate his literary business. His books had been widely reprinted in England and on the European Continent almost from the beginning. Even *Precaution* was pirated (that is, reprinted without payment to the author) in 1821 and appeared in German in 1826 and in French the following year. *The Spy* likewise was pirated in London in 1822, and unauthorized translations appeared in Paris the same year, in Leipzig in 1824, and in Stockholm in 1825–1826. From none of these editions, or their frequent reprints, did Cooper receive a penny. This was not for lack of trying. He had sought to sell even *Precaution* to an English publisher, but with that book and *The Spy* the pirates acted before arrangements could be made for legal foreign editions. Thereafter he had increasing luck. He succeeded in selling the English rights of *The Pioneers* and his next three books to London publishers. These deals brought him some income; however, most of his books still were issued in pirated versions that gave him no direct monetary benefit and often mangled his original texts.

With his sales in America so brisk and remunerative but his financial needs still large, Cooper understandably eyed such foreign markets as potential sources of fresh, perhaps crucial, income. For some time he had been talking about taking his family to Europe for an extended visit. He thought living expenses there might be cheaper than in New York City, where he and Susan, having had a falling-out over money issues with her family, had occupied a series of rented quarters since 1822. He also thought that the couple's five surviving children (they lost their first daughter in 1813 and first son in 1823) might be more thoroughly educated abroad. In addition, there were clear cultural benefits that would accrue to parents and children alike. But Cooper's main motivation for sailing to Europe with Susan and the children in June 1826 was the desire to capture hitherto elusive income from his books. On arriving in Paris the following month, he finished a new book, *The Prairie*, in which Natty Bumppo, now an aged trapper, is living out his last days among the Indians deep in the heart of the North American continent. From Paris, Cooper negotiated a lucrative deal with a new English publisher for the novel. At the same time, he hired a French printer who specialized in English-language texts to set *The Prairie* in type and produce multiple sets of proof sheets that Cooper then could distribute to his American and English publishers and, for additional sums, to various publishers and translators on the Continent. This ingenious procedure allowed him to deliver easily reproducible texts of his new books prior to their official publication, with the result that the piracy market for his works shrank.

With *The Prairie* on the market in London, Paris, and Philadelphia, by May 1827 Cooper turned his attention to several new projects. Although the lawsuits that had devastated his father's estate were now behind him, several related issues remained unresolved during his European sojourn, and his own financial situation was such that he needed to write as many books as he could and sell them for as much as possible. *The Red Rover*, a pirate tale and his second nautical novel, was issued in the fall; *Notions of the Americans* (1828), a fictionalized travelogue supposedly penned by a European count visiting the United States, came out the following summer; and *The Wept of Wish-ton-Wish* (a second settlement tale and Cooper's only story of seventeenth-century Puritan New England) appeared in September 1829. Continuing his established pace, Cooper soon published his eleventh novel in as many years, *The Water-Witch* (1830), another nautical romance, this one set in early eighteenth-century New York and notable for its exploration of the Dutch and French Huguenot backgrounds of that colony, in which his wife's family held a prominent place. Although none of these books matched Cooper's best from the middle of his first decade of writing, their disparate array added to the range and bulk of his work. Taken together, they demonstrated his adaptability and staying power. Across the period since he first threw down that unsatisfying English book and vowed to write a better one himself, Cooper had authored something like 10 percent of all the novels published by American authors. He was the dominant creative force in American fiction across that period.

Cooper was so celebrated in Europe that almost on his arrival in the French capital in 1826 he was sought out by writers, artists, and other celebrities. Scott himself, the greatest novelist of the age, came to call on Cooper unannounced at the latter's Paris lodgings. Lafayette, the great Franco-American patriot whom Cooper had briefly met during that man's triumphal return to the United States in 1824–1825, similarly courted him; indeed, he had been at the Coopers' lodgings, and had sat in the same chair as Scott, earlier on the very morning when Scott called. With Lafayette, about whom Cooper as a boy had heard tales from an Otsego schoolmaster, the tie led to a special intimacy. It was partly to chronicle Lafayette's American return that Cooper wrote (in fact, at the Frenchman's suggestion) *Notions of the Americans*. And later, as turbulent political changes in France raised and soon quashed hopes of important reforms, Cooper sided with Lafayette on the republican side of the divide. He did so in part to bring American principles to bear on European realities. Cooper and Lafayette also served to gather support from Americans resident in Europe for the Polish people when they rose up, also unsuccessfully, against their Russian masters.

In response to these challenges, Cooper began to use his pen to make the case for the principles of liberty and representative government. He did so directly in such publications as *Letter of J. Fenimore Cooper, to Gen. Lafayette* (1831), which countered European reactionary claims that republicanism was a costly form of government. More important, he used fiction itself for polemical ends. In the early 1830s, he published a trio of European tales: *The Bravo* (1831), a novel set in eighteenth-century Venice that explored the corrupting influence of great wealth and power; *The Heidenmauer* (1832), a sixteenth-century Bavarian tale focused on the conflicts among three entrenched institutions—the church, the aristocracy, and the rising bourgeoisie—at the time of the Reformation; and *The Headsman* (1833), whose title character, the hereditary executioner of the canton of Berne in Switzerland, embodies the arbitrary injustice of inherited position and privilege, a key republican target. This trilogy met with unequal response. The first and second books did reasonably well, particularly *The Bravo*, sales of which were especially strong in Europe. Those two books were also notable for the seriousness with which Cooper, at the time so closely identified with New World adventure, shifted theme and technique to accommodate both his new surroundings and the current crisis in European culture and politics.

The European trilogy represented another aspect of Cooper's evolution as a writer in his second decade: the way his experience of European society since 1826 had affected his sensibility. His travels across western Europe were extensive. Having stayed in Paris and its environs (including St. Ouen) from July 1826 until February 1828, Cooper spent the next eight months traveling in England, the Lowlands, Germany, and Switzerland before taking up residence in various Italian locales, especially Florence (October 1828–July 1829), Naples (July–August 1829), Sorrento (August–November 1829), and Rome (December 1829–April 1830). He then sojourned in Dresden in the summer of 1830 (where he worked on the proofs of *The Water-Witch*) before rushing back to Paris, where the July Revolution that so concerned Lafayette was in full swing. From there, he visited Belgium and Germany (September 1831 and again in summer 1832) and Switzerland (August–October

1832). He also made two trips to London (June–July and August–September 1833), the second just before embarking for New York with his family. And he planned, but did not undertake, even more widely ranging trips, to Russia and to Turkey and Greece.

Cooper's explorations of these differing venues fed his large appetite for natural and cultural landscape. Already, in his American tales and his sea novels, he had shown himself intrigued with experience in space as both historical fact and fictional motif. *The Spy* had used the Revolution's neutral ground of Westchester as an apt figure for the moral uncertainties that surround most human action. In *The Pioneers* and *The Last of the Mohicans*, the forest landscapes of Otsego and the Adirondacks were richly described and powerfully employed. In his nautical tales, the ocean was not backdrop but environment, a complex, ever-changing milieu capable of shaping and coloring human experience.

Prior to his European sojourn, Cooper had used Old World settings sparingly and in a largely derivative way, only in *Precaution* and (through John Paul Jones's raiding of the English coast) *The Pilot*. His American readers made it clear that they preferred more familiar settings. His European readers reinforced this imperative by their hunger for those same settings, which for his Old World audience seemed fresh and exotic. Even after going to Europe in 1826, Cooper therefore continued to employ American settings: the upper Midwest in *The Prairie*, the waters off Newport in *The Red Rover*, Connecticut in *The Wept of Wish-ton-Wish*, greater New York in *The Water-Witch*. Only the crisis in contemporary politics across Europe in the early 1830s motivated him to expand the coverage of his fiction.

In turning to Old World settings, he used scenes with which he was personally familiar. In *The Bravo* (the title of which means "cutthroat"), eighteenth-century Venice, a nominal republic but virtual oligarchy, was a perfect vehicle for indicating the dangerous pattern of oppressive fraud he saw everywhere in contemporary European society. Venice was not his actual target—England was, and with special urgency in 1831, so now was France. The Italian city, which Cooper had visited for the first time in the spring of 1830, was settled on for the book because, as he wrote a New York friend in 1831, it had "seized my fancy . . . in a man-

ner not to be spoken of."[10] Its appropriateness for Cooper's
theme was the result of artful elaboration.

In *The Heidenmauer* and *The Headsman*, Cooper similarly exploited other parts of the European landscape that had evoked
strong personal reactions during his travels. The former book
opens with a long introductory narrative of a journey from Paris
through war-torn Brussels to the Rhine, and at last to "Duerck-
heim," the Bavarian town where the novel proper was to be set.
Cooper himself made essentially that journey in the fall of 1831,
when, with his work on *The Bravo* completed, he took Susan and
their two youngest children for a three-week excursion that
included a visit to the famous Heidenmauer ruin near Bad Dürk-
heim. It was during that visit that the local scenery struck
Cooper's fancy and determined him to site the second of his political novels there. With *The Headsman*, a similar visit to Lake
Geneva immediately after work was finished on *The Heidenmauer*
(September–October 1832) inspired Cooper to undertake his
third tale, in which a good deal of what he saw and experienced
at Vevey and its surroundings provided scenic background and
episodes. As had been true of many of his books since *The Spy*,
The Pioneers, and *The Last of the Mohicans*, Cooper's personal investment in a real place helped determine not only where he set
his tales but also how he developed them.

In some ways, Cooper's turn away from the American settings
that had dominated his work from the beginning up to 1830 suggests a certain loss of continuity between himself and his native
land. Perhaps sensing that some such disconnection might occur,
he had intended to stay abroad no longer than five years. Even in
The Water-Witch, which appeared as that deadline neared, he had
been able to *imagine* America, so to speak, from the distance.
With the European trilogy, however, America was no longer a
place for Cooper; partly due to his lengthening absence and
partly due to the surging political events of the new decade in
Europe and their effect on him, it had become an idea. For his
readers in the United States, the importance of the American
idea in these new works did not entirely compensate for the ab-

sence of the place itself. Cooper seemed to some Americans not a defender of their homeland but a renegade whose lingering abroad and involvement in foreign political and social causes were tantamount to abandonment.

There was a plausible appearance to such an interpretation, but something other than plausibility was at work in the consequent plunge of Cooper's reputation. New political forces rising in America that had their counterpart among the retrograde opponents of Lafayette seized on Cooper as a visible and vocal target. In the newly expanding newspaper culture of the 1830s, he became the object of outlandish, highly personal attacks. The appearance of new books provided an excuse for fresh assaults, disguised as literary criticism, on his private character.

Much of the bitterness and vituperation that resulted from Cooper's pillorying in the public press awaited his return from Europe in the fall of 1833, just as *The Headsman* was appearing. Already, however, Cooper had decided to take his revenge on a public he no longer completely understood. His feelings were certainly hurt; perhaps more important, he was tired of the perpetual busyness of authorship, driven as it had been by his need for income. The European trilogy reveals the exhaustion. So does the last book he began in Europe while at work on the trilogy (but finished in America), a Swiftian voyage narrative entitled *The Monikins* (1835). This book was, in a sense, the perfect conclusion to the trilogy: the imaginary monkey nations visited by his Antarctic voyager, Leaphigh (England) and Leaplow (the United States), represent the collapse of landscape as such and the substitution of mere ideas for it. They also express the author's disillusionment with a country for whose values he had fought, in person and as a writer, while in the midst of the corrupt political scenes of the Old World. Small wonder that, even before *The Monikins* was finished, Cooper penned *A Letter to His Countrymen* (1834), in which he seemingly threatened to end a literary career that had quickly led to popularity in the early 1820s but that now left him a figure of attack and ridicule.

In fact, Cooper had no intention of laying aside his pen completely. Not only did he persevere and finish *The Monikins*; he already was thinking of shifting gears even more dramatically, embarking on a series of European travel narratives that would use his personal experience abroad as an overt framework for analyzing the cultural, social, and political realities of the modern world—without the need, which in fiction might well be imperative, to entertain his readers with coy inventions. There followed in quick succession five works of nonfiction: *Sketches of Switzerland* (1836); *Sketches of Switzerland (Part Second)* (1836); *Gleanings in Europe* (1837); *Gleanings in Europe: England* (1837); and *Gleanings in Europe: Italy* (1838). The first of these works, covering Cooper's 1828 travels from Paris through Neufchâtel to Berne, with side trips to such places as Zürich and the Brienzer Zee, represents his early, relatively apolitical stance; it is a picturesque account that owes a good deal to older styles of travel writing. The second part of *Sketches*, which begins in the throes of the 1830 Revolution in Paris, is quite the opposite; as it goes on to narrate the Cooper family's 1832 visit to Belgium, Germany, and Switzerland, the reader is aware that a sharper, more mature social observer is in control of the prose.

The first of the three *Gleanings in Europe* volumes is concerned with the early years in France, from the voyage over in 1826 to early 1828. The English narrative picks up the story at that point in time, recounting Cooper's extended stay in England with his wife, their son, and his nephew William, who was serving as Cooper's amanuensis. It also reaches back in time to Cooper's three earlier visits to the country: two relatively long stays as a young sailor before the mast in 1806–1807, plus a brief stopover while on his way to Paris in 1826. And it inserts other observations drawn from the family's farewell trip in the fall of 1833. Even as it draws together these disparate occasions, the book manages to transcend them, becoming a sharply critical examination of English society and politics as Cooper had reflected on them for most of his adult life. Here, as his long-simmering dislike of English condescension (and aggression) continually surfaces, Cooper's postcolonial voice is most clearly audible.

By contrast, his final travel book, the Italian *Gleanings*, is mostly sunshine and sea views, a wistful recreation of his long Italian residence from the fall of 1828 to the spring of 1830. Italy was, his wife said, the only country he ever left looking back over his shoulder; he himself, writing to sculptor Horatio Greenough in the very year he was composing his Italian travels, longed to go back there: "We may yet meet in Italy. Italy! The very name excites a glow in me, for it is the only region of the earth that I truly love. I tire of Switzerland, France I never liked, and Germany, though pleasant, excites no emotion, but Italy lives in my dreams."[11]

Cooper had left Italy, however, and all of Europe, for good in 1833. Indeed, even before then he was dreaming of his old American home, to which he would endeavor to renew his long-buried emotional attachment. He very much wanted to return to Cooperstown, where he had not set foot in sixteen years; he therefore began negotiations even while in Europe to at last settle his father's estate and, if possible, repurchase the now ramshackle family mansion from its present owner. That man was agreeable, and within a few months of his return to New York City, Cooper would undertake a satisfying pilgrimage upstate through the old, now haunted terrain. Soon he had carpenters at work renovating the vacant Hall, and for the summer of 1834, when he was finishing *The Monikins*, the whole family was back there. He wrote the two Swiss travel books there the following summer, and by May 1836 the finished building, now fashionably Gothic in look, became his permanent home.

The homecoming, to America and to Otsego, was not without its problems. The country had changed, but so had Cooper, and for several years the alienation between them worsened. Cooper did not overcome it with the four American books that, in addition to his Italian travels, he published in 1838: *Chronicles of Cooperstown*, an account of the village founded by his father and developed by his family; *The American Democrat*, a hard-headed analysis of the promise and foibles of the national political system; and *Homeward Bound* and *Home as Found*, two novels about an elite American family (the Effinghams, revived from *The Pioneers*) long resident in Europe but now returning to their old domain in Templeton, Cooper's fictional version of Cooperstown. The first of these books, published anonymously in Cooperstown, was unexceptionable enough. It stirred some local feelings, positive and negative, but did not rise to the level of national attention. The political tract, stimulated by Cooper's struggle to come to terms with the country from which he had been so long absent, was misinterpreted as an attack on democracy when in fact Cooper was defending its potential by excoriating its actualities. H. L. Mencken rightly noted in his edition of *The American Democrat* that Cooper was "probably the first American to write about America in a really frank spirit."[12]

The frankness had its price not only in this instance but also in the "Home" novels, which set the hornets' nest of Cooper's opponents abuzz and resulted in fresh attacks. Here, too, Cooper did not romanticize his native land, but directly attacked both venerated institutions (such as the press, in the person of the shifty journalist Steadfast Dodge) and a host of suspect public attitudes and assumptions. A particular sore point was created by Cooper's decision to import into the fictional landscape of Templeton his actual dispute with his neighbors over public use of the private family picnic ground on Lake Otsego, Three Mile Point, lost in the forced sales long before but since restored to the Coopers. Although Cooper's satire in many instances was well-honed (and just), the fracas that resulted from the "Home" novels, including many public trials over newspaper critiques of the book that were vicious attacks on Cooper, left a negative impression of the author in the public mind.

Similar reactions developed to some of Cooper's opinions in his next, much more serious literary effort, *The History of the Navy of the United States of America* (1839), a work long planned by the old midshipman. Here the issue centered on his view that the dominant interpretation of Commodore Oliver Hazard Perry's famous victory in the Battle of Lake Erie in 1813 did an injustice to another officer, Jesse Duncan Elliott, who was wrongly thought to have pulled back from engaging the enemy. Partisans of Perry and opponents of Cooper attacked the *History* for its courageous championing of Elliott, prompting more lawsuits and, eventually, Cooper's separate account of *The Battle of Lake Erie* (1843).

By that time, fortunately, Cooper had rediscovered his true calling and begun afresh his career as a popular American and international novelist. The renewal came with a final pair of Leather-stocking tales: *The Pathfinder* (1840) and *The Deerslayer* (1841). These books proved that Cooper had not, as his critics had been saying, lost his touch. They were so popular that one of his fiercest opponents, Albany newspaperman Thurlow Weed, read and enjoyed *The Pathfinder* even while in the midst of a bitter courtroom confrontation with the author.

One reason for Cooper's active return to fiction was his never satisfied need for cash; indeed, as book prices fell in the 1840s he wrote more works—a full sixteen novels from 1840 to his death, plus another half dozen titles—as he once more tried out new methods for deriving as much income from them as possible. But the works of his last decade hardly were potboilers. If Cooper admittedly faltered in *Mercedes of Castile* (1840), an attempt at inscribing the first voyage of Columbus, his other books of the period show vigor and innovation. Having experimented with and now brought to seeming conclusion the five-part saga of Natty Bumppo (although Cooper in fact toyed with the idea of writing a sixth Leatherstocking tale, this one to be set during the Revolution), he used the same principle in two fresh sets of novels: two books, both originally entitled *Afloat and Ashore* and focused on the quasi-autobiographical exploits of Miles Wallingford on land and sea in the early years of the nineteenth century; and the Littlepage tales, a trio of books documenting the life of an American family from the 1750s to the 1840s.[13] The first set, stimulated in large part by Cooper's chance reunion with a shipmate from his own days at sea and the subsequent collaboration of author and shipmate on the latter's tale, *Ned Myers*, comes closer than Cooper had since *The Pioneers* to deflecting his own experience into art. The second set could not have been more different in origin, for the Littlepage trilogy was written to prove a point, or rather a series of points, about an issue very much in debate in the early 1840s in New York State. Under laws held over from the colonial era, land ownership there was a complicated matter. Manors such as that of the Van Rensselaers of Albany gave a semifeudal quality to social relations even as the state began a vigorous democratic expansion. Cooper knew the manorial families well (Mrs. Cooper was related to several, and Cooper himself had gone to school with two of the Van Rensselaers while in Albany), but his imaginative reconstruction of the social texture of New York life over the preceding century was more than an apologia for his class, as some have claimed. Cooper saw the unrest over manorial institutions (such as the perpetual leases that bound tenants to the lands they had worked, in some cases, for generations) that swept through New York following the death of the most recent lord of Van Rensselaer manor in 1839 as one more consequence of the cultural invasion of New York by a social group he had distrusted ever since his tumultuous days at Yale: the transplanted New England Yankees who had begun pouring out of their native domain in the 1780s and by the 1820s had effectively taken over New York. That state had had very different social and cultural origins from Puritan New England (it was, of course, Dutch at the start, but it also was not defined by any single dominant ideology), and Cooper's larger effort in the Littlepage books was to explore the claims of regional differences in a nation that was still, in 1845, very much an aggregation of regions. The trilogy was a venture in local color before that mode had been fully accredited.

By virtue of their narrative technique, the Littlepage books likewise represented a significant innovation on Cooper's part. Told in the first person, as were the Wallingford novels and the travel books but very few of the books Cooper wrote prior to 1835, they exploited that narrative perspective with considerable finesse. All of the Littlepage books, even *The Redskins* (in which Cooper brought the Littlepage saga down to the present, importing the antirent riots of the 1840s as a source of fictional episodes), have moments of real energy, although only the first of them, *Satanstoe*, is a work of coherent imaginative power and real interest. Its narrator-hero, Corny Littlepage, returns to the site of Natty Bumppo's forest adventures in *The Last of the Mohicans*, but as a young ex-collegian rather than a hardened warrior. His social escapades in New York City (where he visits a vividly reconstructed Pinkster fair, an Afro-Dutch festival Cooper had witnessed just before the Yankee invaders had suppressed it), his cavorting on the wintry hills of Albany and the frozen Hudson River (exploits Cooper probably recalled form his schooldays there), and his trip north to view and manage family grants in the forest (copying Cooper's own trips to family lands on the Canadian border) all suggest that Cooper's investment in the story had to do with more than his immediate political environment in 1845.

With the three Littlepage tales published, Cooper entered the final phase of his career. His brief biographies of U.S. naval officers, published serially over the previous few years, were gathered in book form in 1846. Then came five last works of fiction: a shipwreck tale, *The Crater* (1847), a dystopian treatment of the weaknesses of democracy set on a volcanic island in the Pacific; *Jack Tier* (1848), a pirate romance set in Florida; *The Oak Openings* (1848), a midwestern reprise of *The Prairie* without Natty Bumppo; *The Sea Lions* (1849), an Antarctic tale drawing on Cooper's days as the owner of a whaling vessel and indebted to the recently completed U.S. naval exploring expedition under Charles Wilkes, nephew of his old New York confidante; and *The Ways of the Hour* (1850), a murder mystery set in New York City and Westchester. Although none of these books rises to the level of the Leatherstocking saga, all of them have interest and power.

Cooper long bore the ill effects of health problems that had originated during the financial trials of the early 1820s, but he was physically sound through this last period of creative effort until he fell seriously ill in 1851. Across that summer he was still at work on a final publication, the first history of the greater New York City area (which was to be mostly lost in a fire at his printer's), when his strength failed him and, on September 14, the eve of his sixty-second birthday, he died in Otsego Hall, as he had come to call the old family home that his art had enabled him to reclaim from the wreck of his father's once great fortune.

Within two weeks, a group of literary, political, and cultural lights of the day gathered in New York City under the direction of Washington Irving to plan an unprecedented memorial service in his honor. That service, held the following February, was led by statesman Daniel Webster. Cooper's close friend, the poet and newspaper editor William Cullen Bryant, delivered a long, admiring address on that occasion. He was followed by historian (and democratic politician) George Bancroft, novelist G. P. R. James, and others. Letters from writers Nathaniel Hawthorne, Richard Henry Dana, Ralph Waldo Emerson, Henry Wadsworth Long- fellow, Francis Parkman, William Gilmore Simms, and John Pendleton Kennedy were read to the assembly. All were warm with memories of how Cooper's works struck and affected them: Emerson, for instance, recalled the wide applause, including his own, that had greeted "that national novel," *The Pioneers*, on its first appearance almost three decades before.

But it was Herman Melville, his greatest sea tale just issued to a generally blank response, who sent perhaps the best tribute to Cooper's example. Everyone knew that Cooper had been a fierce combatant in a dozen causes, sometimes Quixotic but always worthy. Melville reminded them of what else he had been—and of the nation's obligation, now that he was gone, to treasure his memory. Melville offered his personal testimonial. Cooper's nov- els, he wrote, were "among the earliest I can remember, as in my boyhood producing a vivid and awakening power upon my mind." But there was much more to the story than a chance liter- ary encounter between two great writers of the sea. The trou- bles between Cooper and the country were, Melville wrote, only the inevitable result of literary fame. Cooper weathered them and came out unscathed because he "was a great, robust-souled man." Not everyone fully appreciated such things yet. But Mel- ville at this point in his own terminally disappointed career still had hope. A "grateful posterity," he added, would "take the best care of Fenimore Cooper." Perhaps Melville, presciently describ- ing his own future reputation here, was right about Cooper as well. Only now, however, a century and a half after Cooper's death and Melville's tribute to him, are we beginning to take the measure of the man and his accomplishments. The new edition of his works and, at last, the prospect of a full biography give hope that the cloud will lift.[14]

NOTES

1. On Cooper's family background, see Alan Taylor, *William Cooper's Town: Power and Persuasion on the Frontier of the Early Ameri-*

can Republic (New York: Knopf, 1995), and Wayne Franklin, "Fathering the Son: The Cultural Origins of James Fenimore Cooper," *Resources for American Literary Study* 21 (2001): 149–178. Because the novelist forbade his family from allowing access to his papers, a stricture largely honored by his descendents through several generations, Cooper's biographers have labored under unusual burdens. Earlier lives include the following: Thomas R. Lounsbury, *James Fenimore Cooper* (New York: Houghton Mifflin, 1882); Robert E. Spiller, *Fenimore Cooper, Critic of His Times* (New York: Minton, Balch, 1931); Henry W. Boynton, *James Fenimore Cooper* (New York: Century, 1931); Marcel Clavel, *Fenimore Cooper: Sa Vie et Son Oeuvre* (Aix: Imprimerie Universitaire de Provence, 1938); and James Grossman, *James Fenimore Cooper* (New York: William Sloane, 1949). Published versions of primary sources for the study of Cooper's life include James Fenimore Cooper (1858–1938), ed., *Correspondence of James Fenimore Cooper*, 2 vols. (New Haven: Yale University Press, 1922), and James Franklin Beard Jr., ed., *Letters and Journals of James Fenimore Cooper*, 6 vols. (Cambridge, MA: Harvard University Press, 1960–1968). Major manuscript holdings are at Yale University and the American Antiquarian Society. The present writer has in preparation a two-volume biography, which will be the first to thoroughly employ these resources; volume 1 will be published by Yale in 2007.

2. See Ralph Birdsall, *The Story of Cooperstown* (New York: Scribner's, 1925) and James Arthur Frost, *Life on the Upper Susquehanna, 1783–1860* (New York: Columbia University Press, 1951).

3. William Cooper wrote up his own story as a kind of promotional pamphlet shortly before his death in 1809; see *A Guide in the Wilderness* (Dublin, 1810; rpt. Cooperstown, NY: Paul F. Cooper Jr., 1986), 13.

4. This important question deserves careful documentation. For the Cooper family's familiarity with displaced New England Mohicans settled near Cooperstown in the village of New Stockbridge, see Susan Fenimore Cooper, *Rural Hours* (New York: George P. Putnam, 1850), 7/17/1849 (pp. 178–179), which tells of the visit to the Cooper home of a family bearing the name Kunkerpott, who claimed "an hereditary acquaintance with the master of the house." Despite Susan's suspicion that the name in question was a laughable tag applied to this family by the German settlers in the Mohawk valley, in fact these were clearly Stockbridge Indians then located on

Oneida lands. Konkapot was a common Stockbridge family name, and Jacob Konkapot was a settler in New Stockbridge; see Patrick Frazier, *The Mohicans of Stockbridge* (Lincoln: University of Nebraska Press, 1992), 1–3, 21–35; W. Deloss Love, *Samson Occom and the Christian Indians of New England*, ed. Margaret Connell Szasz (Syracuse, NY: Syracuse University Press, 2000), 256, 260. See also the recollection of two prominent Stockbridge leaders by tribe member Levi Konkapot Jr., "The Last of the Mohicans," *Wisconsin Historical Collections* 4 (1859): 303–307). Natty Bumppo's reference in *The Pioneers* to "them Yankee Indians, who, they say, be moving up from the seashore," is to such New England migrants; see *The Pioneers, or the Sources of the Susquehanna*, ed. James Franklin Beard, Lance Schachterle, and Kenneth M. Andersen Jr. (Albany: State University of New York Press, 1980), 452. The novelist clearly had continuing contact with members of these displaced groups; see, for instance, his somewhat skeptical comments in 1840 to President Martin Van Buren regarding a local Brotherton Indian who had reported to Cooper, based on news forwarded east from his kin in Wisconsin, rumors that the British were stirring up midwestern Indians against the United States: *Letters and Journals*, 4: 25–26.

5. A sketch of Cooper's naval experience is offered by Louis H. Bolander, "The Naval Career of James Fenimore Cooper," *U.S. Naval Institute Proceedings* 66 (1940): 541–550.

6. These details derive from legal records and Bridgen family papers I recently discovered.

7. Susan Fenimore Cooper, "Small Family Memories," in *Correspondence*, 1: 38.

8. *Letters and Journals*, 1: 42. My inferential interpretation of Cooper's "secret" ambition rests on a variety of sources, most particularly on his dedication of a copy of *Precaution* in 1825 to British American banker Charles Wilkes. Cooper there revealed that his close friend Wilkes, who was quite familiar with the financial situation of Walter Scott, alone knew "the secret history of [the book's] authorship." The story later told by Cooper's daughter about his spontaneous disgust with that British novel directly contradicted his own contemporary statement. For the Wilkes dedication, see *The Spy, A Tale of the Neutral Ground*, ed. Lance Schachterle, James P. Elliott, and Jeffrey Walker (New York: AMS Press, 2002), xiii.

9. *Pioneers*, 414–415.

10. *Letters and Journals*, 2: 75.

11. James Fenimore Cooper, *Gleanings in Europe: Italy*, ed. Constance Ayers Denne (Albany: State University of New York Press, 1980), 295; *Letter and Journals*, 3: 233.

12. James Fenimore Cooper, *The American Democrat* (New York: Knopf, 1931), xii.

13. Cooper confusingly published both novels with that title in Philadelphia; only after his death did Stringer and Townsend retitle the second *Miles Wallingford*.

14. *Memorial of James Fenimore Cooper* (New York: G. P. Putnam, 1852), 33, 30.

COOPER
IN HIS TIME

"More Than a Woman's Enterprise"

Cooper's Revolutionary Heroines and the Source of Liberty

John P. McWilliams

> And the women he draws from one model don't vary,
> All sappy as maples and flat as a prairie.
>
> *James Russell Lowell (1848)* [1]

James Russell Lowell's smarty couplet with its three flashy puns ("sappy," "flat," and "prairie") has had a very long reach. From Lowell's era to ours, Cooper has been regarded as a particularly male novelist, whether as the creator of the sea tale, as a fabricator of adventure plots suitable for dime novels, Classic Comics and bloody B movies, as a mythic romancer of male bonding (according to D. H. Lawrence and Leslie Fiedler), or as a keen observer of Republican and Jacksonian political persuasions. Harvey Birch, Leatherstocking, Judge Temple, Indian John, and Uncas still retain their resonance, not only in Cooper criticism, but also in ever-changing reconstructions of American literary traditions, such as the recent interest in the social construction of manhood. As Jonathan Arac has observed, relations among Cooper's major male characters, both Euro- and Native American, comprised America's first "national narrative," preceding and influencing the national narratives of both George Bancroft and Francis Parkman.[2]

Cooper's women, however, remain at the vanishing margin of critical interest. The characterization of Alice Munro, that helpless cipher from *The Last of the Mohicans*, encourages the widespread assumption that Cooper's stock heroine is a vapid compendium of propriety and conventionality who simply waits, smilingly or tearfully, through lifeless chapters of stilted dialogue to marry her propertied, handsome lover at novel's end.[3]

The heroines of Cooper's later novels, Anneke Mordaunt and Dus Malbone of the Littlepage manuscripts notwithstanding, often affirm this impression. Until Cooper wrote *The Ways of the Hour* (1850), he remained tacitly dismissive when writing directly about women's issues. It is telling that *The American Democrat*, despite its breadth of insight into American culture and institutions, contains not even one chapter with a title such as "On Women." Because the marital destinies of most women were clearly prescribed, the duties of women could be fleetingly and confidently summarized, as in two sentences of a subsection titled "On the Private Duties of Station": " 'Nevertheless,' says St. Paul, 'let every one of you in particular, so love his wife, even as himself; and the wife see that she reverences her husband.' There is an obligation of deference imposed on the wife, that is not imposed on the husband."[4] It is little wonder, then, that Cooper's fiction has been dismissed, or at best regarded as a blocking force, in much of the feminist criticism of the past thirty-five years. By my approximate count, of sixty-two monographs published on Cooper since 1900, eight have been written by women.

My purpose is to challenge, in one significant way, the critical and scholarly neglect of Cooper's women characters. Throughout the four Revolutionary War novels Cooper wrote during the early 1820s, young women have a critical role in furthering both the fictional plot and the political debate about loyalty, independence, and family on which the valuing of America's new republican culture depends. Cooper returns almost obsessively to variations on one family plot with decidedly national overtones. An aging loyalist, whose property and authority are threatened by patriot revolt, engages in sharp, often bitter exchanges with two young women of the household who are his daughters, nieces, or wards. The two young women, one a loyalist and the other a patriot, possess at least as much courage, intelligence, and sense of individual identity as their lovers, who are, invariably, mid-ranking officers in the British or American military.

The young women's privileged social class influences their choice of marital partners but does not determine their political opinions. The extent to which these marriageable young women defer to their suitors' politics is always at issue but never fully resolved. The convention of pairing "the two daughters" thus assumes that young American women are sprightly, courageous, and surprisingly forward in expressing their opinions. Cooper's two daughters, in sum, embody Linda Kerber's "Republican Motherhood" in the making, but they do not yet inhabit Nancy Cott's "separate sphere."[5] There is nothing "flat" or "sappy" about them; their seaboard colonial upbringing has removed them far from every geocultural connotation the word "prairie" was later to possess for James Russell Lowell's mid-nineteenth-century contemporaries.

To fully understand the innovative significance of Cooper's two daughters, we must consider the fictional texts that introduce their historical prototypes—the once ridiculed, now canonized seduction novels of Susanna Rowson and Hannah Foster. Revolutionary War fictions of a sort, *Charlotte Temple* (1791) and *The Coquette* (1797) are at the polar opposite from Cooper's fictions in their treatment of woman's political awareness. The question to be asked about the difference is less "why was Cooper so willing to portray avowedly political heroines?" than "how, in terms of the development of fictional conventions, did Cooper ever conceive of the two daughters?" There are multiple possibilities. The difference could be ascribed to authorial gender expectations—the earlier woman novelist avoids political questions while the later male novelist expresses subversive political ideas more safely through the presumably less authoritative voices of women. The difference could also result from demonstrable cultural change: because the more literate and better-educated women of Cooper's day had become more outspoken about political matters, Cooper assumed they must have been equally so during revolutionary times. Or the fundamental difference could be traced to the influence of specific literary traditions: Rowson and Foster were developing the apolitical seduction novel of Samuel Richardson's *Clarissa*, whereas Cooper was writing within Walter Scott's decidedly political tradition of historical romance. A fourth and perhaps most plausible answer lies in some combination of the first three. The complexity of this issue is surely a sign of its importance.

In the revolutionary New York world of *Charlotte Temple*, there hardly seems to be a war. Although Charlotte's seduction and pregnancy are traceable to a lovers' crisis provoked when Montraville is transferred from England to the British army in Manhattan, neither current political ideals nor troop movements nor rebel violence penetrate the imagination of Charlotte or her creator. The only explicit sign of the war is one mention of New York women washing clothes for the British troops. Although the glamour of a gallant in a military uniform accounts for Charlotte's initial attraction to Montraville, she cannot ever seem to analyze the source of her feelings. To her, sexual passion, elopement, seduction, and bastardy remain exclusively moral questions that aggravate her dishonor and her shame. The intensity of her exclamatory sentiments depends directly on her obliviousness to all social and political contexts. Accordingly, the outer social world, which she believes to be perpetually scrutinizing her moral disgrace, can have, for Rowson's reader, absolutely no definition and no embodiment. Before relegating Susanna Rowson's avoidance of politics to the status of a gender-determined period piece, however, we would do well to remember that *Charlotte Temple* was to be published in more than two hundred editions, only forty-five of them during Rowson's lifetime.[6] Even in the 1820s it thus seems probable that at least as many republican readers (men as well as women?) were attracted to Rowson's *Charlotte Temple* as to Cooper's *The Spy*.

Although the epistolary form of *The Coquette* would seem to allow for greater multiplicity of voices, the same apolitical pattern persists, and to almost the same degree. Eliza Wharton's so-

cial instincts and coquettish ways lead her to associate primarily
with American military officers in Connecticut, but we learn so
little of the current military or political situation that we cannot
be sure whether the tale takes place near the end of the Revolutionary War or slightly after it. Neither Major Sanford, General
Richman, nor Captain Pribble seems to have had any experience
of war, nor do any of them have political convictions. Eliza is not
curious about their past lives. General Richman's wife may ostensibly include Eliza in her advocacy of republican motherhood
("Why then should the love of our county be a masculine passion only? Why should government, which involves the peace
and order of the society, of which we are a part, be wholly excluded from our observation?"),[7] but Eliza herself never expresses anything remotely similar to these words. As a general's
wife, Mrs. Richman knows that Major Sanford's reputation as a
rake is well deserved, and tells Eliza so, but Eliza ignores the information. She clearly prefers to imagine Major Sanford through
an apolitical, asocial haze that isolates and glamorizes him in hy-
pothetical solitude. For author, reader, and heroine, to isolate individuals from all political contexts renders the moral issues of
sexual seduction all the more significant, all the more titillating,
as a wellspring of sentiment. Eliza cultivates a sensitivity that
makes her increasingly blind to the import of her seducer's meta-
phors; Major Sanford regards seduction merely as "a long and
tedious siege" full of parleys, in which a lady who seeks "to enter
the lists" armed only with her honor is doomed to surrender
(139–140).

In both novels, author and heroine are ultimately in a double
bind. Although there is implicit criticism of the heroine's unwill-
ingness to consider political, social, and class realities, including
the power of money in the marriage market, the emotional force
of the seduction novel depends on ignoring, or at least mini-
mizing, those very same realities. For author and heroine, the
shedding of tears, the bitter pleasures of melancholy, rise more
readily in an insular world of moral feeling. A young woman's innocence of society and politics, though it is crucial to her down-
fall, must ultimately be valued because it provides the emotive
engine of the novel itself.

One might argue that such limitations placed on women's political awareness reflect the historical reality of expected gender roles. In 1773, when John Trumbull imagined a formidable, protective aunt explaining the "rule for education" to her niece, Miss Harriet Simper, Harriet's aunt settles the matter with absolute answers to rhetorical questions: "And why should girls be learn'd or wise?/Books only serve to spoil their eyes." Harriet's aunt concludes with words likely to keep her niece simpering forever: "In vain may learning fill the head full:/'Tis Beauty that's the one thing needfull; /Beauty, our sex's sole pretense/The best receipt for female sense."[8]

Similarly, at century's end, Brockden Brown imagined an equally formidable. middle-aged woman named Mrs. Carter who is resentfully resigned to woman's intellectual bondage:

> What! ask a woman—shallow and inexperienced as all women are known to be, especially with regard to these topics [federalism vs. republicanism]—her opinion on any political question! What in the name of decency have we to do with politics? If you inquire the price of this ribbon, or at what shop I purchased that set of china, I may answer you, though I am not sure you would be the wiser for my answer. These things, you know, belong to the woman's province. We are surrounded by men and politicians.[9]

These two passages suggest that, during the revolutionary era, prominent male authors were likely to use the forthright voice of an experienced woman to satirize the limitations circumscribing women's minds—limitations of which they, as male authors, did not entirely disapprove.

To take Trumbull and Brown as the historical bookends of an era's changelessness would, however, be misleading. The historical findings of Linda Kerber, Cathy Davidson, and Mary Beth Norton provide abundant examples of women, usually married, whose political convictions, loyalist or patriot, emerged just before or during the Revolutionary War and were expressed in writing, in person, and by public petition. Abigail Adams and Judith Sargent Murray were only the most outspoken among them.

The difference between women's Revolutionary War experience and Trumbull's and Brown's formulations is attributable to the historical quelling of an emerging women's voice. As Cathy Davidson summarizes it, "The War ambiguously emphasized to women both their private capability and their public powerlessness."[10] For many women, the war aroused political convictions that could have no public outlet save in the humble, silent act of signing a petition.[11] John Trumbull and, to a lesser degree, Brockden Brown, see no emergence of a woman's political principle arising under conditions of revolutionary warfare. Neither, be it said, do Susanna Rowson or Harriet Foster, who led their readers to conclude that feeling women remained oblivious to contending for national independence. In the world perceived by their heroines, revolutionary politics does not even exist.

As characterizations of *jeunnes filles à marier*, Charlotte Temple and Eliza Wharton are a far cry from Katherine Plowden, the plucky, admirable heroine of Cooper's *The Pilot*, who sneeringly reminds her loyalist guardian, Colonel Howard, that only "the glorious British constitution" that "gives liberty to all" could possibly explain why almost all of Colonel Howard's former slaves in Carolina have "fled on the wings of the spirit of British liberty!"[12] Katherine is playing a dangerous game here, not only because she voices her anti–Common Law beliefs in England in front of an entire household, including British military officers, but because Colonel Howard, whose Tory loyalties she is frontally attacking, presently retains all legal power over her purse and her person.

What can account for so sweeping a change in the depiction of the marriageable heroine in revolutionary times? It would surely be fruitless, in proposing an initial answer, to seek out evidence of James Fenimore Cooper's nascent feminism. Cooper was no defender of the bluestocking; his mother, wife, and daughter are not known to have expressed personal political opinions.[13] In the 1820s, the public voices of Lydia Maria Child, the Grimké sisters, and Margaret Fuller were at least a decade in the future, to say nothing of Seneca Falls or the legalization of women's property rights in the revised 1846 Constitution of the State of New York. Given this contextual vacuum, I propose that the important changes accounting for the rise of Cooper's out-spoken revolutionary heroines are two literary interventions: the publication of Mary Wollstonecraft's *Vindication of the Rights of Woman* (1792) and of Walter Scott's *Waverley* (1814).

Mary Wollstonecraft knew exactly why young women like Charlotte Temple and Eliza Wharton could quickly spiral down-ward from unmarried pregnancy to shame, guilt, despair, and suicide. Because women are still being educated, if at all, in su-perficial accomplishments designed to attract men (drawing, music, and French), their minds can only "dwell on effects and modifications without tracing them back to causes."[14] Woman's "slavish dependence" and "enslaved understanding" deprive her of the powers of generalization and comparison, forcing her to live mentally in an eternal present of would-be lovers and imme-diate family relations (131). To rely on the marriage market in the absence of skills needed for self-support is to allow one's worth to be defined by premarital chastity: "A woman who has lost her honour imagines that she cannot fall lower, and, as for recovering her former station, it is impossible; no exertion can wash this stain away" (165). The current fashion for reading novels only ex-acerbates a woman's mental limitations; romance readers in search of a husband are left "hanging their heads surcharged with the dew of sensibility that consumes the beauty to which it first gave lustre" (262).

Wollstonecraft argues, with great acuity, that there is a close educational and mental affinity between women and soldiers. Both the young soldier and the marriageable woman seek to fill their lives with fashionable clothes, dancing, "crowded rooms," and "gallantry" primarily because their education consists of "a little superficial knowledge, snatched from the muddy current of conversation" (106, 105). "Soldiers, as well as women, practice the minor virtues with punctilious politeness" (105). Just as women are educated to submit to men, so young officers are trained to submit to their elder superiors in rank. What then, must be the consequence for both groups? "Taking all their opinions on credit, they blindly submit to authority" (106). Although Woll-stonecraft suspects that the mind of the soldier has been perma-nently corrupted, she holds forth hope for the young woman.

Henceforth, women and men must be educated together, as potential friends and mental equals, first in day schools (emphatically not in the British public school) and then in select coeducational academies where they will "continue the study of history and politics, on a more extensive scale" (287). In the northeastern United States, the many all-women academies, day school or boarding school, that were to open their doors after 1800 clearly represented a modest but real half-step toward Wollstonecraft's goal. By Cooper's day, literacy rates among women were rising rapidly, and birth rates were beginning to fall. It would have been considerably more difficult, in 1825, to imagine an admirable woman of the revolutionary era as mentally docile. For at least a minority of Cooper's contemporaries, the gradual spread of Wollstonecraft's ideas had surely undermined the seduction novel as a means for evoking tears for victimized heroines or pity for vulnerable coquettes.

From Cooper's perspective in the early 1820s, the publication of Scott's *Waverley* in 1814 upended the fictional convention that women during revolutionary times were assumed to be apolitical by instinct and education. Scott bifurcates the victimized heroine of sensibility into the fair and dark ladies who would reappear in seemingly endless variations in nineteenth-century fictions by Cooper, Poe, Emily Brontë, Dickens, Hawthorne, Stowe, Thackeray, and James.[15] The stunningly beautiful, dark-eyed, dark-haired Flora Mac-Ivor—fluent in three languages, adept at the Highland harp and royal genealogies, fervently Catholic yet committed to freedom of religion, as familiar with Paris as with Edinburgh—proves to be the most outspoken and most disinterested Jacobite supporting Bonnie Prince Charlie's claim to the throne. Her political allegiance to the Stuarts, Scott insists, consists of equally formidable degrees of "fanaticism" and "purity"; for Flora, unlike her brother Fergus, "the zeal of loyalty burnt pure and unmixed with any selfish feeling."[16]

Through the force of Flora's person and personality, the ever-wavering Edmund Waverley is finally induced to join the Jacobite army despite his English and Hanoverian upbringing. Whatever the historical reality of the 1745 rebellion may have been, the power of political persuasion in Scott's fictional narrative clearly can reside within, and emerge from, a marriageable young woman. In *Waverley* it is the titular male hero, not the heroine, who proves to be passive and vacillating, in great measure because of his desultory, undirected education.

Scott's desire to give his narrative a progressive ending leads him to emphasize that Waverley must eventually choose to leave the Highland army (much as he had earlier left the Hanoverian army) to marry Rose Bradwardine and settle down into prosperity on her family's newly renovated estate in the Lowlands. The purpose of Scott's endowing Rose with a "Scotch caste of beauty," "hair of paley gold," and "skin like the snow" involves far more than physical description providing a fair lady foil to Flora (86). Her sobriquet, "the Rose of Tully Veolan," reminds us that Rose is in the perilous position of a Lowland Scottish lord's daughter who wears white, if not the white cockade. Rose knows, however, that her impulsive, opinionated father, Baron Cosmo Bradwardine, will always be a rigid, ridiculously reactionary Jacobite. From the outset, Rose has had the political savvy to discern that, however pure the Stuart cause might be, Jacobites are history's losers. If she were to alienate her father, or directly challenge Waverley's thoroughly *sentimental* fascination with Highland culture, she might lose both her estate and her man. At novel's end, Rose's waiting game secures her her estate, her marriage, and acceptability for them both within the victorious Hanoverian order. To Scott, Rose's quiet kind of woman's politics, combining common sense about public policy with a keen eye for domestic self-interest, is evidently a force to be heeded.

In the main, Cooper adopts Scott's contrast of fair and dark ladies but reverses Scott's associations of revolutionary allegiance and personal temperament. Cooper's golden-haired daughters and wards (Sarah Wharton, Alice Dunscombe, and Cecil Dynevor) are repeatedly associated, not with Rose Bradwardine's cautious progressivism, but with a heartfelt, backward-looking loyalty to England. Conversely, Cooper's dark-haired daughters and wards are sprightly, outspoken advocates for American liberty and American independence. By novel's end, they, too, like Rose, win their man, but their man has invariably been a committed American patriot from the outset. Moreover, until the postrevolutionary era Cooper describes in *The Pioneers*, retaining her father's estate forms no part of the happy patriot bride's marital bliss. For Cooper, therefore, narrative resolutions shift with historical contexts. During the American Revolution, but apparently not thereafter, new political beginnings could portend new alignments of family property between father and daughter.

Outspoken Daughters, Revolutionary Inheritances

We have long known that the divided politics of Cooper's parental heritage (paternal patriots, maternal loyalists) made him acutely if reluctantly aware that the American Revolution must be viewed, not as virtuous republican farmers casting off the British imperial father, but as a brutal civil war in which political truth and moral conduct were not the possession of any one nation, people, army, legislative body, or social class. Nowhere more so than in Westchester County, New York, the "neutral ground" of *The Spy*, a region contested by both armies but possessed by neither, a no-man's land wasted by irregular forces (Cowboy loyalists and Skinner patriots) who have been secretly paid for their vigilantism by British and American authorities (ultimately, Henry Clinton and George Washington). Although *The Spy's* avowed controlling theme is American patriotism, nearly every atrocity in the novel is committed by the ostensibly pro-American Skinners, who are roundly denounced by Virginia patriot Captain Lawton as "fellows whose mouths are filled with liberty and equality, and whose hearts are overflowing with cupidity and gall."[17] Under such circumstances, unsullied patriotism can be embodied only in Harvey Birch's lifelong self-sacrifice to the abstract cause of American liberty, a cause that Harvey psychologically needs to personify in the revered outsider figure of George Washington.

Given such a darkly complex view of the American Revolution, it is understandable that, in both his title and his text, Cooper should have foregrounded the issue of defining a spy while keeping the legitimacy and virtue of republican revolution a real but subsidiary concern. The second paragraph informs us that, in the neutral ground, "a large portion of its inhabitants, restrained by their attachments, or influenced by their fears, affected a neutrality they did not feel" (23). While the majority kept silent out of self-interest, a few endured the stigma of a Tory spy to serve the American cause at the very moment other "divers flaming Patriots" were securing "royal protections . . . concealed under piles of British gold" (23). When, therefore, Cooper concludes that "great numbers . . . wore masks" (23), masking serves as a metaphor for nearly everyone's public behavior, as well as for the clothing that defines a spy. The treacherous conditions of the neutral ground compel the men who fight for or against the Revolution, not so much to lie about their political beliefs as to disguise them under masks of gesture, innuendo, or silence. Only the women, sometimes to the peril of their men, seem willing openly to declare their beliefs and allegiances.

The tension maintained during the novel's long opening sequence underscores this contrast of gender and political speech. Henry Wharton (British captain), Mr. Harper (George Washington), and Harvey Birch (peddler spy)—all of them masked literally and metaphorically—confront one another at the Locusts, the summer home of Mr. Wharton, an aging gentleman of Tory sympathies who, to protect his property and his children, is presently affecting a neutrality he does not feel. While the men try to discover each other without revealing anything of themselves, the speaking silence is broken by Mr. Wharton's two golden-haired daughters, Frances, age fifteen, affianced to patriot Peyton Dunwoodie, and her sister, Sarah, one or two years older, infatuated with British Colonel Wellmere. Frances begins the exchange in her characteristically sprightly manner:

> "You know it is liberty for which Major Dunwoodie is fighting."
> "Liberty!" exclaimed Sarah, "very pretty liberty—which exchanges one master for fifty."
> "The privilege of changing masters at all is a liberty."
> "And one you ladies would sometimes be glad to exercise," cried the Captain.

"We like, I believe, to have the liberty of choosing who they shall be in the first place," said the laughing girl. (60)

Frances advances the Jeffersonian assumption that liberty involves both individual rights and the collective will to change the government; Sarah has a prescient fear, famously expressed by Tocqueville, of the tyranny of the majority. Neither sister, however, wins the exchange. Instead, Captain Henry Wharton intervenes, seeking to deflect the emerging political discussion by reducing the presumably male issue of political liberty to the presumably female issue of remaining free to choose one's master in marriage. He succeeds in forestalling the threat of political confrontation only because Frances, perhaps recognizing the danger of the situation, allows him to do so, while laughingly insisting on retaining her power to choose.

Henry Wharton wishes to assume that his sisters' political beliefs can be nothing more than emotion-driven extensions of love for their men: " 'Women are but mirrors, which reflect the images before them' cried the captain, good-naturedly.—'In Frances I see the picture of Major Dunwoodie, and in Sarah—Colonel Wellmere' " (63). Although both Sarah and Frances laughingly grant their brother's supposition, it proves questionable at best. Again and again the two sisters express what seem to be their own strong political convictions. Frances: "On many accounts, I certainly do [long ardently for peace] . . . but, not at the expence of the rights of my countrymen" (31–32); "With what hopes of success could the Americans contend, if they yielded all the principles which long usage had established, to the exclusive purposes of the British?" (62). Sarah: "Whose rights can be stronger than those of a sovereign; and what duty is clearer, than to obey those who have a natural right to command!" (32). Black men, Sarah observes, are "frequently much better" than their white masters, be they patriots or loyalists (50). Assessing the constitutional legality of revolution, Sarah bluntly observes, "Being rebels, all their acts are illegal" (63).

The most telling interchange between the two sisters occurs when they walk together on the piazza at the Locusts, with no man within earshot. Although their conversation begins with remarks on the propriety of transforming the Locusts into a hospital for wounded gentlemanly patriots as well as wounded gentlemanly loyalists, it concludes with Sarah's summary of the immediate, felt consequences of the Revolution: "You now have the fruits of rebellion brought home to you; a brother wounded and a prisoner, and perhaps a victim; our father distressed, his privacy interrupted, and not improbably his estates torn from him, on account of his loyalty to his king" (166).

Sarah's summary is couched entirely within the terms of family as metaphor for nation and not within terms of the political loyalty determined by one's suitor. Tellingly, Frances can offer Sarah no rejoinder; Sarah is allowed the last word while Frances "continued her walk in silence" (166). Sarah's summary should, by novel's end, be remembered as a Tory nightmare become reality. Although her brother Henry escapes being hanged for a spy, his release does not occur because the American military court accepts his innocence (Henry is condemned to be hanged, rather than shot) but because Harvey Birch heroically rescues him, even though Henry is a British military officer. Her father's fate proves to be more dire than Sarah can imagine: Mr. Wharton's estate is confiscated, the Locusts is burned (by the Skinners), he is reduced to a state of "perfect imbecility" (276), and he dies before being sure of his children's survival.[18]

Vivacious, golden-haired Frances Wharton is prepared to voice her allegiance to liberty even if it might put herself, her father, and his estate at risk from the British army. Aging Katy Haynes, who has served as Harvey Birch's housekeeper for decades, is puzzled by revolutionary politics, but would readily adopt any political belief Harvey might hold, if only she could discover what Harvey's beliefs are and then marry him. After the Skinners have burned and leveled both the Birch and Wharton households, Katy and Frances walk north together beside Mr. Wharton's tattered armorial carriage, protected as women refugees by Peyton Dunwoodie's Continental dragoons:

> "If I could but see any thing to fight about," said Katy, renewing her walk as the young lady proceeded, "I shouldn't mind it so much—'twas said the king wanted all the tea for his own

family, at one time; and then again, that he meant the colonies should pay over to him all their earnings.—Now this is matter enough to fight about—for I'm sure that no one, however he may be lord or king, has a right to the hard earnings of another.—Then it was all contradicted, and some said Washington wanted to be king himself, so that, between the two, one doesn't know which to believe."

"Believe neither—for neither is true, I do not pretend to understand, myself, all the merits of this war, Katy; but to me it seems unnatural, that a country like this should be ruled by another so distant as England." (310)

Katy's one sure conviction—that everyone has a right to his or her earnings—certainly had its political implications in 1780, but the reader knows by this time that Katy's real concern is not political but her right to her personal earnings, which would include her due portion of Harvey's lost gold as well as Harvey himself. Frances's response to Katy, however, represents a surprising shift. The atrocities Frances has witnessed in the neutral ground have clearly led her to acknowledge that she cannot pretend to understand "all the merits of this war." The one argument Frances then cites to sustain her revolutionary patriotism has nothing to do with the virtue of liberty. It is rather the wholly pragmatic, geopolitical argument central to Edmund Burke's cogent "Speech on . . . Conciliation with the American Colonies" (1775): no continent can be permanently ruled by an island; no colony can be permanently ruled across an ocean. Is not Frances acknowledging, convincingly if momentarily, the one hard, irreducible fact beneath all the rhetoric of liberty and loyalty—including, of course, Cooper's own rhetoric?

With her hair of "raven blackness" (167), Isabella Singleton serves as Frances Wharton's foil. Isabella is all enthusiasm and sentiment, sensibility atremble. In love with Peyton Dunwoodie, as is Frances, Isabella acknowledges that her "ungovernable feelings" (201) have led her—as if she were in a seduction novel—into the "impropriety" of being consumed by her need for one man. Killed by the stray bullet of a Skinner, Isabella had in spirit already died of long-unrequited love. Her final words show that she is but half aware that her vulnerability derives from her assumptions about the aim of a woman's life: "Woman must be sought, to be prized—her life is one of concealed emotions; blessed are they whose early impressions make the task free from hypocrisy" (301). Unlike every other woman in the novel, Isabella Singleton (single tone?) has no political beliefs, no political interests, no interest whatever in the struggle for independence. Cooper's never stated implication is that women who, like Isabella, seem to pride themselves on being indifferent to politics reap only the miseries of unalloyed feeling. Frances, by contrast, earns Peyton's devotion in part because she has political convictions she is willing to adapt to circumstances. To Cooper, as to Wollstonecraft and Scott, the sensibility that rules the world of the seduction novel seems dangerously naïve.

Near novel's end, Cooper's narrator declares, "The good treatment of their women, is the surest evidence that a people can give of their civilization; and there is no nation which has more to boast of in this respect than the Americans" (368). This commonplace assertion, shared by Jefferson, John Adams, and Washington Irving among male American writers, seems in context to be more boast than fact. Its chief supporting evidence is negative: Colonel Wellmere's betrayal drives Sarah Wharton into an insanity of grief when his bigamy is revealed at their marriage altar. American women as a whole, however, do not fare well. Gentlemanly courtesies toward women at the dinner table and in the drawing room do not extend to men's welcoming women to engage in political discussion. Katy Haynes earns nothing for her lifetime of service to Harvey Birch and Harvey's father. Betty Hollister, nomadic sutler to Washington's army, gains only the momentary gratitude of dragoons for the liquor, food, and laundry she so cheerfully dispenses. Isabella Singleton is mistakenly shot to death by a Skinner. Aunt Jeannette Peyton and Sarah Wharton survive to live as childless spinsters on Dunwoodie's Virginia plantation. There is not one mother-daughter relationship in the novel; in Cooper's Revolutionary War novels, mothers remain conspicuous by their absence. If a society's degree of civilization is measured by good treatment of its women, the Americans' record in *The Spy* is decidedly mixed.

How was Cooper to resolve such divisive complexities for the many American readers who, in 1820, sought confirmation of their revolutionary patriotism in the conclusion of the War of 1812, in the chauvinism of texts like Parson Weems's extraordinarily popular *Life of George Washington* (1800), and in the forthcoming fifty-year celebration of national independence? Surely no novel has ever been more in need of a palliative patriotic ending. Cooper foregrounds Harvey Birch's death during the War of 1812, providing restitution to the spy through disclosure of Washington's note of tribute, while suggesting the progress of young America through the emergence into manhood of Wharton Dunwoodie, who gazes into the sublime future visible in Niagara Falls.

But what of the women? Given the melancholy that tinges the happy survival of so many of Cooper's women characters, woman's status as the protected cynosure of republican civilization must rest entirely on the future of Frances Wharton. In scenes whose plausibility can only be symbolic, Frances accosts the narrow literalism of the military court's definition of a spy and then climbs a mountain alone at night in search of her escaped brother, only to meet George Washington (whose disguise as Mr. Harper is wearing thin) in Harvey Birch's hut. Washington is so impressed by the integrity with which Frances has combined personal courage, devotion to American liberty, and loyalty to her genteel Tory family that he proclaims, before pressing "a paternal kiss upon her forehead":

> "God has denied to me children, young lady, but if it had been his blessed will that my marriage should not have been childless, such a treasure as yourself would I have asked from his mercy. But you are my child: all who dwell in this broad land are my children, and my care, and take the blessing of one who hopes yet to meet you in happier days." (379–380)

Washington's words transfer the paternity of Liberty's daughter from the impotent past of her loyalist blood father to the powerful future of the metaphoric father of the nation. Frances's stature as the republican mother emerges as the true treasure replacing Harvey Birch's lost gold. Blessed by America's Virginian father, Frances can now prepare for a new life with her Virginian husband. As the entire Wharton household except Henry prepares to remove to Peyton Dunwoodie's plantation in Virginia, the anarchy and contentiousness of the neutral ground seem left behind. For the Wharton family as for the new nation, the locus of political power shifts to the planter class of Virginia in whose hands, as the sequence of Virginia presidents suggests, political power was historically to reside between 1788 and 1824. Through the birth of Wharton Dunwoodie, Frances's body thus becomes the source of a power of liberty that, at novel's end, makes the bleak futures of Katy Haynes, Sarah Wharton, and Betty Hollister seem comparatively negligible, if not quite forgotten.

For *The Pilot* Cooper devises a variant of the two-daughter plot to befit the troubling, sullied patriotism of his Byronic historical hero, John Paul Jones. The novel's aging Tory father figure, Colonel Howard, is as blunt in declaring his honest loyalist prejudices as Mr. Wharton had been fearfully silent. The two sprightly young patriot women whom Colonel Howard has virtually imprisoned in his English household, Katherine Plowden and Cecilia Howard, are Howard's raven-haired wards and nieces rather than golden-haired daughters. The two patriot military officers whom Katherine and Cecilia eventually marry, Richard Barnstable and Edward Griffith, seem vacuously conventional— little more than eligibly handsome—because their fiancées prove to be provoking in politics, saucy in courtship, and courageous in action. No one in the novel displays as much moral courage as the fair-haired, blue-eyed Englishwoman Alice Dunscombe, who loves, criticizes, and ultimately rejects John Paul Jones, not because Jones fights against England on behalf of American liberty, but because his libertarian politics are increasingly driven by a need for celebrity and a limitless revolutionary ego that isolate him from the very people he claims to serve. Replacing George Washington with John Paul Jones thus requires that the evidence for American political integrity must rest even more squarely on the characterization of Colonel Howard's nieces than it had on the characterization of Mr. Wharton's daughters.

Katherine Plowden fulfills the needed role. She possesses, she

herself says, "more than a woman's enterprise"; she is prepared
to do "more than my sex will warrant."[19] She provokes Colonel
Howard into a rage by discrediting his boastings about British liberty, pointing out "in plain English" (112) that his Carolina slaves
have fled his service and that he has confined his wards, guarded
by soldiers, in an abbey that is little more than a comfortable
prison. When Colonel Howard darkly hints that Katherine and
Cecilia's rescuers (Barnstable and Griffith, aided by Jones the
Pilot) may be lost at sea, Katherine retorts, "In whose behalf
would a just Providence sooner exercise its merciful power, than
to protect the daring children of an oppressed country, while
contending against tyranny and countless wrongs?" (113). It is
Katherine Plowden who, with "infinite contempt" (117), denounces the cowardly schemes of the British villain Christopher
Dillon, who prefers to uses the law to seek an inheritance rather
than to serve his king.

Even more than Frances Wharton, Katherine Plowden proves
to be a woman of action. She has acquired navigational skills.
She devises a coded system of silk ship's flags by which she secretly informs her rescuers of her whereabouts and of the best
stratagems for escape. She leads Barnstable and Long Tom Coffin through the maze of the abbey's passageways to safety. After
Barnstable and Griffith have drawn swords over a silly point of
honor, she bodily separates them. Because Cecilia is Colonel
Howard's sole heir, Katherine at novel's end inherits no land and
no money, but spends her childless life as a navy captain's wife
serving actively at sea. Small and nimble, with a "dark but rich
complexion" and "dancing eyes of jet-black" (105), Katherine
Plowden upsets the literary applecart of conventional sex coding
among the fair and dark ladies of the American romance tradition. How Captain Barnstable will deal with his wife's provoking
nature aboard ship, Cooper does not say; it is perhaps telling,
however, that Cooper envisions no place for Katherine Plowden
in America's landed or urban communities, based as they were
on family inheritance of property.

Neither Cecilia Griffith nor Katherine Plowden will allow
Colonel Howard, Tory reactionary though he is, to be personally
insulted, demeaned, or wronged. They protest against any threat

to his person or property, against any plan that would desecrate the abbey, and against any escape strategy that would disavow his rights as their guardian. Such protests derive, in part, from the nieces' loyalty to family and from the belief that any liberty that tramples on the rights of one's opponents is not worth a bloody revolution. But their overriding concern in offering such protests is their notion of personal honor. Challenging another's political beliefs and strategizing an escape are one thing; betrayal and condoning revenge are another. Dishonoring their uncle would be dishonoring themselves.

The practical difficulties such high-mindedness poses for managing their own rescue are, to be sure, finally washed away by the nearly simultaneous death of Colonel Howard and the nieces' double marriages aboard ship. But the issue of whether a person's moral worth is ultimately to be measured by honor irrespective of political allegiance remains long after the nieces' happy escape. It is Alice Dunscombe's function in the novel to express the supreme value of personal honor by repeatedly discrediting John Paul Jones at the expense of her own love for him. No matter what navigational and naval heroics Jones might perform, he has become increasingly ruthless in pursuit of mere personal glory. The very last time Alice challenges him, "her sentiments awakened in his own breast those feelings of generosity and disinterestedness, which had nearly been smothered in restless ambition and the pride of success" (362). Jones's awakening, however, proves but momentary; he has been too long the roving isolato to be made new.

Women thus serve as the troubling voice of moral conscience in assessing the appropriateness of adopting bloody deeds to revolutionary ends. Like Katherine Plowden, Alice intervenes to stop needless bloodshed between Borroughcliffe and Griffith by exclaiming, more than a little stagily:

> "Hear me, men! if men ye be, and not demons, thirsting for each other's blood; though ye walk abroad in the semblance of him who died that ye might be elevated to the rank of angels! Call ye this war? Is this the glory that is made to warm the hearts of even silly and confiding women? Is the peace of

families to be destroyed to gratify your wicked lust for conquest; and is life to be taken in vain, in order that ye may boast
of the foul deed in your wicked revels! Fall back, then, ye
British soldiers! If ye be worthy of that name, and give passage to a woman." (335)

The next line is "The men, thus enjoined, shrunk before her
commanding mien" (335). Like Shakespeare's Rosalind, Cooper's
Alice Dunscombe ironically performs male deeds of virtue based
on her womanly sense of a transcendent morality.

When Cooper's women publicly protest on behalf of private
honor, they assume that the candor and magnanimity due to
family relations must be extended to political relations. Alice tries
to persuade Jones to direct his pursuit of independence toward responsible civic purpose by questioning him with Burkean meta-
phors: "Are not the relations of domestic life of God's establishing,
and have not the nations grown from families, as branches spread
from the stem, till the tree overshadows the land!" (151). No male
in the novel expresses so searching an opinion about the nature of
a nation. Jones's immediate and characteristically callous response
("The Pilot smiled disdainfully") is the most glaring example in
Cooper's fiction of the male revolutionary's need to dismiss
women's troubling political morality. Alice's question is, however,
one that Cooper is no more able to answer than was Jones.

Cooper published *Lionel Lincoln* during the fiftieth anniversary
year of New England's independence as the first of a projected
series of novels to be called "Legends of the Thirteen Republics."
The celebratory moment, we may surmise, induced Cooper to
attempt an even more patriotic variant on his Revolutionary War
plot. Neither of his two young women (first cousins once removed this time) would be avowedly loyalist. The British military
suitor would be a comically inappropriate captain rather than a
bigamist colonel. The aging loyalist father figure (Mr. Wharton,
Colonel Howard), who had aroused pity if not outright sympathy,
would be replaced by a proud, greedy, and deceitful Tory grandmother (Priscilla Lechmere). Accounts of the battles of Lexington, Concord, and Bunker Hill and of the fortification of Dor-
chester Heights would affirm the defensive courage of America's

embattled farmers without violating known evidence of American failings and British valor. The title figure, surely modeled on Scott's Waverley, would be an American-born but British-educated major in the infamous Royal 47th Regiment, whose exposure to the oppression of the colonists following the Boston Port Act would make a change of allegiance at least plausible. This plot design was both promising and internally consistent. Why, then, was Cooper so unable—and finally even unwilling—to render it convincingly?

Nineteen-year-old Agnes Danforth, who bears a New England name famous for Puritan resistance, tells Major Lionel Lincoln immediately upon his disembarkation that he should promptly resign his British commission. Like Frances Wharton and Katherine Plowden, Agnes is, we soon learn, "plain and direct, though a little blunt."[20] In her Tory great-aunt's household, she denounces both the Intolerable Acts and the Writs of Mandamus, calls tea a "detestable herb" and a "subtle poison" (38), and insists that good times will never come again to New England "under the guise of a scarlet coat" (207). She refuses British Captain Polworth's offer of marriage so many times that he remarks, "This girl treats me like a cart horse!" (127). Agnes reconnoiters on undisclosed missions at night. When Lionel Lincoln is wounded after the Battle of Bunker Hill, it is Agnes Danforth who nurses him back to health. Because of her pluck and intelligence, Lionel is immediately drawn to her; in her presence, Cooper notes, Lionel never exhibits "that air of pique which the British officers were often weak enough to betray, when the women took into their hands the defence of their country's honour" (37).

Cecil Dynevor, Agnes's cousin and Mrs. Lechmere's granddaughter, never seriously questions her loyalty to king and "Government," but her Toryism lacks even a trace of the satiric bite of Sarah Wharton. The Tory daughter now publicly approves a cautious, restorative position about emerging revolutionary warfare: "Let the Parliament repeal their laws and the King recall his troops" (311). Cecil may seek the peace of the status quo ante, but she is not, like the sentimental heroines of the seduction novels, oblivious to the politics of allegiance. When Lionel Lincoln volunteers to accompany the British troops on their inland march to Concord, Cecil sharply urges him not to do so, even as a "witness" (94). Such an expedition, she declares, is likely to be "unholy in its purposes, and disgraceful in its results" (94). "If you go only as a curious spectator of the depredations of the troops . . . are you not wrong to lend them even the sanction of your name?" (94). She, like Agnes, believes that Lionel Lincoln's American birthright must always compromise his British military service: "As a man your own feelings should teach you to be tender of your countrymen" (95). Although Cecil never explicitly says so, her words suggest that the horrors of war outweigh any justifying cause. By ascribing such sentiments to the loyalist daughter, Cooper withholds authorial sanction from the possibility that advocacy of both rebellion and repression are ultimately founded on rationalizations.

Priscilla Lechmere's Tremont Street mansion, fitted out with dark furnishings, heavy silverware, and the Lincoln coat of arms, is the perfect metaphor for her inner self. At age seventy, her face has become a mask of propriety no longer able to conceal her manipulative avarice and her yearning for aristocratic family power in England as well as New England. Sensing that British power in Boston is rapidly waning, she has become consumed by her desire to marry her granddaughter Cecil to Lionel Lincoln. To do so would serve three purposes: (1) bring the Lincoln money and noble title into her (female) family line; (2) secure a British wartime asylum for Cecil, her soon-to-be-unprotected granddaughter; and (3) lend the social armor of full respectability to Cecil, who was conceived out of wedlock (224, 338).

During her lifelong pursuit of title, money, and power, Mrs. Lechmere has had Lionel's father imprisoned as a maniac, has smeared the reputation of Lionel's mother, and has paid off Abigail Pray to prevent recognition of the bastardy of Mrs. Lechmere's grandson, Job Pray. A cross between Shakespeare's Lady Macbeth and Dickens's Miss Havisham, Priscilla Lechmere is not as credible as either one of them. Both in her characterization and in the unraveling of her dark plots, Cooper clearly sought to create a symbol of every conceivable evil associated with male primogeniture, with the ancien régime, and with colonial aping of British aristocracy. In literary effect, however, Mrs. Lechmere remains a caricature. The reason is surely not, as in *Great Expectations*, a matter of the author's intent. Perhaps Cooper simply could not imagine a convincing loyalist who had been relentlessly and irredeemably evil.

The problems in Mrs. Lechmere's characterization pale beside those of Cooper's denouement. Because the outspoken Ralph remains a maniac and the equally outspoken Job Pray remains an idiot, male revolutionary patriotism becomes increasingly, though not intentionally, associated with insanity. Lionel Lincoln never seriously considers changing his allegiance, though he has good reason to do so. Despite moments of unexplained family distemper, he serves honorably with his British regiment during the Battle of Bunker Hill, marries Cecil Dynevor, retires with her to the Lincoln estates in England, and eventually is awarded an earldom. Priscilla Lechmere thus obtains, in Cooper's happy ending, her fondest wish! Worse yet, Agnes Danforth marries an American military officer (as had Katherine Plowden) but then lives, apparently blissfully, in Mrs. Lechmere's Tremont Street mansion, which Cecil Dynevor, now Lady Lincoln, has given to Agnes as a dowry. In an abrupt ending, like the close of *The House of the Seven Gables*, the simple virtue of the republican maiden earns its due reward by being showered with the remains of ill-gotten, aristocratic wealth.

Why the collapse into such inconsistencies? Is it a result, as has been alleged, of sheer haste or of Cooper's inability to manage the conventions of the gothic novel? Is it because Cooper constructed for Cecil Dynevor the perfect Jamesian dilemma (caught between her love for Lionel, her grandmother's wish to marry her off for money, and her own sense of honor) but lacked Henry James's psychological insight and the skill in dialogue needed to properly develop it? Does Lionel Lincoln fail to change allegiance because Cooper believed that human beings do not readily transform themselves in times of crisis by casting away their education and heritage? Or was Cooper more inwardly committed to the security and contentment of inherited property than he professed to be? We do not know. What we do know is that Cooper ended his novel with the curious words "It is more than probable, that the prosperous and affluent English peer, who now enjoys the honours of the house of Lincoln, never knew the secret history of his family, while it sojourned in a remote province of the British empire" (365). The novel's closing perspective thus becomes entirely British. The American Revolution suddenly recedes into a family legend, little more than a tearing away of the veil over the forgotten sins of British aristocracy. Is so dismissive an ending a sign of Cooper's impatient desire to rid himself of his novel's failings?

Of these possible causes of inconsistency, Cooper's desire to secure inherited property was, I suspect, the most important. *The Pioneers*, published prior to *Lionel Lincoln*, concerns the aftermath of the Revolution, rather than wartime, and contains not two daughters but one. Elizabeth Temple, with her "jet black eyes," black ringlets, and upright stature, retains many of the qualities of previous revolutionary patriot heroines.[21] She has a pert sense of independence (a "dark proud eye") that makes her confrontational to the verge of being "a little severe" (66). She curtly puts down her garrulous cousin Richard Jones and her father's jealous housekeeper, Remarkable Pettibone, whenever they attempt the slightest touch of overfamiliarity. She has an instinctive sympathy for the natural right of John Mohegan and Natty Bumppo, prior occupants of her father's lands, to remain outside the institutional legal system that Judge Temple has brought to the wilderness. Like Frances Wharton and Katherine Plowden, Elizabeth performs acts of courage that illustrate her freedom to choose to support those she believes to be oppressed. She approves and abets Leatherstocking's escape from jail, procures him his gunpowder, and risks her own death by climbing Mount Vision as it begins to be consumed in fire.

Elizabeth's interpretation of the laws of nature and of nature's God leads her, like Indian John and Leatherstocking, to challenge both her father's legal right to possess his lands and his authority to enforce conservation laws that violate Leatherstocking's right of prior occupancy. Fully aware that her father's lands were originally possessed by the Delawares and that she herself is likely to be her father's sole heir, Elizabeth declares, "I own that I grieve when I see old Mohegan walking about these lands, like the ghost of one of their ancient possessors, and feel how small is my own right to possess them" (280). After Judge Temple orders Leatherstocking to be imprisoned for a month, to pay a $100 fine, and to spend one hour in the stocks for having killed a deer out of season and for having assaulted Hiram Doolittle, she bluntly confronts her father: " 'Surely, sir,' cried the impatient Elizabeth, 'those laws, that condemn a man like the Leather-stocking to so severe a punishment, for an offence that even I must think very venial, cannot be perfect in themselves' " (382). When her father responds that Leatherstocking was in legal fact guilty of resisting a search warrant by force of arms, Elizabeth indignantly responds, "In appreciating the offence of poor Natty, I cannot separate the minister of the law from the man" (382). Knowing that Doolittle's motives were venal, and that Leather-stocking's hut existed long before Judge Temple saw the land on which it stands, Elizabeth has concluded, quite plausibly, that her father's jurisdiction over Leatherstocking is questionable, that Deputy Doolittle has abused the law, and that her father's insis-tence on the letter of the law killeth.

Elizabeth's position on these issues can easily be seen as an outgrowth of revolutionary ideology. She challenges the civil statutes in the name of the law of nature; the freedoms of right-minded individuals are, to her mind, a higher law than estab-lished patriarchal authority. The problem for Cooper, however, is that the father his heroine is challenging is no longer an aging Tory but a vigorous patriot land entrepreneur. To the extent that Judge Temple is a fictive representation of Judge William Cooper, the problem arises for the novelist in acute personal form: How far will Cooper be willing to allow the daughter's rebellion against her father to extend?

In a scene that has no predecessor in the Revolutionary War novels, the father vigorously curtails his daughter's rebellion. As soon as Elizabeth has protested against the imperfections of the law, Judge Temple tells her, "Thou talkest of what thou dost not understand, Elizabeth" (382). When she continues to protest that Hiram Doolittle with a badge is the same venal Hiram Doolittle underneath, her father attempts to quell her through an appeal to a father's gender supremacy: "There thou talkest as a woman, child" (382). But when even this rebuke fails to suppress Elizabeth ("It is immaterial whether it be one or the other," she replies), Cooper as narrator steps in to comment that Miss Temple has spoken "with a logic that contained more feeling than reason" (382). To pit male reason against female feeling in this manner reverses the pattern of the Revolutionary War novels, in which Cooper's sprightly patriot heroine had spoken with both feeling *and* reason.

Like the continued presence of Leatherstocking and Indian John in the vicinity of Templeton, Elizabeth's arguments threaten the validity, and possibly the survival, of Judge Temple's extensive land holdings. After the judge disparages his daughter's challenge as mere womanly feeling, Elizabeth's protests conveniently subside and Cooper resolves his plot in exact accord with Judge Temple's values. Major Effingham and John Mohegan die; Leatherstocking and Doolittle depart westward; whether Oliver Edwards has Delaware blood or not, his marriage to Elizabeth, together with Judge Temple's probated will, accord the right of land ownership to the owner of a signed and purchased paper title. At novel's end Elizabeth is mistress of the mansion house, "issuing her usual orders for the day" (447), having either forgotten or changed her mind about her "small right" to inherit her father's lands. As Elizabeth and Oliver Edwards Effingham stroll along cleared fields beside the lake, Oliver remarks, "Bess! you amaze me! I did not think you had been such a manager!" " 'Oh, I manage more deeply than you imagine, sir,' said the wife, archly smiling again" (449). Scott's Rose Bradwardine, at the moment when she marries Edmund Waverley and repossesses Tully Veolan, could hardly have said it better!

In all four novels, the curtain is hastily dropped on the heroine's postmarital future. There are, however, no signs that the newly married patriot wife will ever challenge her husband as she had challenged her father or her guardian. Cooper even tells us that his most forward heroine, Katherine Plowden, "passed merrily, and we trust happily, down the vale of life . . . making, every thing considered, a very obedient and certainly, as far as attachment was concerned, a most devoted wife" (*The Pilot* 420). In such hasty, sun-drenched prose does the rebelliously minded *femme sole* become a conveniently and conventionally submissive *femme couverte.*

Deference to one's patriot husband is not, however, the dominant note struck in Cooper's characterizations of his revolutionary heroines. Before marriage and property become a reality of their middle age, we remember these young women's sudden, unexplained outbursts of political reason and patriotic feeling. If Cooper conceded much to social stability in his revolutionary heroine's marriage, he also contributed to republican ideology through his account of her rebellious youth. When Frances Wharton, Katherine Plowden, and Agnes Danforth declare their love of republican liberty in defiance of personal and political patriarchy, they do not do so because they have read John Locke, or because they have studied the history of Rome, or because their fathers are cruel oppressors, or because they condone the tactics of the Sons of Liberty. They stand for liberty because, as thinking individuals, they somehow instinctively know that liberty is mankind's natural right. Their revolutionary American faith is wholly unsourced; it simply *is.* The unexplained origin of woman's faith in freedom is, for Cooper, both the commendable mark and the eventual limitation of woman's political power.

NOTES

1. James Russell Lowell, *A Fable for Critics* (1848), in *Fenimore Cooper: The Critical Heritage*, ed. George Dekker and John P. McWilliams (London: Routledge & Kegan Paul, 1973), 239.

2. Jonathan Arac, *The Emergence of American Literary Narrative, 1820–1860* (Cambridge, MA: Harvard University Press, 2005), 5–15.

3. A significant exception is Signe O. Wegener's *James Fenimore Cooper and the Cult of Domesticity* (Jefferson, NC: McFarland, 2005), which was published after this chapter was written. Wegener's focus is on the complexity and importance of Cooper's renderings of "Victorian domesticity and family dynamics"(3), not—as is mine— on the political beliefs that Cooper's marriageable heroines voice about the American Revolution. We emphasize different novels and place them in different contexts. Nonetheless, my chapter would

have benefited from Wegener's findings, especially those in her last chapter titled "Daughters."

4. James Fenimore Cooper, *The American Democrat* (1838), ed. George Dekker and Larry Johnston (London: Penguin Books, 1989), 144–145.

5. See Linda K. Kerber, *Women of the Republic: Intellect and Ideology in Revolutionary America* (Chapel Hill: University of North Carolina Press, 1980), 11, and Nancy Cott, *The Bonds of Womanhood: "Woman's Sphere" in New England, 1780–1835* (New Haven: Yale University Press, 1977), 62.

6. Cathy N. Davidson, introduction to *Charlotte Temple* by Susanna Rowson (New York: Oxford University Press, 1986), xxvii–xxviii.

7. Hannah Webster Foster, *The Coquette*, ed. Cathy N. Davidson (New York: Oxford University Press, 1986), 44.

8. John Trumbull, "The Progress of Dulness" (1773), in *The Satiric Poems of John Trumbull*, ed. Edwin T. Bowden (Austin: University of Texas Press, 1962), 50.

9. Charles Brockden Brown, *Alcuin: A Dialogue* (1798), ed. Lee R. Edwards (New York: Grossman, 1971), 9–10.

10. Cathy N. Davidson, *Revolution and the Word: The Rise of the Novel in America* (New York: Oxford University Press, 1986), 120.

11. See Mary Beth Norton, *Liberty's Daughters: The Revolutionary Experience of American Women, 1750–1780* (Boston: Little, Brown, 1980), especially 170–194.

12. James Fenimore Cooper, *The Pilot: A Tale of the Sea*, ed. Kay Seymour House (Albany: State University of New York Press, 1986), 132.

13. The language in which Cooper described the joyful success of his courtship is revealing. In an 1810 letter to his brother Richard, Cooper wrote, "Like all the rest of the sons of Adam, I have bowed to the influence of the charms of [a] fair damsel of eighteen." James F. Beard, *The Letters and Journals of James Fenimore Cooper* (Cambridge, MA: Belknap Press of Harvard University Press, 1962), 1: 17. In his footnote to this letter, Beard remarked that Cooper's characterization of his bride, Susan De Lancey, as "amiable, sweet tempered and happy in her disposition" was to prove "singularly perceptive and just" (1: 17). Cooper wrote very few letters to any woman other than his wife, whom he was to address for forty years as "My Sue," "My Beloved Sue," "My dearest Sue," or simply "Dearest."

14. Mary Wollstonecraft, *Vindication of the Rights of Woman* (1792), ed. Miriam Brody (London: Penguin Books, 1985), 105.

15. Within the broader history of narrative, the convention of juxtaposing fair and dark ladies reaches back at least as far as the contrast of Una and Duessa in the first book of Spenser's *The Faerie Queene* (1589).

16. Sir Walter Scott, *Waverley; or, 'Tis Sixty Years Since* (1814), ed. Andrew Hook (London: Penguin Books, 1985), 168, 169.

17. James Fenimore Cooper, *The Spy: A Tale of the Neutral Ground* (1821), ed. James P. Elliott, James H. Pickering, Lance Schachterle, and Jeffrey Walker (Brooklyn, NY: AMS Press, 2002), 305.

18. Cooper's term "imbecility" is often glossed as "helplessness." One wonders, however, whether the word does not retain more than a tincture of today's meaning. Cooper applies the word "imbecile" or "imbecility" to Mr. Wharton repeatedly.

19. Cooper, *The Pilot*, 27.

20. James Fenimore Cooper, *Lionel Lincoln, or, the Leaguer of Boston* (1825), ed. Donald A. and Lucy B. Ringe (Albany: State University of New York Press, 1984), 40–41.

21. James Fenimore Cooper, *The Pioneers, or the Sources of the Susquehanna; A Descriptive Tale* (1823), ed. James Franklin Beard, Lance Schachterle, and Kenneth M. Andersen Jr. (Albany: State University of New York Press, 1980), 18.

Cooper's Europe and His Quarrel with America

J. Gerald Kennedy

Gleanings in Europe, the massive five-volume project completed in 1838 by James Fenimore Cooper, marks the most ambitious effort by an antebellum American author to scrutinize the new nation from a critical, transnational perspective. Cooper's ostensible subject, the curiosities of western Europe, facilitates a comparative analysis of his own country and its emerging national character. Having contemplated early American experience in such narratives as *The Spy*, *The Pioneers*, *Lionel Lincoln*, and *The Last of the Mohicans*, Cooper went abroad in 1826 to ensure that his daughters learned foreign languages, to arrange European publishing agreements, to seek relief from physical ailments, and to acquire a cosmopolitan understanding of cultural differences. Through DeWitt Clinton and Henry Clay he secured a nominal appointment as U.S. consul to Lyon, France, to "avoid the appearance of going over to the enemy" as an expatriate.[1] His only prior glimpse of Europe had come two decades earlier during a youthful tour of duty with the U.S. Navy. When he returned as a celebrated novelist, Cooper made the grand tour, studied the human scene, and socialized as a literary lion, meeting the great and near great, all the while drawing inferences about manners, beliefs, politics, and national traits in the countries he visited.

Cooper had a keen sense of the historical moment, which he associated with the spread of modern nationalism and the advent of republican government. In some ways his *Gleanings* anticipate the objectives of current transnational studies: he wanted to develop a global (or at least transatlantic) perspective to surmount the parochial nationalism of his American contemporaries. His timing could not have been better for observing the surge of popular, revolutionary sentiment against aristocratic rule that arose inchoately in fifteenth-century Switzerland, gained impetus during the English Civil War, erupted in America in 1776, and reached an international tipping point in the French Revolution of 1789. Cooper studied the contemporary situation to evaluate alternative forms of government in a dawning era of national self-determination. Yet his years abroad also disposed him to view his own country in an increasingly critical perspective; he bristled at the growing tyranny of American popular opinion while valuing in European society a taste and decorum missing in the United States. Marked (in one friend's opinion) by a frank tone more like Cooper's manner of speech than anything else he wrote, his *Gleanings* have nevertheless suffered critical neglect.[2] Mostly adapted from his journals and letters, the volumes teem with topical perceptions that lead to pointed cultural reflections. Their significance here lies in Cooper's insights into national identity and his determination to write against the American nation in order to reform it. Unmistakably, the journey to Europe precipitated the author's notorious quarrel with America.

Cooper arrived in Europe stoked with patriotic sentiment and armed with a nationalist agenda. *The Prairie*, *The Red Rover*, and *The Wept of Wish-ton-Wish*—all completed abroad—reflect his continuing preoccupation with national subjects. So, too, does *Notions of the Americans*, a collection of travel letters ostensibly written by a European bachelor for a British audience. Responding to America's English critics, Cooper in 1828 concocted a series of admiring sketches based on imaginary travels in the United States, affecting the delight of a European stranger at scenes of progress and civility. Through this persona Cooper drew the distinctive features of localities he knew personally, emphasizing those public improvements that signaled energy and foresight. But licensed by nationalistic indignation, he also affected more extensive knowledge: his narrator speaks of traveling "over an immense surface of the southern and western States," regions that Cooper knew only through report.[3] In a work marking the zenith of Cooper's uncritical enthusiasm for his native land, his roving bachelor concludes, "The spirit of greatness is in this nation."[4]

Compared to the jingoism of *Notions*, however, the later *Gleanings* exhibits discriminating rigor. Cooper came to understand nationality as a complex of collective memories, practices, and myths; while he was exploring Europe, he witnessed revolutionary changes in France, impending insurrection in England, and conditions that impelled the Italian Risorgimento. He observed popular unrest in Germany and learned of mounting discontent in Poland from poet-revolutionary Adam Mickiewicz. In Europe Cooper did not simply indulge in touristic escapism; he monitored and sympathized with sociopolitical change. Nor did he become Europeanized—though that, ironically, was how compatriots saw him on his return—but rather maintained a prickly nationalistic assertiveness. The "truckling to foreigners and eagerness to know what other nations think of us . . . that always disgusted me when at home," he wrote to Luther Bradish, "is a hundredfold more disgusting now that I know how utterly *worthless* are the [European] opinions they [American newspapers] republish."[5]

In the process, however, Cooper came to regard the United States from a critical viewpoint. His clashes with the American press before and after his return home doubtless contributed to his disillusionment, but expatriation itself provided the perspective of otherness that revealed the oddities and deficiencies of American life. Cooper's *Gleanings* thus reflect the evolution of a more complicated understanding of nationhood and nationality. If the exercise began with an earnest desire to know Europe and to correct its misapprehensions about America, it ended, somewhat surprisingly, with Cooper's dismantling of his nation's most cherished illusions about itself. Comparing the traditional, ethnic cultures of the Old World, Cooper discovered that the national community hardest to locate or define was his own. For him the

American nation remained (to borrow Paul Giles's formulation) a "virtual construction," more a "signifier than a signified," a potentiality already jeopardized—in Cooper's judgment—by American provincialism and self-deception.[6] The disturbing conclusion that American national culture was doomed to greed and vulgarity dampened his homecoming and initiated a professional crisis, for his *Gleanings* offended the American public. Cooper had broached the unspeakable, disconcerting possibility that in its brash assertiveness, U.S. nation building was an act of cultural imposture.

Cooper's reconstruction of his European experience followed a course unrelated to the itinerary of his travels, which began and ended in France. The author and his family—which included his wife, infant son, four daughters, and nephew William as traveling secretary—took up residence in Paris in June 1826 and remained there or in nearby St. Ouen until early 1828. In Paris the American novelist met the aging revolutionary hero, the Marquis de Lafayette, as well as the Great Unknown of British literature, Sir Walter Scott. In March 1828, literary business took Cooper to London, where he completed *Notions*, saw Scott, and met Samuel Taylor Coleridge, William Godwin, and other writers. But after returning to Paris in June via Holland and Belgium, the family set out in mid-July for Switzerland. Renting a villa near Berne, Cooper (then beginning *The Wept of Wish-ton-Wish*) organized several Alpine excursions during the late summer, gathering notes on the country and material for *The Headsman*. Then in October, racing the onset of winter, the family traversed the Simplon Pass into Italy, where extended residences in Florence, Sorrento, and Rome highlighted nineteen months in the sunny land where Cooper wrote *The Water-Witch* and collected impressions for *The Bravo*. The desire to afford his daughters German language instruction prompted their departure for Dresden in May 1830, but unfolding political events in Paris abbreviated that stay. In August Cooper returned alone to France, where the July Revolution had deposed the last Bourbon king, Charles X, and enthroned Orléanist Louis Philippe. Resettling his family again in

Paris, the writer there studied the manipulations of a government touted as a constitutional monarchy. Cooper enjoyed an ideal vantage point on the revolutionary nationalism erupting across Europe in the early 1830s, as well as on conservative resistance to change. Apart from a second tour of Belgium, the Rhineland, and five weeks in Switzerland in 1832, Cooper and his family remained in the Faubourg St. Germain to the end of their European tour.

In Paris, Cooper completed *The Bravo, The Heidenmauer,* and *The Headsman,* a trilogy testing his abilities in the European historical romance. Into narratives variously illustrating the abuses of aristocratic rule, the author infused unmistakably American ideals, contriving transparent critiques of contemporary Continental politics. About these novels Udo Nattermann surmises that "Cooper's goal is to present European societies as underdeveloped versions of the United States and as systems in the process of embracing the American model; America is to appear as the end-point of the historical process, as what nature wills human society finally to become."[7] Though the convoluted *Headsman* still boggles even Cooper aficionados, most modern critics have judged *The Bravo* and *The Heidenmauer* as passably engaging narratives. Yet adverse reviews of the trilogy in American newspapers so closely echoed derisive European judgments that an exasperated Cooper threatened to renounce the writing of novels.

Such is the import of his angry *Letter to His Countrymen* (1834), composed soon after his return to the United States in 1833. Domiciling his family in New York while workmen renovated the repurchased family home in Cooperstown, he confronted the estranging effects of a residence abroad. The "raven-like prediction" of a man who had prophesied at his departure in 1826, "You will never come back," was in a sense true: the Cooper who returned to the United States in 1833 was a very different man.[8] And the country, to his dismay, seemed likewise altered, consumed by greed and partisan rancor. When he began *Gleanings,* Cooper fancied himself embarking on a new career as a cultural critic. He hoped his nonfiction writing would enjoy success, but above all he meant to combat ignorance at home and abroad, correct-

ing American self-delusions and enlightening native readers
about Europe while aiming (through foreign editions) to provide
European readers with revealing views of the countries he had
visited.

For the initial volume, Cooper focused not on France, the base for
his travels, but on Switzerland, where he kept a meticulous daily
journal for three months in 1828. The account would emphasize
spectacular Alpine landscapes to capitalize on the vogue for the
picturesque; political and cultural observations would comple-
ment and humanize the natural scenery. Tracing his route to
Berne, the author of *The Last of the Mohicans* notes that they have
passed through Dijon on the heels of a small band of Osage Indians who were "making a sensation" in France.[9] Cooper incor-
rectly supposed that the Osages had been invited to discuss an alliance with the French against the United States, and he looked
forward to Switzerland as a retreat from political intrigue, an opportunity for "a sublime communion with nature" (5).

In four excursions to the country's various cantons, Cooper
managed to visit most of Switzerland's legendary sites and natural attractions. Rocky gorges, soaring peaks, and scenic waterfalls
repeatedly induce in the family a condition of "touzy-mouzy"
(19) or touristic rapture. The author regards his expedition to the
canton of Schweitz as a "pilgrimage to the cradle of Helvetic liberty" (101), a place associated with the "memorable exploits"
(108) of William Tell, who had led ten Swiss cantons against an
Austrian tyrant in the fifteenth century. Ostensibly this alliance
for freedom marked the remote origin of modern nationalism in
western Europe. Cooper likewise seeks out the ancient abbey of
Einsiedeln, finding his "Protestant insensibilities" (169) almost
moved by a statue of Mary. He visits and compares Zürich,
Lucerne, and Geneva, detouring from the last to inspect the
home of Voltaire in Ferney.

In these pursuits, Cooper behaved like many a foreign traveler
in Switzerland, and he studies his fellow tourists, invariably interpreting their manners as symptoms of national identity. The English nettle him most consistently, whether by ignoring him at

the breakfast table or failing to return his courteous bows, or scribbling satirical comments about America opposite the names of American tourists in hotel registers (67–68). However critical Cooper becomes of American vulgarity, he seems invariably to take umbrage at witticisms directed at his country. "This thing called national pride is a queer sentiment" (235), he justly notes, perhaps sensing the perverse contradictions of his own nationalism. The English are especially prone to "attach wrong conclusions" (241) to American facts, and it does not help that Cooper is recurrently taken for an Englishman by Continental types.

But what distinguishes the first volume of *Gleanings* from other guidebooks is Cooper's determination to analyze Swiss national culture and its political system. He judges the confederation of cantons chaotic and inefficient: "For a nation of limited extent, and tolerably identified interests, the confederated form possesses scarcely an advantage, while it necessarily brings with it many peculiar disadvantages. Diversity of laws, want of unity, embarrassments in the currency, the frequent recurrence of frontiers, organized means for internal dissensions, and a variety of similar sources of evil are, beyond a doubt, the ordinary price that is paid for the confederated form of government" (144). The author estimates that, despite Tell's legacy, little political liberty actually exists in Switzerland: some cantons dominate others, and aristocratic families still control certain municipalities. Cooper also believes that "true liberty [has] no abode" (146) in Catholic cantons, where religion and education are closely regulated. Linguistic heterogeneity also obstructs Swiss nation building. "This is the country of languages" (200), he remarks, observing that in the canton of Grisons alone, three languages and several local dialects impede national development. "The great influx of strangers" looking to "turn the picturesque into profit" (92) also provoke national disunity and demoralization. In Switzerland Cooper confronts a condensed version of the challenge already facing the United States: how a multiethnic, multilinguistic population might overcome geographical and cultural barriers to create a fully representative republic.

Yet Cooper misses the analogy. Indeed, he contrasts the diversity of the Swiss population with the homogeneity of the American people, suggesting that there is "less real difference . . . between a skipper of Kennebunk and a planter of the Arkansas, than there frequently is to be found between two Swiss peasants whose cottages may be seen in the same valley" (130). The comparison reveals that, like most of his contemporaries, Cooper envisioned the emerging American nation as inherently Anglo-Saxon. The uniformity among Euro-Americans nevertheless troubles the author, who in a footnote characterizes the United States in 1835 as "a country where the mass has become so consolidated that it has no longer any integral parts; where the individual is fast losing his individuality in the common identity" (128–129 n). If his attenuated gaze at Switzerland sharpens his appreciation of "American principles" (2) and motivates his biased comparison of American and English forms of government (124–129 n), it also provokes certain withering judgments about his compatriots. For example, when Cooper portrays the unfortunate cretins of St. Maurice and registers the provincial belief that obscurity, ignorance, and poverty are essential to happiness, he adds with savage irony, "It might not be amiss to effect a little infusion of American blood into them, which, I think, would thoroughly eradicate the latter singularity. Poor wretches! They have not yet learned to term a lust for money, a virtue; the desire to live in a better house than their fellows, ambition; overreaching a neighbor, genius; and the restlessness of covetous desires, energy!" (271). Such biting asides explain the mixed response of American reviewers to Cooper's *Switzerland*. Poe noticed Cooper's "splenetic ill humor" toward "both himself and his countrymen," though on balance he judged the author's national critique accurate enough.[10] The picturesque views of the Alps ultimately carried the volume to moderate success as the first installment of Cooper's comparative transnational studies.

The subsequent volume, *Sketches of Switzerland, Part Second*, now available as *Gleanings in Europe: The Rhine*, culminates in an emotional return to the Alps in 1832. The journey represents an escape from the dangers of Paris, still gripped by cholera and revolutionary violence, and the book's opening section depicts the charged atmosphere in the capital at the beginning of Louis Philippe's reign. Cooper reports hearing sporadic gunshots and describes a morgue filled with bodies, of which "twenty or thirty dead" have been pulled from "a citadel of the disaffected" after a militia assault.[11] The "money-power system" (28) of the new regime has already alienated supporters of the July Revolution expecting a genuine republic to emerge, and Cooper heaps scorn on Louis Philippe. For example, he mocks the monarch for "condescending with all his might" to the "rabble" during a stroll in the Tuileries staged for "republican effect" (70). Intriguingly, Cooper portrays himself as a nocturnal *flâneur*, standing alone on the Pont des Arts at midnight, "while contending factions were struggling for the mastery [of the capital], and perhaps the fate of not only France, but of all Europe was hanging on the issue!" (51). He remarks on the portentous strangeness of the "brooding calm" that prevails over "an empire in jeopardy" (52).

The opening section also features a portrait of Lafayette containing revelations about his role in the recent Revolution. The novelist esteems Lafayette as a paragon of republican virtue, a living link to the heroic generation that fought the American Revolution. But because Lafayette has been removed as head of the National Guards by Louis Philippe, the general also figures (in Cooper's view) as "the dupe of his own good faith and kind feelings" (13). Lafayette acknowledges his role in suppressing violence during the Revolution and admits that he could have formed a new, republican government but suspects that the monarchies of Europe "would have united to put us down" (69). For Cooper, the general personifies the virtuous man disinterested in power, the countertype of the calculating monarch he has reluctantly enthroned.

When Louis Philippe declares a state of siege to consolidate his authority, Cooper and family depart for a tour of the Rhineland. By carriage they journey north to Brussels, then east to Liège and Spa, but Belgium holds little interest. Cooper crassly remarks that the Flemish have the reputation of being "the most ignorant population of Europe" (95). Germany, on the other hand, abounds in interest as "the land of sensations, whether music, poetry, arms, or the more material arts be their object," a nation of artists unlike "the great bulk of the American people," who have little "real reverence for letters, arts, or indeed cultivation of any kind" (114). Cooper visits the extraordinary, unfinished cathedral at Cologne but finds the city itself the "dirtiest and most offensive" (117) he has toured in Europe. Learning of "political disturbances" in Frankfurt, he comments on the "serious discontent, all along the Rhine" where the "*nouveaux riches*" are attempting to limit the sway of "the old feudal and territorial nobility" (135). Among Germany's well-ordered towns, Stuttgart impresses Cooper as "more *European*" and less "peculiar" (140) or provincial. Beyond Tübingen, the crumbling Hohenzollern castle seems the "epitome of royalty" (144), the detritus of a self-indulgent aristocracy that has divided the land into "*quasi* kingdoms" (141), setting the stage for German national unification.

From Germany the Coopers embark on a "new pilgrimage to the mountains" (147) of Switzerland. The route brings them back to La Lorraine, their home in 1828, evoking a nostalgia colored by the recent death by consumption of Cooper's nephew, who had accompanied them earlier: "The old abode was empty, and we walked over it, with feelings in which pain and pleasure were mingled, for poor W[illiam], who was with us, full of youth and spirits, when we resided here, is now a tenant of *Père la Chaise*" (160). An intellectual purpose also impels the return: Cooper wants to investigate reports that "great political changes have occurred in Switzerland since 1830" and that "democracy is in the ascendant" (159). The dozen letters (XV–XXVI) on Switzerland thus deal less with nature and more with national culture.

The changed political climate prompts repeated comparisons with the United States. Revising his earlier view that the cantons lacked real freedom, Cooper now perceives a deep affinity between Swiss and American values, based on a shared devotion to republican principles. Among European states, Switzerland seems moreover unique in its concern about the American nullification crisis, then perceived as "menacing disunion" (186). Writing in 1836, he downplays the seriousness of South Carolina's secession threat yet remarks bitterly that most European newspapers in 1832 were predicting the "speedy dissolution" of the

United States, displaying their "political antipathies," whereas the Swiss "with very few exceptions, wish[ed] us well" (229). Perhaps Cooper's most acute observation on Switzerland and the United States, though, concerns the fundamentally different origins of national identity. Whereas Americans imagine themselves a nation largely because they share common democratic ideals, the Swiss sense of nationhood is more profoundly rooted in geography and landscape. "It would be curious to inquire how far the noble nature of the country has an influence in producing their strong national attachments," Cooper writes, noting that although necessity sometimes obliges a Swiss to "tear himself from his native soil . . . yet very few of them absolutely expatriate themselves" (221). American national feeling suffers from the opposite tendency:

> The migratory habits of the country prevent the formation of the intensity of interest, to which the long residence of a family in a particular spot gives birth, and which comes at last, to love a tree, or a hill, or a rock, because they are the same tree, and hill, and rock, that have been loved by our fathers before us. These are attachments that depend on sentiment rather than on interest, and are as much purer and holier, as virtuous sentiment is purer and holier than worldly interestedness. In this moral feature therefore, we are inferior to all old nations, and to the Swiss in particular. (221)

In their restless, rootless habits, Americans betray a lack of sentiment for place or homeland. Uprooted himself from Cooperstown by the selling of Otsego Hall in 1819, the author envies the Swiss devotion to their native mountains, a consciousness heightened in the mid-1830s by his troubled return to the family home.[12]

Cooper's travels in Switzerland provoke observations on other disconcerting features of American life. His effort to persuade a Bürgerschaft member that men without political experience can cultivate leadership leads him to admit of America that "so long as the impetus of the revolution, and the influence of great events lasted, we had great men, in the ascendant, but now that matters were jogging on regularly, and under their common-place aspects, we were obliged to take up with merely clever managers" (161). Further evidence of this decline comes from a diplomatic corps populated by sycophants of "indomitable selfishness"; they personify the degeneration of "national pride and national character" (236) in their willingness to derogate American democracy to curry favor in foreign courts. As letter XXV makes clear, the author's scorn for American representatives abroad stemmed from the "finance controversy" of 1832, in which he suspected that William Cabell Rives, the American minister to France, had sanctioned a French refutation of Cooper's essay on the economic advantages of republican government.

The last letter in *The Rhine* traces the family's return to Paris. When they stop at Lafayette's country home, La Grange, Cooper's conversation with the general turns on South Carolina, and Lafayette confesses that the dissolution of the Union would "break his heart," adding poignantly, "'I hope they will at least let me die . . . before they commit this *suicide* on *our* institutions'" (256, Cooper's italics).[13] An impending compromise between free and slave states has, Cooper believes, quashed the secessionist impulse, but his further observation seems prescient: "There is but one interest that would likely unite all the South against the North, and this was the interest connected with slavery" (257). He remarks on the "notorious" fact that "neither the Federal Government, nor the individual states, have any thing to do with [slavery] as a national question" (257). Set against his earlier reflections on Swiss national attachments, Cooper's closing attention to the unresolved problem of slavery emphasizes the pragmatic rather than ethnic or territorial basis of American nationhood: "The Union was a compromise that grew out of practical wants and *facts*." Although he insists that "this was the strongest possible foundation for any polity" (258), he does not address the concomitant question of whether a union by compromise can indefinitely bind a people deficient in national feeling. It was a question that would increasingly haunt Cooper's ruminations on Europe and America.

Because France had become Cooper's "second home," his next book ventures cultural comparisons more informed—and piquant—than those of previous volumes.[14] Because he had just devoted a portion of *The Rhine* to postrevolutionary Paris, the author focuses in *France* (originally titled *Gleanings in Europe*) on unrest during the last years of Charles X. The book thus delivers a political autopsy: the violence of 1830 has (at the time of writing) already exploded, and Cooper writes with a retrospective awareness of impending insurrection, although he also maintains the eager perspective of an American coming to Paris for the first time. Singularly composed, according to Thomas Philbrick, without reference to correspondence or journals (xxvi), the volume derives intensity from Cooper's insights into the delusions of temporal power. "*Nations* are not easily destroyed," he observes in *The Rhine*, but they inevitably suffer "mutations" effected by upheavals of government.[15]

Cooper's narrative reconstructs the beginnings of his self-exile by retracing the family's Atlantic voyage, their landing on the Isle of Wight, and his mission to London in quest of a publishing agreement. He ranks his tour of Westminster Abbey as the greatest "sensation" (*France* 61) among his European experiences of 1826, although unlike the Anglophile Irving, Cooper feels no sense of homecoming: "For myself, I have always felt as a stranger in England. . . . In the whole of that great nation, there is not a single individual, with whom I could claim affinity. And yet, with a slight exception, we [Coopers] are purely of English extraction" (28). This uneasiness would produce an inevitable confrontation with his own conflicted sentiments in *England*.

Cooper's *France* confines itself mostly to Paris, with one section devoted to nearby, bucolic St. Ouen, where he spent several months in 1827. Cooper judges Paris "the centre of Europe" (270) and recommends it as the ideal training ground for expatriate Americans. He finds France "a great and an intellectual nation" (184), its people marked by "*bonhomie*" and "touches of chivalry" (55). He most values "good breeding" in the French, a term Cooper seems to equate with tolerance, manners, and ease.

Although he criticizes the concentration of wealth and power in Paris, he savors the delights of the great city. One day Sir Walter Scott calls to introduce himself; his visit nearly coincides with another by Lafayette. Cooper devotes letter XX to Lafayette and La Grange, which the novelist visited on three occasions prior to 1830. Soon after arriving in Paris, the author finds himself unexpectedly caught up in its social life: "I am acquainted with no town," he explains, "in which . . . there is more true hospitality, than in Paris" (211–212). Much of *France* focuses on social etiquette and the intricate system of aristocratic distinctions that determined protocol. Cooper positions himself as a cosmopolitan Mr. Manners, instructing compatriots on social usages while lamenting the "provincial and rustic" (76) practices of American society. Two entire letters, VI and XI, treat forms of *politesse* and offer a veritable guide to French manners and conventions. Cooper dutifully explains the value and use of visiting cards, the practice of allowing new arrivals to initiate social visits, the niceties of personal calling, and even the spatial configuration of Parisian *hôtels particuliers* (presumably to avoid arriving at the wrong door). He also treats proper forms of address to titled guests and advises Americans to affect "simplicity" in acknowledging nobility (81). He admonishes fellow citizens to avoid elegance in dress; they should "go to court as they go to the President's House, in the simple attire of American gentlemen" (120). They should by all means maintain reserve and dignity: "Let us at least show that we are not mannikins to be pulled about for the convenience and humours of others, but that we know what honest words are, understand the difference between civility and abuse, and have pride enough to resent contumely, when, at least, we feel it to be unmerited" (87). This defensiveness hints at one of Cooper's deepest anxieties: being mocked by Europeans simply for being an American. It suggests that his fastidious delineation of French social practices stems from a compulsive need to protect the national honor by preparing transatlantic travelers for the subtleties, complexities, and even dangers of European society. A few decades later Henry James would transform this delicate predicament into a major literary genre.

In one extraordinary letter (XVIII), Cooper displays his own savoir faire, tracing his course from one social engagement to another, beginning with a dinner at the home of the French chancellor and ending with a glittering late-night ball hosted by the Russian ambassador. In between, he makes courtesy calls at four other gatherings, each representing a distinct social milieu. From one, he beats a strategic retreat rather than suffer the "big looks" (222) of unfriendly dukes. The ambassador's ball, attended by fifteen hundred, offers a lesson in exclusivity: hundreds of others applied for invitations and were refused. But a poor French girl has been invited, Cooper discovers, on account of her ravishing beauty; another attendee is identified as the daughter of a marquis beheaded during the Reign of Terror. The author also hears gossip about the infidelities intimated by the complex social tableau around him. He narrates this adventure not to demonstrate his suavity but to dramatize the social challenges facing an American expatriate in Paris—and to illustrate that the French are (as he observes elsewhere) "notoriously addicted to intrigue" (178), whether political, social, or sexual.

Cooper's fascination with the beau monde extends to the monarchy. Explaining that tradition obliges the kings of France to dine in public twice annually, he tells in letter IX of receiving an invitation to observe the dinner from behind a railing, while less privileged spectators shuffle past the scene. From his vantage point Cooper finds himself surprisingly close to royalty: "Thus, I stood for an hour, within five-and-twenty feet of the king, and part of the time much nearer, while, by a fiction of etiquette, I was not understood to be there at all. I was a good while within ten feet of the *Duchesse de Berri*, while, by convention, I was no where" (116). His puckish acceptance of social invisibility typifies his wry depiction of festivities staged for the sake of public access to the king but in fact serving to reinforce the chasm between royalty and the masses. About Charles X Cooper observes that "his countenance betrayed a species of vacant *bonhomie*" and lacked the "majesty of character and expression" (123) indispensable to a monarch. Cooper cannot imagine a "droller *mélange*" than the commoners who form the procession of "queer faces" all turning "like sunflowers, toward the light of royalty" (124). He notes the ennui of titled dinner guests, the absence of conversation, and the apparently disappointing cuisine, confessing his relief at the end of the affair.

The disdain for royalty evident here recurs throughout *France* and explains Cooper's attentiveness to signs of aristocratic insecurity or public unrest. "Notwithstanding the present magnificence of the court," he writes, "royalty is shorn of much of its splendor in France, since the days of Louis XVI" (72). At a military review in the Champs de Mars, shouts of "à bas les ministres" (106) provoke the king to disband the Parisian National Guards, who have been accused of subversion. Cooper remarks that "a more unjust decree" could not have been imagined, provoking a "deep," perhaps "lasting discontent" (106) among the people. The king's reliance on the regular army, "with the intention of keeping the people in subjection to tyranny" (102), has in fact entailed huge expenditures of public funds, and according to Lafayette, the monarch has further exploited "the machinery of power" to pervert the legal system, meting out "the grossest injustice, illegality, and oppression" in "political cases" (98). This pattern of subjugation that incited the Revolution of 1830 suggests obvious parallels to the regime of Louis Philippe. Assessing the French political scene in 1828, Cooper opines, "Further revolutions are inevitable. The mongrel government which exists, neither can stand, nor does it deserve to stand. It contains the seeds of its own destruction" (233). Replete with a scathing survey of extravagances at Versailles (letter X), *France* cumulatively exposes not just the self-indulgence and corruption of Charles X but the systematic injustice of dynastic monarchy itself. For Americans wrestling with the politics of "King Andrew" and his successor, Martin Van Buren, Cooper's postmortem analysis of the Bourbon regime provides a tonic perspective. Cooper freely acknowledges the defects of democracy but believes that given "a choice of evils" (253) among forms of polity, Americans benefit from their chosen system.

Cooper's admiration for French culture prompts unsettling contrasts, however, between his second home and his native land. He raises the problem of meddling in the sphere of personal privacy to suggest that the pressure to conform to public mores is far greater in the United States than elsewhere: "I greatly question if there be any civilized people among whom the individual is as much obliged to consult the habits and tastes of *all*, in gratifying his own, as in free and independent America" (200). Despite the king's perversion of political justice, his use of the army to intimidate the populace, and even his deployment of spies (Cooper writes in letter XXI of being covertly investigated), the French nevertheless enjoy greater "personal independence" (257) than Americans, he asserts. Attributing the "prominent love of meddling" (247) to America's Puritan legacy, Cooper suggests that the very idea of freedom in the United States is a delusion: "The American goes and comes when he pleases, and no one asks for a passport; he has his political rights; talks of his liberty; swaggers of his advantages, and yet does less as he pleases, even in innocent things, than the Frenchman. His neighbors form a police, and a most troublesome and impertinent one it sometimes proves to be. It is also unjust, for having no legal means of arriving at facts, it half the time condemns on conjecture" (257). By implication the moral policing of neighbors in the United States more deeply undermines personal freedom than authoritarian surveillance. The indictment shatters a national illusion hallowed in the United States and helps to explain the "lukewarm" (xxx) American response to *France*.

Cooper's singular vehemence about meddling ultimately exposes the circumstance that perhaps precipitated his move to Europe. To illustrate his belief that "society meddles much more with the private affairs of individuals . . . in America than in Europe," he tells of a man with several daughters who had intended to hire an instructress for their collective education but was warned by a minister *"that the community would not bear it, and that it would infallibly make enemies!"* Cooper adds, "I was myself the person making the application" (255, Cooper's italics). Together with his insistence on the provincialism of manners in the States, his vehemence about the limits of privacy, the pressures of conformity, and the constraints on American personal freedom gives his portrait of France an unexpected bite.

Yet there is another area in which Cooper discerns a radical difference between French and American attitudes. Although the former are, in his view, "singularly alive to the advantages of money" (213), they also manifest a certain disdain for wealth and find nothing shameful about poverty. The latter, on the other hand, "consider money the very base of all distinction"; it has become in America "every man's goal," causing individuals daily to *"corrupt themselves*, in the rapacious pursuit of gain" (213). Acutely responsive to money, the French nevertheless refuse to worship it and thereby secure a certain self-possession, whereas Americans readily succumb to the lure of wealth and in the process lose themselves.

Behind these delineations of what Cooper supposes to be "nation character" lie two distinct yet unspecified ideas of nationhood. The French possess a rich culture (one letter concerns the Académie Française and French theater), a distinctive and poetic language, a long and vivid history (despite the trammels of monarchy), and a sense of hereditary kinship. Cooper can generalize about the French as a nation because of the innumerable commonalities they share. He writes about America and Americans, conversely, mostly in terms of missing qualities: the lack of manners, the want of real liberty, the absence of that cultural self-reliance crucial to authentic nationhood. But before America can achieve that autonomy, it must confront its deficiencies. Two things necessary to the nation, in Cooper's view, are a powerful navy to protect "our national rights" (169)—an old sailor's analysis of homeland security—and a "National Gallery" to enlighten aesthetic tastes. But the greatest obstacle to national self-development, in his view, is "the disposition to resent every intimation that we can be any better than we are at present." He adds, "This tendency to repel every suggestion of inferiority is one of the surest signs of provincial habits" (170). To realize its potential greatness, the American nation must open itself to criticism, Cooper suggests. He quotes with approbation a French saying that implies a crucial difference between the United States and France: " *'On peut tout dire à un grand peuple.'* 'One may tell all to a great nation.' "

Cooper's compulsion to tell all, to confront the urgency of national intellectual self-reliance, impelled the writing of *England* from late 1836 through the spring of 1837. The American edition, delayed by the Panic of 1837, reached bookstores only days after Ralph Waldo Emerson urged Phi Beta Kappa scholars at Harvard to write their own books and listen less to the "courtly muses of Europe." Cooper's preface announces a purpose that the younger Emerson might have applauded:

> The American who should write a close, philosophical, just, popular, and yet comprehensive view of the fundamental differences that exist between the political and social relations of England and those of his own country, would confer on the latter one of the greatest benefits it has received since the memorable events of July 4, 1776. That was a declaration of political independence, only, while this might be considered the foundation of the mental emancipation which alone can render the nation great, by raising its opinion to the level of its facts.[16]

America's "mental emancipation" was the theme of the hour. By "facts" Cooper means the country's geographical size and remoteness from Europe as well as its burgeoning population and political independence. By "opinion" he denotes its capacity for independent judgment. He intends to root out the "colonial subserviency" (233) that blocks American national self-realization. The great, remaining obstacle, slavish deference to English opinion, can be overcome only by frontal assault: by facing the "unpalatable truth" (267) of this incongruity and also exposing England's grand illusions about itself.

Nowhere in *Gleanings* is Cooper more scornful of the United States than when he elaborates his criticisms of England. There seems to be almost too much at stake. Clearly, he yearns to exorcize personal demons and confront the hostilities that underlie his own morbid sensitivity to English derision. As he portrays himself in *England* moving from one social event to another, he hardly conceals his vexation at real or imagined slights, his annoyance at being always under inspection *as an American*. More than once he watches the supercilious English watching him, awaiting a gaucherie or provincial malapropism; at a dinner party he chafes at being seated at the foot of the table on account of his nationality.[17]

The pervasive, even obsessive theme of the volume is English enmity for America. In the preface he categorically avers that "the English do not like the Americans" (2), and variations of this charge recur early and often. Late in the narrative he reaches a kind of Anglophobic frenzy: "The prejudices of the English, against us, against the land in which we live, against the entire nation, morally, physically, and politically, circulate in their mental systems, like the blood in their veins, until they become as inseparable from the thoughts and feelings, as the fluid of life is indispensable to vitality" (263). In contrast to Irving, who had celebrated Anglo-American consanguinity in *The Sketch-book*, Cooper emphasizes the bad blood between the two nations, here virtually imputing to the English a monstrous taint. The problem of England afflicts him viscerally; his own English blood amounts to a congenital affliction, complicated by his wife's ultra-English, Tory origins. In 1806 he had watched the English arbitrarily seize a fellow American sailor, and in 1828 he resented English talk about "recolonization" (287) of the United States. Ultimately, perhaps, Cooper despised the inescapable nature of English influences in his own life and in that of the American nation.

While undertaking a balanced comparison of "national manners" (131), Cooper nevertheless aims to uncover what he perceives as the dependency of America's "better classes" (180) on English opinion and to challenge an inexplicable "national deference" (205) to nobility. He attacks the tyranny of British pundits by suggesting that even as they "exulted in their power over the American mind" (208), their reviews go unnoticed in England. Yet by virtue of their sway over U.S. public opinion, these commentators nevertheless control the fate of American literature and the reputations of individual authors. England "writes up all who defer to her power," he insists, "and writes down all who resist it" (245).

Despite his admiration for certain noblemen—Whig acquaintances such as the redoubtable Lord Grey—Cooper condemns the English aristocracy for its system of "extreme exclusion," a "diseased excrescence" (178), that allows a privileged few to control government. He blames plutocrats for circulating "atrocious misrepresentations" (154) of the United States, and he even assails Sir Walter Scott (who died prior to the writing of *England*) as deferential to hereditary rank, a titled Tory whose novels possess a "deep insinuating current" (121) of antidemocratic feeling.[18] More damningly, he characterizes England itself as a "country of the wealthy" (73), not consumed by profit (like America) but crushed by a privileged elite. The English perversely revere "proprieties" (71) and "the ethics of station," traits instilled by "social drilling" (236), thus perpetuating them by subservience to an oligarchy of wealth that has legitimized injustice, produced rampant "pauperism" (146), and denied political representation to the majority. The aristocracy manipulates "national feeling" in a "fraudulent, and even wicked" (151) way, consolidating its own power and wealth through Parliament. Cooper's scathing critique in letter X of the "antics" (105) of the House of Commons accompanies his revelation that the vast majority of that body derive from the same "social caste" (138) as the House of Lords and so represent identical interests.

Cooper thereby locates in the "perfect order" (19) of England an insidious conservatism. The national attachment to "established proprieties" (73) that charmed Irving appalls Cooper, who perceives exclusion as a mechanism of political control. "The affluent dread revolutions" (139), he observes trenchantly. Letter XIII outlines mounting problems caused by the concentration of wealth in Parliament, which include (in addition to poverty) the flight of industry and capital from the country. Under England's archaic legislative system, most members of the House of Commons were hand-selected by wealthy landowners who controlled fiefdoms called "boroughs." The common folk, whom Cooper regards as "the body of the nation" (112), can resist parliamentary tyranny only through formal petition or by public outcry. "I am of [the] opinion that the present system in England is to undergo radical alterations" (145), he writes, warning that "reform must move fast in England, or it will be overtaken by revolution" (59). Such may have been Cooper's sentiment in 1828, but by 1837 history had overtaken prophecy. By the time he returned to the

United States, England had already enacted several initiatives that included the Reform Act of 1832, which significantly curtailed representation by boroughs and added seats for real commoners from industrial districts. Cooper alludes to 1830–1831 as a period when England "was menaced with revolution" (153 n), yet in November 1830, his friend Lord Grey had led the Whigs to power and accomplished what Linda Colley describes as "the first major reconstruction of the British representative system since Oliver Cromwell's rule in the 1650s." The Reform Act did not create universal male suffrage, but it significantly increased the representative character of British government, for a time making it (as Colley says) "one of the most democratic nations in Europe."[19]

What England most requires, according to Cooper, is an American-style, elected republic: "Our system must, in principle at least, be the next great change of England" (*England* 64). In the face of American deference to English nobility and English scorn for American democracy, his insistence that England must, to ensure its survival, copy the U.S. model of government audaciously reverses the dynamics of influence and asserts the superiority of American political principles. Leavened by many appreciative comments about the English scene, Cooper's deconstruction of "propriety" as the defining national peculiarity thus counteracts American Anglophilia, compelling his compatriots to question their "colonial habits of thought" (210). Such defamiliarization contributes to the "process of alienation" (286) from England necessary to strengthen American self-respect.

Cooper's blazing exposé of inequalities and prejudices in England also establishes his right to judge American national shortcomings. His final verdict is succinct: "The prevailing characteristic of America is mediocrity" (200), he declares, because whether accepting or denying European ridicule, the nation had failed to confront its real faults. The most pernicious American tendency, he suggests, is the "rapacity for money" (135), the "pecuniary cupidity" that incites the "propensity to blackguard those who thwart the rapacity of the grasping" (207). That craving for money has fostered a "dishonesty of sentiment" (213) in the nation itself. Rapid growth and sudden prosperity also affect American manners, which seem "decidedly worse now" (270) than thirty years earlier. The freedom of speech vaunted in the United States is becoming increasingly "one-sided" (267), permitting praise of all things American but quashing discussion of unpleasant realities. Despite their boastfulness, Americans nevertheless lack self-confidence, while social and economic striving has left them no longer a "happy people" (281). Some of these themes had surfaced in earlier volumes of *Gleanings*, but their reiteration here leads Cooper to confront an even more disturbing possibility.

If the "prejudices" of the English—their servile regard for station, propriety, and exclusion—constitute "the base of the nationality of her people" (247), he concludes that Americans are "national" from "a consciousness of living under a system that protects their rights and interests" (248). Yet he also wonders whether belief in the principles and institutions of civil polity can sustain a sense of nationhood among a fractious population united mostly by "national conceit." For the "upper classes" have taught the masses to "repress" their regard for U.S. institutions, causing a conspicuous want of "national pride" (248). Cooper seems to suspect that American nationhood, rooted not in myth, memory, heredity, or heritage but in contingent loyalties to imponderable abstractions, might be chimerical. Having gone abroad to study the national cultures of western Europe, the writer returns with the disconcerting apprehension that America is still far from becoming a nation in any legitimate or demonstrable sense.

Cooper himself resists this dire conclusion, and his frequent references to an American "nation" mask the dread to which he alludes but briefly in *England*. Yet he approaches this void again when he explains the role of metropolitan centers in solidifying nationhood:

> It is not easy for any but close observers, to estimate the influence of such places as London and Paris. They contribute, essentially, to national identity, and national tone, and national policy: in short, to nationality—a merit in which we are almost entirely wanting. I do not mean national sensitiveness,

which some fancy is patriotism, though merely provincial jealousy, but that comprehensive unity of feeling and understanding, that renders a people alive to its true dignity and interests, and prompt to sustain them, as well as independent in their opinions. We are even worse off, than most other nations would be without a capital, for we have an anomalous principle of *dispersion* in the state capitals. . . . An Englishman or a Frenchman goes into distant countries, with a consciousness that he leaves behind him, a concentrated and powerful sentiment of nationality, that will throw its protection around him, even to the remotest verge of civilization, but the case is altogether different with the American. (264–265)

This extraordinary passage captures the radical uncertainty of American nationhood in the 1830s. Cooper's experience in London and Paris has enabled him to see those capitals as (literally) concrete articulations of national identity, which in comparison with Washington—then a small city lacking any rudiments of national culture except a handful of grand buildings—reveals the perceptible difference between the "comprehensive" and "concentrated" nationalities of Europe, conferring portable national identities, and the dispersed, heterogeneous, unformed character of the U.S. population. For the American abroad determined to assert national self-reliance, this poses a deeply disconcerting predicament.

The confessed superficiality of American nationality makes the clamor for a national literature nearly ludicrous, in Cooper's judgment. Surprisingly, the author of revolutionary and border romances shares Poe's scorn for the "impudent . . . pretension that the American reading public requires American themes," and Cooper views the preference for foreign subjects as at least "excusable" because there seems so little that can confidently be called American, at least among the literate "social aristocracy": "As to distinctive American *sentiments* and American *principles*, the majority of that class of our citizens hardly know them when they see them" (248). Americans are more "wrong-headed" and "deluded" (248) about national ideas than any other people because of their provincial isolation from the more fully articulated nations of Europe.

If, in criticizing America for lacking "national pride" yet flaunt-ing national egotism, Cooper seems to be demanding a contradic-tory collective mentality—a bold, self-reliant modesty—the para-doxical desideratum seems a function of the conflicting pressures of English influence. America and England are alike, he main-tains, in that "no other people praise themselves so openly, offen-sively and industriously"; implicitly, emulation of the mother country accounts for the U.S. habit of "self-glorification" (268). Yet England's relentless scorn for American culture and America's deference to English opinion explain the concomitant fragility of U.S. national pride. Caught between these conflicting impulses, the American nation must learn to trust its own self-estimate while resisting the temptation of unmerited self-praise. Cooper's blunt criticism of American foibles scarcely boosted the popu-larity of *England* among U.S. readers.

Cooper left Great Britain in 1828 regretting his own conflicted sentiments. He describes England as "a country that I could fain like, but whose prejudices and national antipathies throw a chill over all my affections" (308). His ambivalence at the conclusion revealingly replicates the "very conflicting sensations" acknowl-edged on arrival: "It was the land of our fathers, and it contained, with a thousand things to induce us to love it, a thousand to chill the affections" (11). Cooper cannot solve the problem of England in part because he can never acknowledge the deep, personal as-pect of his national prejudices or recognize how his family his-tory and marriage complicate his intellectual judgments. But he remains convinced that American national self-respect and self-confidence hinge on exorcizing England as a possessive presence.

Cooper's concluding volume, *Gleanings in Europe: Italy* (1838), sig-nals a retreat from the lacerating conflicts of *England*. The family's extended stay in Italy from 1828 to 1830 had yielded al-most unalloyed enjoyment, and the author confesses, "I have never yet quitted any country with one half the regret that I quit-ted Italy."[20] *Italy* differs from its predecessor both in its attention to the pleasures of landscape and architecture and in its subtle re-contextualizing of the problem of nationhood. An excursion to an island near Naples reveals an exquisite "fairy picture" that discloses to Cooper the effect of Italy's topography on his emotions: "Until that moment I was not fully sensible of the vast superiority of the Italian landscapes. . . . Italian nature wins upon you, until you come to love it like a friend" (132). Everywhere he travels, magnificent scenes produce unanticipated effects; the built environment proves no less impressive than "Italian nature." Cooper's first sight of St. Peter's stirs unbidden emotion: "As I stood gazing at the glorious pile, the tears forced themselves from my eyes" (192). The Piazza San Marco in Venice reminds him of a scene from the Arabian Nights, and he writes that "no other scene in a town ever struck [him] with so much surprise and pleasure" (279). More than any other volume in the series, *Italy* savors of guidebook notations, many of them happily invested with Cooper's critical intelligence and unaffected delight.

While declaring himself no antiquary, Cooper encounters antiquity everywhere in Italy. The ubiquitous classical ruins provoke predictable meditations on the collapse of empire, although he concludes that this postimperial condition also explains the mellowness of the Italian temperament. "I fancy that nations in decline enjoy more true happiness than nations in their advance" (21), he writes, aiming the comment at American readers. The ancient Greek temple of Neptune at Pæstum inspires a reflection on time and change that culminates in a fresh awareness of the brief history of Cooper's own nation. The site already lay "buried in vines and brambles" when Columbus discovered the New World; even the ancient Romans saw it as "an object of wonder" and "a curious relic of distant ages" (164). In Pompeii he lingers over vestiges of houses buried by lava in the first century A.D. and muses that an American regards as old a chimney built fifty years earlier. Italy's past determines its everyday life.

In this perspective, the country provides an illuminating contrast to the United States, almost a theoretical antithesis, not simply in its antiquity but more broadly in its national culture and ethnicity. From the outset, Cooper looks at America from an Italian perspective, even as he regards Italy from an American viewpoint. Rather than repeating Italian opinions about the United States, he identifies so closely with Italy that he sees his own country as a foreigner might. Still ruminating on the significance of a national metropolis, he compares New York invidiously with the principal cities of Italy. "When a European speaks of New York as a provincial town," he insists, "rely on it, such is peculiarly the character and appearance of your Gotham" (82). In relation to Florence, where his family lived for nine months, New York reveals its relative cultural poverty: "New York, which is four times as large as Florence, and ten times as rich, does not possess a tithe—nay, not a hundredth part of its attractions. To say nothing of taste, or of the stores of ancient art, or of the noble palaces and churches, and the other historical monuments, the circle of living creatures here affords greater sources of amusement and instruction than are to be found in all the five great American towns put together" (22–23). Florence epitomizes an exuberant cosmopolitanism, an "extraordinary blending of nations" (46) that hints at what Europe may someday become. The Bay of Naples, on the other hand, exposes the aesthetic shortcomings of New York; the harbor of the latter city is "barely pretty" (93), whereas Naples possesses "glorious and sublime scenery, embellished by a bewitching softness" (94). The palaces and villas lining the Mediterranean stand in contrast to the "Grecian monstrosities, and Gothic absurdities in wood" (94) ranged along the New York shore.

Rome, however, inspires Cooper's most extended contrast with New York. The two cities are "absolutely the moral opposites of each other" in temporal orientation: "One is a town of recollections, and the other a town of hopes. With the people of one, the disposition is to ruminate on the past; with the people of the other, to speculate eagerly on the future" (244). Rome is composed of "palaces, monuments, and churches, that have already resisted centuries," whereas New York discloses "architectural expedients" (245) razed a few decades later. While the Roman is "proud of his birthplace, proud of his past," the New Yorker lacks comparable attachments: "In New York, so little is ancestry, deeds, or anything but money esteemed, that nearly half of her inhabitants, so far from valuing themselves on family, or historical recollections, or glorious acts, scarcely know to what nation they properly belong" (245–246). New Yorkers constitute a rootless "congregation of adventurers" (246) concerned not with past greatness but with inventories and dollars. Between these two cities "so completely the converse of each other" (247), Cooper declares his scandalous preference: "I would a thousand times rather that my own lot had been cast in Rome, than in New York, or in any other mere trading town that ever existed" (246). He juxtaposes these cities to elucidate salient national distinctions, arriving at a declaration that could only have infuriated American readers.

This identification explains Cooper's sympathetic attention in the closing chapter to the future of Italy. In a book surprisingly reticent about politics, the author predicts that the "divided" (296) Italian nation will "inevitably become a single State" (299). Cooper then summarizes influences favorable to national solidarity: "Nature appears to have intended Italy for a single country. With a people speaking the same language—a territory almost surrounded by water, or separated from the rest of Europe by a barrier of grand mountains—its extent, ancient history, relative position, and interests, would all seem to have a direct tendency towards bringing about this great end" (297–298). Cooper recommends the study of Italy as "profitable to an American" (298) not only because the greatest obstacle to Italian unity— residual enmities among its ten separate states—provides a cautionary lesson for a country already divided by sectionalism, but also because the components of nationality represent precisely the shortcomings that the United States must surmount. Cooper hopes that Italy will accomplish unification by reform rather than violent revolution but sees the formation of a single Italian state as a political certainty.

Eight years after his sojourn there, Italy provided Cooper with a mirror by which he could examine more clearly the problem of American nationhood that had haunted previous volumes of *Gleanings*. Italians living in different cities and states feel themselves to be united as a people by their distinctive common language, by their peninsular geography, by the Roman past, and by mutual economic interests. They also share in Catholicism a common religion, of which Cooper had become warmly appreciative, and an ennobling "knowledge of the arts" (297) through the cultural heritage of Italian painting, music, sculpture, and literature. Overturning stereotypes, Cooper opines that "a large portion of the common Italians are as much superior to the Anglo-Saxon race as civilization is superior to barbarism" (297), thus acknowledging elements of race and ethnicity that also fostered a sense of kinship. None of these elements alone will make Italy a nation, but collectively they conduce to national community.

In 1830, Italy was a virtual nation in quest of political sovereignty and statehood. Conversely, the United States enjoyed independent statehood but had yet to achieve nationhood. In what Lydia Maria Child called "the great game of nations" being played out in two hemispheres, the increasingly multicultural, multiethnic United States was still clinging to a vestigial Anglo-Saxon ethnic nationalism associated with its Puritan origins and exceptionalist assumptions while at the same time trumpeting a civic nationalism rooted in supposedly universal laws and principles that transcended race, religion, or ethnicity.[21] Cooper did not entirely grasp the complexity of the contradiction inherent in American nationhood, but he recognized its symptoms in the flimsiness of national culture and the absence of national pride. His comparative, transnational reflections on Switzerland, Germany, France, England, and Italy revealed the difference between articulated national cultures and the confused, nascent nationalism of the United States. Cooper's *Gleanings* marked a stubborn, even perverse effort to effect cultural reform, to tell the American nation the truth about itself.

In contemporary works such as *The American Democrat* (1838), Cooper continued the national critique initiated in his series on Europe, although, bowing to public demand, he shortly returned to the less polemical genre of the historical romance, resurrecting his frontier hero, Natty Bumppo. His *Gleanings* eventually slipped from public notice, and despite the publication of a scholarly modern edition, few contemporary readers have actually accompanied Cooper through Europe or encountered the bracing texts by which he meant to challenge and correct the emerging nation's distorted notions about itself. His penetrating judgments on American greed, rootlessness, social conformity, unfree speech, and compromised privacy seem as pertinent today as they were in the 1830s. And his astute perception that Americans resist self-criticism, boasting national greatness (and now global destiny) while denying their own conflicted, problematic nation-hood cuts to the heart of a problem still unresolved in millennial, multicultural America.

NOTES

1. James Fenimore Cooper, *Gleanings in Europe: France*, ed. Thomas Philbrick and Constance Ayers Denne (1837; Albany: State University of New York Press, 1983), 270 n. Cooper's appointment to Lyon was a diplomatic fiction: he never set foot in the city.

2. George Washington Greene, who met the novelist in Paris, later noted that the voice in Cooper's *Gleanings* sounded "exactly as he talked." See *Biographical Studies* (New York: G. P. Putnam, 1860), 52–53. The tendency to gloss over the series is illustrated by Stephen Railton's provocative *Fenimore Cooper: A Study of His Life and Imagination* (Princeton, NJ: Princeton University Press, 1978), which mentions Cooper's years in Europe and discusses *Notions of the Americans* but ignores *Gleanings in Europe* altogether. No prior, detailed study of *Gleanings* is available in print.

3. James Fenimore Cooper, *Notions of the Americans*, ed. Robert E. Spiller (1828; New York: Frederick Ungar, 1963), 2: 256. Cooper's letters on the South contain disquieting rationalizations of slavery and U.S. Indian policy.

4. Ibid., 2: 347.

5. James Fenimore Cooper, *The Letters and Journals of James Fenimore Cooper*, ed. James Franklin Beard (Cambridge, MA: Belknap Press of Harvard University Press, 1960), 1: 287 (Cooper's italics).

6. Paul Giles, *Virtual Americas: Transnational Fictions and the Transatlantic Imaginary* (Durham, NC: Duke University Press, 2002), 20.

7. Udo Nattermann, "Ahistorical Histories: Ideological Persuasion in Cooper's European Novels," *Modern Age* 42 (2000): 279.

8. *France*, 6.

9. James Fenimore Cooper, *Gleanings in Europe: Switzerland*, ed. Kenneth W. Staggs and James P. Elliott (1836; Albany: State University of New York Press, 1980), 10. Subsequent page references to *Switzerland* are cited in parentheses and correspond to this modern

edition. Cooper had two other near encounters with the Osages: they passed through Florence just before he arrived there in October 1828, and then later in Paris Lafayette staged a soiree to raise funds for their return to the United States. Cooper later learned (as his volume on Italy suggests) that the group had been brought to Europe as a traveling show by a French entrepreneur.

10. Edgar Allan Poe, "Cooper's *Switzerland*," *Southern Literary Messenger* 2 (1836): 401.

11. James Fenimore Cooper, *Gleanings in Europe: The Rhine*, ed. Thomas Philbrick and Maurice Geracht (1836; Albany: State University of New York Press, 1986), 57–58. Subsequent page references to *The Rhine* are cited in parentheses and correspond to this modern edition.

12. By 1837 Cooper was involved in the notorious Three Mile Point controversy, when he exercised his rights as a landowner to deny local residents access to a picnic site.

13. Lafayette died in 1834, the year after Cooper's return to the United States.

14. *France*, xvii. Subsequent page references to *France* are cited in parentheses and correspond to the modern edition.

15. *The Rhine*, 175.

16. James Fenimore Cooper, *Gleanings in Europe: England*, ed. James P. Elliott, Kenneth W. Staggs, and R. D. Madison (1837; Albany: State University of New York Press, 1982), 1. Subsequent page references to *England* are cited in parentheses and correspond to this modern edition.

17. Cooper had been accused of giving himself airs and of refusing English civilities but vigorously defended himself in an 1829 letter to Mrs. Peter Augustus Jay. See *Letters and Journals*, 1: 354.

18. He thus anticipated the later judgment of Mark Twain (author of the hilarious "Fenimore Cooper's Literary Offenses"), who famously blamed Scott for popularizing chivalric, feudal attitudes in the South and thus inciting the Civil War. See Mark Twain, "Fenimore Cooper's Literary Offenses," *North American Review* 161 (July 1895): 1–12.

19. Linda Colley, *Britons: Forging the Nation, 1707–1837* (New Haven: Yale University Press, 1992), 345, 349. Colley points out that with Catholic emancipation in 1829, the Reform Act of 1832, and the abolition of slavery in 1833, Britain seemed to reclaim its role as a de-

fender of freedom after the ignominious loss of her American colonies in their battle for independence.

20. James Fenimore Cooper, *Gleanings in Europe: Italy*, ed. John Conron and Constance Ayers Denne (1838; Albany: State University of New York Press, 1981), 295. Subsequent page references to *Italy* are cited in parentheses and correspond to this modern edition.

21. See Lydia Maria Child, *Hobomok*, ed. Carolyn L. Karcher (1824; New Brunswick, NJ: Rutgers University Press, 1986), 101. For a discussion of this question, see my essay, "National Narrative and the Problem of American Nationhood," in *A Companion to American Fiction, 1780–1865*, ed. Shirley Samuels (Oxford: Blackwell, 2004), 7–19.

Cooper's Leatherstocking Conversations

Identity, Friendship, and Democracy in the New Nation

Dana D. Nelson

What is an American, this new man?" Farmer James famously queries in one of the most anthologized passages of early American literature. In *Letters from an American Farmer* (1782), Hector St. John de Crèvecoeur offers, through a series of fictionalized letters, a look into the social, political, and emotional life of American colonists. He charts for the inquisitive European the extraordinary changes in attitude, lifestyle, family structure, and personal belief that the wider availability of land—and property's guarantee of citizenship—made possible for more white commoners in the northern colonies.

Though Crèvecoeur composed his *Letters* when the United States were still British colonies, his question would resonate in the early nation. The movement for independence had a long reach into the lives and beliefs of many in the new United States. Not just the political leaders who framed the Declaration of Independence and Articles of Confederation, and then, years later, the Constitution, but also artisans in the city, settlers on the frontiers, wheat farmers in the backcountry, itinerant ministers and their congregations, fathers, mothers, daughters, and sons, were moved by its ideals. The Revolution challenged traditional hierar-

chical patterns of deference toward Britain and also within
America, between classes and social orders, in congregations and
families. But a challenge does not always contain an answer: if
Americans no longer felt compelled to mind their place in a hier-
archal social order, what would their place *be*? How would men
and women in the new nation ideally comport themselves in the
great experiment of self-government? What were the best models for patriotic manliness and womanliness? Whom should citizenship include, and exclude? What would democratic American
relationships look like?

One of the first plays performed after independence in the
Northeast was Royall Tyler's *The Contrast* (1787). Tyler tackles
these issues of American identity and democratic interrelation
directly in an urbane comedy of manners, naming his hero
Colonel Manly, a no-nonsense leader whose first loyalty is to the
men he has commanded in the War. This ever serious character
plays hilariously off the charming Billy Dimple, a foppish, man-
nerly playboy. Tyler frames his questions about new American
social identities through a series of contrasts, and despite the hu-
morous moral tone, the play leaves open as much as it answers.
For instance, Manly is the play's spokesman for the equalitarian
fraternalism that informed the new nation's democratic aspirations. But Manly hasn't really found any men to be friends with
by the end of the play: instead of forging friendships with men,
he marries the play's heroine, the sensitive (or sappy) Maria, who
pines for the romances she reads about while making herself
obedient to her father's terrible choice for a husband (Dimple).
How independent is *she*? Is her obedience good or stupid? Do her
reading passions demonstrate her silliness or her seriousness? Is
Maria's womanhood the model for the new Republican Motherhood? Is it a proper substitute for Manly's fraternity? And really,
shouldn't he loosen up a *little*?

These kinds of questions, as generations of literary historians
have remarked, preoccupied early generations of U.S. writers.
They would continue to occupy James Fenimore Cooper
throughout his Leatherstocking series. And despite differences of
interest, setting, and concern, Cooper's method is very similar to
Tyler's. In each of the Leatherstocking novels, groupings of male

and female characters across lines of class, habitude, and race provide readers a series of contrasts that foreground the problems of creating new identities that can support and sustain the democratic aims of the early United States. And as in Tyler's play, Cooper's contrasting characters ask more questions than they comfortably answer, while offering a window into changing models of identity and interrelation in the early United States.

Much has been made of Cooper's ambivalence or self-contradiction—his supposed inability clearly to resolve moral and political issues for the readers of his Leatherstocking series. Is civilization bad or necessary? Is too much lost with its advance across the continent? Do Indians have anything to contribute to U.S. culture, or are they essentially beyond the pale? Is it bad or good that they are being removed from their homelands into the invisibility of reservations and remaindered to visibility only in U.S. history? What about the United States' multicultural heritage? As Cooper shows in *The Pioneers*, Americans were of Dutch, French, German, African, Native American, and British descent: Is this something to be celebrated or suppressed? And what about women: Are women only a drag on manliness, the domestic, civilizing foil to men's more natural independence? Finally, the unique Natty Bumppo: Does he represent a viable alternative to the (sub)urban models of manhood he is contrasted to in several of these novels? Or is he, like the last of the Mohicans, fated to fade into the sunset, having reluctantly guided the civilizers west?

It is possible that Cooper was not so much ambivalent as that he found such questions more interesting than any single answer. This essay explores some of the questions he raises about women and men, as well as the questions he opens up about the possibility of relationship across race, gender, and class differences, and examines their connections to the historical period in which he was writing. Cooper has long been credited with developing a timeless myth in the character of Natty Bumppo and his friendship with Chingachgook. Appreciating that myth should not keep readers from understanding how Cooper also posed some immediate social and political questions about identity and social possibility in the new nation. These questions resonated

with his original readers because of their immediacy, and though historical circumstances have changed the way readers respond to their various terms, these questions continue to resonate with contemporary social and political issues for many readers today.

"The Weakness of the Females"

Cooper is probably best known today for *The Last of the Mohicans*.[1] The novel famously opens by pairing the fair and dark sisters, Alice and Cora Munro, a pairing D. H. Lawrence long ago denominated an "inevitable" (67) strategy in Cooper's portrayal of women. Critics long agreed that his women were stick characters, who symbolized what real men needed to escape from (domesticity or society), or stood for the eternal battles between Good and Evil that tested men's character.[2] More recent generations of critics, influenced by academic feminism, have given the female characters another look, finding greater character complexity, plot centrality, and sociohistorical relevance.

Beginning with *The Pioneers*, Cooper does not just employ, but tweaks a durable strategy of pairing women into what, for readers in the early nineteenth century, was becoming a familiar trope. He tinkers with it mildly in this first Leatherstocking novel by reversing its terms: Elizabeth Temple is the lovely, educated, wise, brave, jet-eyed, and brunette counterpart to the more retiring, timid, less bright, and flaxen-haired Louisa Grant.[3] They may both want the man (Oliver Edwards/Effingham), but only the dark Elizabeth understands him (she understands specifically that he is not the Native American he passes for throughout the novel) and is brave enough to earn his admiration. Here the dark lady gets the man as the blonde fades from view and memory. Cooper deploys this pairing with a great deal more seriousness in the second novel of this series, *The Last of the Mohicans*. Nina Baym has observed in her reading of this novel, "It is a pity that" the fair/dark lady pairing has been so popularly encapsulated in Freudian theory, where the "difference" is one of sexuality. Baym insists that "its uses are far more various than that theory permits us to see" (704), highlighting how Cooper complicates the more

facile readings of Cora and Alice that the trope might initially suggest.

Cooper complicates the pairing here by introducing a theme that he only feigned in his first Leatherstocking novel. Racial mixing was a subject of immediate political and social relevance in the early United States because of the challenges it offered to the "white only" criterion of citizenship established by the first U.S. act of naturalization in 1790. Given the charge of these issues in the 1820s, as state legislatures across the United States moved toward enfranchising all free white men regardless of property holdings, as technological innovations like the cotton gin guaranteed the continued economic intensity and human suffering of slavery in the United States, and as Congress enacted a gag rule against the petitions of abolitionists, the dark/fair pairing would initially seem to offer a clear line on the subject. But Cooper doesn't quite deliver that clarity. Cora, who is partially of African descent and who in her first description is denominated only (and repeatedly) "the other" (see 1: 488), has, as it will turn out, by far the finer sensibility and intelligence of the two sisters. Alice, the "One" (1: 488), is finally hard to read as anything but a caricature of True Womanhood. She lacks depth and spends half the novel in a faint.

Though Alice's fainting might seem wimpy to a modern reader, her passivity in the novel would have been a mark of her superiority to Cora for at least some readers in the early United States by the emerging standards of true womanhood.[4] This new prescription for female identity differed markedly from the active, civically (and therefore politically and economically) minded republican motherhood described by the historian Linda Kerber in the years of the early nation (1776–1812). True womanhood, in Welter's description, was guided by "four cardinal virtues: piety, purity, submissiveness and domesticity" (21). Rather than organizing the tea boycotts of republican mothers, true women would submit piously to any difficulties, trusting that their Christian faith and the example of their martyrlike passivity would eventually convert their oppressors to kinder behavior.

Women saw complex sociological and political shifts in the transition from the eighteenth to the nineteenth century in the

United States. Although a number of states had counted women as citizens in the late colonies, the move toward universal white male enfranchisement in the early United States definitively disenfranchised women from the vote nationwide. Where women of wealth in the early nation had negotiated prenuptial agreements with their husbands in the 1770s and 1780s, by the turn of the century, this was increasingly castigated and disfavored as the legal doctrine of "feme covert [sic]" from the British Common Law became more durably enforced (the legal ideal that a married woman has no legal presence in the eyes of the law except through the "covering" legal "body" of her husband). And, as the nation moved from a primarily agricultural base toward urban industrialization, the workplace shifted from the home to sites distant from the home, thereby cutting women off from practical and economic access to the family livelihood: "work" became increasingly understood as what *men* did away from home. These various changes corroborated the shift from republican motherhood to true womanhood, whereby women's sphere was reduced from the national scene to the domestic sphere, and "good" women embraced this vastly narrowed sphere and their vastly reduced agency within it. This by no means implies that women in fact forfeited *all* agency, and a variety of historians have documented how middle-class women were able to use piety, submissiveness, and domesticity to effect not just power in the home, but in national and even international politics.[5]

The characterization of Cora and Alice Munro in *The Last of the Mohicans* thus strains against its implied categories. Cora, the novel's spokesperson for racial tolerance and race-blind justice, is attractive to the Indian men who meet her and beloved by Uncas, and yet she carries those possibilities to her grave at the end of the novel, mourned by all in a spectacular, multicultural funeral. Alice, the emblem of racial purity in all her blonde glory, gets the British hero Duncan Heyward in the end, but also unthinkingly reveals her own lack of sisterliness and sympathy when she exclaims, as the women and Heyward are rescued from their first captivity, "We are saved! We are saved! . . . And you too Cora!" (1: 602).

Cooper's depiction of Cora raises questions that were only

just beginning to concern the race scientists of the early nineteenth century. One of the things that makes this novel so historically interesting is that it points a direction for this emerging pseudo-science in its central debate over racial mixture.[6] Natty embodies the cultural aspects of interracialism as an Indianized frontiersman. He is deeply committed to his friendship with Chingachgook (more on this later) and does not hesitate to admire Delaware achievements and adopt their skills when he does not find them in conflict with his own morals. But he spends the novel disavowing interracialism as a *physical* possibility. He is a "man without a cross" in his blood, as he insists throughout with annoying (even slightly hysterical) frequency. More pointedly, Natty refuses categorically to translate for Munro at the funeral held for Cora and Uncas when Munro prophesies a race-blind heaven: "To tell them this . . . would be to tell them that the snows come not in the winter, or that the sun shines fiercest when the trees are stripped of their leaves" (1: 874).

Natty invokes natural laws as though they offer proof against interracial life *and* afterlife. But Cora stands for precisely those possibilities in the novel, precisely those categorical combinations. It's not just that she's physically mixed, but she also speaks the language of color-blind justice, flatly contradicting Natty's own insistence on race-based "gifts." For instance, she checks her own instinct to prejudge Magua based on his physical appearance and then chides Duncan rather severely for so doing: "Should we distrust the man, because his manners are not our manners, and that his skin is dark!" she "coldly" demands from Heyward in the novel's opening scene (1: 491).[7] Cora's position here would not have been seen as peculiar: her admonition is charged by the cult of sympathy, the doctrine that informs the Declaration of Independence and U.S. democratic ideals. Take, for instance, the "self-evident" assertion there that "all men are created equal." This was an idea that was by no means common sense to Europeans and colonists, who grew up in traditions that insisted men were created *unequal*. But eighteenth-century Scottish school moral philosophers made it an attractive philosophical and political ideal, and they did so based on a moral argument built on the premise of natural human sympathy.[8] This ideal insists that, using their own experiences to identify with each other across gulfs of social and experiential difference, humans can thereby build equalitarian political and social community. This ideal fueled the growth of U.S. democracy and contributed to the Second Great Awakening, penitentiary reform, the growth of philanthropy in the early United States, the expansion of abolitionism, and a variety of utopian social, economic, and religious experiments across the nation in the antebellum years. The novel discredits those sympathetic ideals with one hand and supports them with another: Cora is killed by the very Indians she tries sympathizing with, but Natty's impassioned speech to Chingachgook about their undying friendship stands as the novel's fervent closing testament to interracial friendship *and* sympathy.

If it is hard to arrive at easy conclusions about this novel's message on race, it's a bit easier to sort out its message about sympathy. Cora is indiscriminate—and flatly *wrong*—in her sympathetic identifications. Magua *is* the archvillain, and it would have been better for everyone, not just for Cora, if she had not insisted he be treated fairly at the outset of the novel. Natty, on the other hand, who can be unabashed in his own sentimentalism (for instance, readers see him crying as he listens to David Gamut's hymns), knows when to stop empathizing. Men, the novel suggests, are better guardians of sympathy than women, who don't know when to shut the doors of their hearts and homes.

Cora's death at the end of the novel arguably signals more than Cooper's castigation of women's promiscuous sympathetic identifications: it seemingly confirms Natty's insistence that racial "blood" not be "crossed." Cora's death, her inability to survive the frontier, and the death of the two Indian men who are romantically or sexually interested in her—Magua and Uncas—lends much symbolic force to an argument against racial intermarriage that was just becoming prominent in the late 1820s and early 1830s, thanks to the abolitionist movement in the United States. Here, Cooper seemingly counters the frontier novels of his female predecessor, Lydia Maria Child, whose 1824 novel *Hobomok* features a young Puritan girl entering into a loving marriage and bearing a child to the eponymous Indian character.[9] Interestingly, too, Cooper seemingly predicts a direction for the racial science that would soon emerge around the question of hybridity: for the theory of polygenesis, or separate racial origins, to pass its own test, scientists needed to demonstrate, contrary to widely visible evidence, that the races could not successfully interbreed. The arguments that emerged over the next two decades were more and more convoluted, the most popular insisting that, somewhat like mules, people of mixed races would over time be less and less fertile and eventually unable to reproduce.[10] Like Cora and Uncas, they would "fall off."

One critical wisdom is that you can learn much about a novel's sociopolitical agenda by paying attention to which characters get to marry and produce children in the end. In marrying off Alice Munro to Heyward, the novel seemingly supports the notion of the nation's white, Anglo-Saxon destiny (despite Cooper's notable interest in the multiculturalism of the early United States), as it apparently confirms a far less sympathetic model of womanhood than Cora's.[11] He thereby affirms the symbolic and racial white purity of true womanhood, a social description of and prescription for womanhood that was only just beginning to emerge into cultural prominence in the late 1820s and 1830s. True womanhood, in historian Barbara Welter's description, was built on the notion of woman's spiritual piety and moral purity, combined with her submissiveness and willing self-restriction of her interests and emotional energies solely to the domestic sphere. But as that cultural ideal found stronger and broader articulation in the United States during the 1830s and 1840s, Cooper appears to back away from its entailments. For instance, even by the time he writes *The Prairie* a year later, in 1827, his upper-class model of true womanhood, the Creole Spanish Louisianan Inez Middleton, carries almost no narrative interest beyond a twist that brings her husband, a descendant of Duncan Heyward, into the plot. Instead, Ellen Wade, a Kentuckian whose lineage is far less secure or impressive, is the plucky, no-nonsense, unreserved heroine. With her proclivity for sneaking off to meet her beau, Paul Hover, and her insistence on making her own decisions, and even wielding a gun, Ellen would never be considered up to the par of true womanhood. Yet in Cooper's handling she seems to embody the democratic future of the country.[12] By foregrounding Ellen over Inez, Cooper seems to counter, if not repudiate, True Womanhood with an alternative feminine ideal, Real Womanhood, which insisted that women should cultivate intelligence, physical fitness, and economic self-sufficiency, and certainly *not* passivity and submission.[13]

In the last two installments of the Leatherstocking series in the early 1840s, Cooper continues this motif of assigning the greater narrative interest to active women of marginal class (if not racial or ethnic) backgrounds. In his portrayals of Mabel Dunham and Judith Hutter, Cooper again foregrounds women who reject the passivity of true womanhood in favor of real womanhood's more physically active, emotionally independent, and intellectually capable model. As usual, though, Cooper does not make these choices entirely clear, especially in the last novel, where Judith, the "dark lady," is far more interesting than her feeble-minded sister, Hetty, but is also sexually compromised by her rumored flirtations with men.

In a fascinating twist on heteroromantic norms in the nineteenth century, Judith proposes marriage to the young Natty in *The Deerslayer* (she does so after broad hints don't register with him). This is a fascinating agency to grant to Judith, made even more pointedly impressive as she renounces her patronym, Hutter, because she is ashamed of the avaricious behavior of her adoptive father. Her self-making agency—an agency that was associated in the nineteenth century with middle-class *men*—has seldom been noted by critics, who have preferred instead to emphasize Natty's rejection of her marriage proposal, correlating that to her compromised sexual purity and dismissing her character as a "temptress" and a "despoiler."[14] Leland Person is one of the few exceptions: his more careful reading finds in Judith "a remarkably perceptive analysis of woman's experience on the frontier."[15] Rejecting the critical tradition that positions her as a Lilith foil to Natty's Adam, Person argues that she serves in the novel as "an ethical barometer: rejecting Hurry Harry and Tom Hutter (and with them their exploitive valuation of nature), she approves Natty and his preservationist values."[16] In this sense, she serves as a durable representation of the experiences of women on the frontier so capably outlined by Annette Kolodny in her germinal study, *The Land Before Her*, where, in the face of representations of the West as a "virginal paradise" fit for conquering by men, women struggled to find alternative ideals that made a positive and productive space for their more nurturing and domesticating presence on the frontier. And it's clear that her character resonated positively with many nineteenth-century readers; as Person documents, Cooper's audience expressed indignation that Natty didn't marry her![17]

The women in the Leatherstocking novels engaged readers in familiar cultural debates about competing social imperatives for womanly behavior across a range of classes and settings, as it made them think about the very issues of race relations that true womanhood especially sought to occlude by making white purity the metaphorical norm.[18] Cooper's women all practice some form of self-assertion, and his most interesting women often critique male behaviors, not only toward women but also toward other men. However, beyond the obligatory relationships with sisters and the thinly rendered interracial friendship that emerges in *The Pathfinder* between Mabel and June, Cooper does not develop substantial relationships *between* women.[19] As Leslie Fiedler perhaps overgeneralized, Cooper was a "writer for boys" (181), and to examine Cooper's deep interest in friendship, it is necessary to turn to his male characters.

"Your Manitou and My God"

Recent social and literary historians have become very interested in the overlapping ideals and practice of democracy and friendship. Though we have long associated sympathy and sentimentalism with women in the nineteenth century, a school of study has emerged that has outlined a wide-ranging exploration among eighteenth-century philosophers, economists, social planners, and religious reformers in the ethics of sympathy.[20] These historians have documented a broad experimentation with various modes of equalitarianism, from property redistribution to philanthropy to more personal practices of friendship, practices that were invested with profound political possibilities. In the late colonial and early national years, friendship among both women and men came to stand for the principle of national fraternity, for new democratic possibility across older gulfs of class and gender. Friendship, as Caleb Crain has observed, stood both as "metaphor and model for citizenly love" (5) in republican ideology, an equalizing relation that could bring very different kinds of people into close bonds of chosen affiliation.

It's clear that Natty Bumppo's enduring friendship with Chingachgook was and remains a friendship that resonates symbolically for American men. Leslie Fiedler long ago classified Cooper's rendition of their friendship as "an archetypal relationship which also haunts the American psyche: two lonely men, one dark-skinned, one white, bend together over a carefully guarded fire in the virgin heart of the American wilderness; they have forsaken all others for the sake of the austere, almost inarticulate, but unquestioned love which binds them to each other and to the world of nature which they have preferred to civilization" (192). This friendship certainly resonates in ways that seem timeless and mythic; it also refers in direct ways to important social and political questions that concerned Cooper's readers. Cooper published *The Last of the Mohicans* in 1826. The 1820s were an important era in white-Native relations in the United States. The Cherokee were in the middle of their grand experiment in New Echota, working to prove their ability to assimilate to the Anglo-American model of civilization by adopting a constitution, creating an alphabet and publishing newspapers, and converting from what historian Francis Jennings summarized as a "commuter lifestyle"—a life divided between seasonal agriculture and then hunting and gathering—into strictly agricultural settlement. Thus demonstrating their communal desire to be recognized within the U.S. democracy, the Cherokee challenged white America to imagine civic friendship more broadly than ever. Indian speakers such as William Apess traveled the Northeast, speaking against white racism and on behalf of Native America's political inclusion in the United States as formal policy seemed to move toward direct exclusion.[21] The "Indian question" was a topic being broadly debated by white Americans in the early nineteenth century, and this discussion was inextricably linked to the question of U.S. racial politics, and the race symbolism of U.S. identity more generally.[22]

And so when Cooper paints his famous friendship—a friendship in this second novel that is by no means "inarticulate" but is portrayed as a deeply respectful, intellectual, and expressive exchange between two men committed to maintaining their respect for each other across great cultural differences—it is worth attending to how this novel weighed in on a pressing national debate. When we first meet Natty and Chingachgook in the novel, at the outset of chapter 3, they are locked deep in discussion as they await the return of Chingachgook's son, Uncas. As the reader encounters them, they are arguing over their differing explanations for the ocean and river tides, which shortly turns into a discussion of the politics of European colonization. Though the men at points vehemently disagree with each other, even revealing a frank impatience with each others' beliefs, their exchange is marked throughout by a steady respect and sympathy; as the narrator observes, Natty was "a good deal touched at the calm suffering of his companion" (1: 505). This novel elaborates the depth and quality of their relationship far more fully than any other of the Leatherstocking Tales; it is here that we have an active and three-dimensional picture of the friendship. And in the novel's closing pages, after the spectacular funerals of Uncas and Cora, it is Natty's passionate testament to his friendship with the bereft Chingachgook on which the novel closes. "I am alone," the Great Serpent mourns, only to be interrupted: " 'No, no,' cried Hawk-eye, who had been gazing with a yearning look at the rigid features of his friend, with something like his own self-command, but whose philosophy could endure no longer; 'no, Sagamore, not alone. The gifts of our colours may be different, but God has so placed us as to journey in the same path. . . . The boy has left us for a time, but, Sagamore, you are not alone!' " (877). Chingachgook greets this protestation with a handshake that turns into an embrace as "these two sturdy and intrepid woodsmen bowed their heads together while scalding tears fell to their feet, watering the grave of Uncas, like drops of falling rain" (877). This mingling of tears at the novel's end documents the passionate, even romantic, nature of this friendship as it evokes (or mourns) alternative civic possibilities for white America. In this way, the novel provides a forceful counter to its own stringent race-purity arguments, seemingly aiming at provoking a discussion among readers on the subject.

But the novel is so powerful not just because of its provocatively countervailing messages on the subject of race. It speaks obliquely, as do all the novels in the series, to a growing tension among European-descended white men in the early United States, as the competitive forces of market capitalism came to bear on their lives and relationships among men. Thoreau would shortly and famously summarize this tension and its entailments in *Walden*: "The laboring man has not leisure for a true integrity day by day; he cannot afford to sustain the manliest relations to men; his labor would be depreciated in the market. . . . The finest qualities of our nature, like the bloom on fruits, can be preserved only by the most delicate handling. Yet we do not treat ourselves nor one another thus tenderly" (8). Thoreau laments the way the intensifying competition of market relations strains friendlier, more tender, less work-focused relations among men. From Thoreau's slightly later vantage, we can see why it's significant for nineteenth-century readers that Natty, much like Tyler's Colonel Manly, can't find an equal relation, a friendship with a white male character, across the five novels and the two decades it took Cooper to write them.

Cooper begins a theme of intrawhite male competition in his first installment, *The Pioneers*. Its central plot revolves around how Marmaduke Temple's capitalist striving after the war blocks the renewal of his friendship with Effingham—and it blocks it permanently because Effingham dies before they are able personally to reconcile. This theme pervades the novel and is developed in multiple characters, such as the competitive sheriff, as well as in subplots, for instance, the one concerning Natty's alleged mining claim. The novel shows how these new competitive economic relations forestall friendships between men. To drive the point home, the novel ends with Natty mourning at the grave of his last deceased friends, Major Effingham and Chingachgook, before he takes off alone into the forest. At the end of the book, friendship among men in the settlement seems to be dead.

The Deerslayer makes a similar point, beginning Natty's career and ending the series with a similar plot about Natty's inability to find friendly communion among white men. He can't make a connection with Harry or Hutter, because these men are so much more interested in making money off Indian scalps and booty than in making friends.[23] This would have resonated with male readers coming increasingly under the pressures of what I have elsewhere described as capitalist citizenship: the imperative to identify politically through the model of fraternity but to strive to succeed competitively by *besting*, not befriending, fellow men.[24] The tensions of the accelerating marketplace and the emerging imperatives of professional careers boosted the expansion of secret fraternal orders, where, as historian Mark Carnes has shown, men substituted formal rituals for informal friendship, a substitution that allowed them a more anonymous sensation of friendship without having to feel badly about competing against that brother the next day at work.

Thus Cooper's depiction of Natty and Chingachgook's friendship as something that happens outside the confines of civilization makes a certain historical sense without necessarily being true (of course white men formed profound personal friendships in the marketplace, and of course there were uncountable true instances of interracial friendships among men, and women, across colonial and national histories). But the fact that it's not true doesn't mean it's not historically grounded: this famous white-Indian friendship develops an archetypal resonance in U.S. literature out of specifically historical circumstances. Within the decade after readers mourned the death of "the last of the Mohicans," they witnessed or traveled the notorious Trail of Tears, just the most famous of many Indian removals begun during the Jackson era, and the Black Hawk and Seminole Wars, presaging the uncompromising military campaigns that would be waged by the U.S. government against Native America after the Civil War. This friendship, with its real historical possibility, necessarily becomes mythic as a way of disavowing the democratic foreclo-

sures of Indian removal *and* capitalist citizenship, while recording, however melancholically, the trace of those abandoned possibilities. In other words, the sense of impossibility that Cooper
traces in Natty's enduring friendship with Chingachgook in *The
Last of the Mohicans* stands both for the constriction of brotherhood under competitive capitalism and the limiting of democratic community under the all-white banner of Manifest Destiny.[25]

Beyond *The Last of the Mohicans*, Cooper experiments with two
kinds of resolutions for the loss of friendship that Natty and
Chingachgook's blood brotherhood memorializes. In the third
installment, *The Prairie*, Cooper once again poses Natty among a
series of white men who offer a range of contrasts to his character but no possibility for enduring friendship. Ishmael Bush, the
squatter patriarch who executes his brother-in-law for murdering
his son, represents patriarchal law outside civilization's legal
order, a law that doesn't exactly support male friendships. Duncan Uncas Middleton stands for a kind of natural American aristocracy, descended of British aristocracy, whose ancestors fought
for the Patriot Cause. Middleton has the breeding and command
that Natty can never match but only serve. Paul Hover represents
a working-class republican manhood romantically fixated on
getting his girl and settling down. Dr. Obadius Battius, a roving
naturalist, represents the battiness of book or formal learning in
contrast to Natty's backwoods experiences in nature. In one way
or another, each of these men represents the settlements that
Natty castigates. He has affable relationships with each of them,
yet none of these men offers the kind of companionship that he
craves. Even as he testifies yet again that "my feelings as well as
my skin are white" (1: 1300), Natty takes leave of all his regretful
white companions at the novel's end to spend his last days in the
Pawnee village. He apparently finds the companionship he needs
there, adopting Mahtoree, or the ironically denominated "Hard
Heart," as his *son*. This novel climaxes with Natty dying, facing
west just like his old friend Chingachgook did in *The Pioneers*.
Thus Cooper replaces the possibilities of white fraternity with
interracial affiliation—not just friendship, but *family*. But this is a
possibility that seemingly goes to the grave with Natty at the end
of the novel, an alternative whose day is already past.

Cooper revisits this theme of interracial affiliation with a new twist fifteen years later in *The Deerslayer*. In this chronologically first novel of the series, written last, he again creates grounds for serious conversation on the subject of race, sympathy, democracy, and identity. Natty and Chingachgook's friendship is a fact that runs throughout the novels. Natty appears in the Lake Otsego (or Glimmerglass) setting of *The Deerslayer* only because he is helping his dear friend track his beloved Wah-ta-wah (or Hist-o-hist in English), who has been taken captive by the Hurons. But this famous friendship is not foregrounded here as it was in *Last of the Mohicans*; in this last novel, it receives almost no narrative development. There are two possible reasons for subordinating the friendship in this novel. First, readers and critics have widely noted the series' diffidence about heterosexual romance. Though characters pair off romantically in every novel, Natty remains all but indifferent to the prospect of marriage (the sole exception to this is his courtship of Mabel Dunham in *The Pathfinder*, where he is rejected in favor of a younger man). Although, or perhaps because, he helps Chingachgook retrieve his betrothed in this novel, Natty—or Hawkeye, as he is newly denominated in this novel—takes a certain distance from his Delaware friend in this plot. But whatever distance he takes from this "blood brother," he more than makes up for in protestations of loyalty to the Delaware people more generally. And here is the second possible reason for the narrative's subordination of the friendship: in this novel, Deerslayer-Hawkeye emerges as the heroic Indian *himself*.

After all the novels' famous proclamations of Natty's racial purity—a "man without a cross"—this is surely a surprising assertion. At many points, *The Deerslayer* seems as adamant about racial categories as ever. But the spokesperson for racial purity is *not* Natty in this novel. Instead, it is Hurry Harry, a character who is discredited by his avarice and low ethical standards. Harry explains his racial schema at the beginning of the novel: "This is what I call reason. Here's three colours on 'arth; white, black and red. White is the highest colour, and therefore the best man; black comes next, and is put to live in the neighborhood of the white man, as tolerable and fit to be made use of; and red comes last, which shows that those that made 'em never expected an Indian to be accounted as more than half a human" (2: 528). He is directly and immediately countered by Natty: "God made all three alike . . . no doubt he had his own wise intentions in colouring us differently. Still he made us, in the main, much the same in feelin's; though I'll not deny that he gave each race his gifts" (2: 528). In the midst of Natty's familiar lecture on racially separate abilities, an interesting counterpoint emerges: the interracial power of human *feeling*. This returns us to a theme raised in *The Last of the Mohicans*. But here, rather than serving as an explanation for a single friendship only, it is elevated into an ethical inquiry; in other words, interracial feeling becomes a *gauge for character*.

In the course of the novel, Natty makes a series of explicit statements on interracial feeling and democratic human brotherhood. For instance, he directly counters his position on the race segregation of heaven in *The Last of the Mohicans* when he explains to Harry, "I look upon the red men to be quite as human as we are ourselves, Hurry. They have their gifts, and their religion, it's true, but that makes no difference in the end, when each will be judged according to his deeds, and not according to his skin" (2: 537). Natty elaborates on this theme in his only intimate conversation with Chingachgook, late in the novel during Natty's furlough from his Huron captivity. Here they are (most articulately, contra Fiedler!) debating Christian doctrine as Natty contemplates his impending torture and death. He exclaims to Chingachgook, "Of all the doctrines, Sarpent, that which disturbs me, and disconsarts my mind the most, is the one which teaches us to think that a pale face goes to one heaven, and a red skin to another; it may separate in death them which lived much together, and loved each other well in life!" (2: 938). The love he references is his love for his Delaware friend, a great feeling that, he soon insists, will carry Chingachgook into Christianity, despite his own reservations about doctrinal fine points: "The time will come I hope, when you'll *feel* these things; for, after all, they must be *felt* rather than reasoned about" (2: 939, original emphasis). Feelings, rather than knowledge—the unifying force of sympathy, rather than the compartmentalizing force of reason—becomes the motivating message of this plot.

When Natty explains himself to his white companion, Harry accuses him of a philosophy "downright missionary." But it is more than philosophy for the young woodsman: it is a living commitment. Quite differently from the middle-aged "man without a cross" in *The Last of the Mohicans*, Deerslayer here denominates himself "a man with a Delaware heart," professing, "I hope to live and die in their tribe" (2: 774). He shortly elaborates (in a way that muddies more than it clarifies), "I'm white in blood, heart, natur' and gifts, though a little red skin in feelin's and habits" (2: 775). The narrator attributes Natty's passionate identification with the Delaware people to the accident of his own history among them: "Though he took a pride in showing his white blood, by often deviating from the usages of the red men, he frequently dropped into their customs, and oftener into their feelings, unconsciously to himself, in consequence of having no other arbiters to appeal to, than their judgement and taste" (2: 947).

However Natty arrives at his commitment to Delaware feeling, his "Delaware heart," the fact is that it earns him the admiration of even his deadliest Indian foes. His Delaware heart makes him unambiguously the hero of this book: he is as noble an Indian as ever could be imagined, and even more so for his "white gifts": his Christian scruples about the cautious taking of life in warfare. Natty becomes in this novel for the first time a "white Indian" exemplar. In this Cooper does not invent so much as emblematize a long tradition in the European colonies and early United States, the tradition of white men playing Indian, for recreation and fraternization (the Tammany Societies, and later, the International Order of Red Men, founded in the United States in 1834, but claiming as its founding date 1492), but also for the more serious pursuit of political protest (e.g., the Boston Tea Party, the Maine land protesters known as the "White Indians").[26] Playing Indian is often associated with claiming a notably isolated manly independence, the posture of standing nobly alone (like "the last of the Mohicans"). But Natty's identification with the Delaware in *The Deerslayer* adds an explicit responsibility for intercultural community to the posture of personal independence. "I would never bring disgrace on the Delawares," Natty explains to the Hurons as he returns from his furlough (2: 951).

Cooper makes this pitch for multicultural sympathy in a period of U.S. history when racial attitudes were becoming widely debated. Polygenesis was triumphing as scientific common sense over monogenesis, the theory of a single human origin, and scientists and politicians were using this debate over racial origins to justify U.S. territorial expansion into Texas and Mexico and to articulate the theory of Manifest Destiny as the rightful domination of the continent—perhaps the hemisphere—by white, Anglo-Saxon Americans. At this same time, abolitionists were garnering wider support across the United States, rousing people with their depictions of slavery's cruelty and, for at least some, with a more inclusive vision for a multiracial democratic polity. By paying attention to history, then, we can see that the friendship between Natty and Chingachgook, and Natty's passionate affinity with Chingachgook's people in 1842, is not so much timeless as it is *timely*. Natty's interracial identification has important political implications; indeed, this kind of passionate interracial feeling served as the basis for some of the most radical ideals and actions of black and white male abolitionists in the 1840s and 1850s, as the historian John Stauffer has so carefully demonstrated in his recent award-winning book, *The Black Hearts of Men*. In that study, Stauffer focuses on four key abolitionists—Gerrit Smith, John Brown, Frederick Douglass, and James McCune Smith—who were experimenting with just the kind of cross-racial identification and friendship that Cooper describes for Natty in *The Deerslayer*: their goal was not just to eliminate slavery but also to end racism.

If in *The Last of the Mohicans* Natty seemingly called for the more careful maintenance of racial boundaries, in *The Deerslayer* he calls for the overlooking of racial boundaries in favor of an ability to recognize a common brotherhood, the kind of brotherhood that can endure like his friendship with Chingachgook at the end of the novel. This ability to identify interracially becomes the novel's standard for heroism. Differently from *The Prairie*, then, where Natty recreates interracial community only to die at the end, in this final installment of the series, the possibility remains alive with him.

"My gifts are white so far as wives are consarned; it is
Delaware, in all things touchin' Injuns"

Almost a decade before the nineteenth-century's blockbuster
sentimental novel, Harriet Beecher Stowe's *Uncle Tom's Cabin*
(1851), Cooper preaches a message about the power of interracial
feeling. Though *The Deerslayer* has never to my knowledge been
considered a sentimental novel, the reading I have presented here
suggests that we might usefully consider it as such. Disdained by
literary critics and historians since the 1950s, sentimental novels
have received a fresh consideration in the past twenty years, following Jane Tompkins's influential argument that they be judged
not by the formalist aesthetic criteria of literary modernism, but
"as a political enterprise, halfway between sermon and social
theory, that both codifies and attempts to mold the values of its
time" (126). Critics have long understood Cooper's novelist enterprise to be sociological, or political; for example, Richard Chase
concludes, "If Cooper is of only secondary importance as an
artist, he is of the first importance, both as a creator and a critic
of culture" (46). Taking the sentimental aspect of his novel seriously, then, is not to discredit but more fully to comprehend its
sociopolitical aims.

Comparing how these two writers navigate this famous question over how far democratic sympathy should take U.S. readers
is instructive in at least two ways. First, they seemingly differ
over the arena for sentimental practice. Stowe deploys interracial
feeling, in scenes like those between Senator and Mrs. Bird and
the escaped slave Eliza, or between Uncle Tom and little Eva, not
just to build character but to influence national politics—indeed,
to *change the nation* by ending slavery. However apocryphal the
story may be that on meeting Stowe President Lincoln pronounced, "So this is the little lady who wrote the novel that
started the Civil War!," it is nevertheless believable because of
the openly political intervention she uses feeling to make. For
Cooper, there is seemingly no such public agenda: for him, interracial feeling does certainly change and define individual people,
but he does not explicitly engage it to change national destiny by
showing us characters using it to influence political outcomes.

Second, this comparison allows us to reconsider an old critical assumption and to understand the history of gender practices with more precision. Readers and scholars have long associated sentimentalism in the nineteenth century with *women* writers and readers. A more careful reading of Cooper's Leatherstocking Tales suggests that view is far too reductive, and even misleading. Cooper engages sympathy—and engages a gendered argument about sympathy—across the span of the novels. His novels suggest that both men and women practice sympathy and are impacted by sentiment. But they also suggest that men are the wiser because they are the more disciplined guardians of sympathy. The difference between Cora in *The Last of the Mohicans* and Hawkeye of *The Deerslayer* is that Cora made the mistake of attempting to sympathize with *all* Indians. Hawkeye, on the other hand, always knows which Indians are the right ones to open up his heart to. He does not make the mistake, for instance, of seeking sentimental exchanges among the Hurons. Like Stowe, then, Cooper asks his readers to invest in sympathy. Differently from Stowe, Cooper offers sympathy to rebuild the limited practice of friendship and community *between men*, a more private, discriminating practice that leaves its political, or world-changing, possibilities an open question.[27]

This proclivity for open questions may contribute to readings that posit a mythic quality for Cooper's Leatherstocking Tales; their very historical open-endedness contributes to making them feel timeless, rather than dated, as Stowe's famous novel came to seem to many after the abolition of slavery. But as I've tried to demonstrate in this essay, we find in the Leatherstocking Tales something far more specific than myth: we encounter an insistent engagement with key contemporary questions about democratic identity and interrelation in the early United States. It may be that what makes the novels seem so timeless for our own generation is their persisting historical relevance. They raise, without providing clear answers, questions about the nature, problems, and promise of democratization for personal identity, gender relations, friendship practice, and multicultural community that continue to be central for readers in the United States today.

NOTES

1. Cooper, *The Leatherstocking Tales*, 1: 1294. Subsequent citations are noted parenthetically in the text.

2. This is a critical tradition dating back to Cooper's contemporaries, such as James Russell Lowell in his 1848 *Fable for Critics*. In the twentieth century, see, for example, Lewis, *The American Adam*; Chase, *The American Novel and Its Tradition*; Fiedler, *Love and Death in the American Novel*; Porte, *The Romance in America*. A notable exception is Donald Ringe, who in *James Fenimore Cooper*, points out that it is only in Cooper's earliest novels that the female characters are weak; these characters become more "convincing" as his career develops (20).

3. In this essay, I discuss the novels in the order Cooper wrote them: *The Pioneers* (1823), *The Last of the Mohicans* (1826), *The Prairie* (1827), *The Pathfinder* (1841), and *The Deerslayer* (1842). By the chronology of Natty's life, the novels would be read in this order: *Deerslayer, Last of the Mohicans, Pathfinder, Pioneers,* and *Prairie*.

4. Barbara Welter describes True Womanhood in *Dimity Convictions* as an ideology for middle-class female behavior that, though in competition with other ideals, became increasingly dominant by midcentury.

5. For historical descriptions of ideals of womanhood in the early nation, see Kerber, *Women of the Republic*; Norton, *Liberty's Daughters*. For historical descriptions of changing ideals of womanhood in the nineteenth century, see Welter, *Dimity Convictions*; Cott, *Bonds of Womanhood*; Ryan, *Empire of the Mother*. Hazel Carby's *Reconstructing Womanhood* contains a particularly concise elucidation of the racial politics of true womanhood in chapter 2, "Slave and Mistress: Ideologies of Womanhood under Slavery" (20–39), and Christine Stansell's *City of Women* helps readers consider its class politics. For discussions that foreground the political agency of women who subscribed to or participated in the ideals of true womanhood, see, for example, Tompkins, *Sensational Designs*; Wexler, "Tender Violence"; Kaplan, *The Anarchy of Empire*. For a helpful critical alternative to the either/or dichotomy that emerges in these later discussions (women did/did not have agency; the agency they exercised was bad/good), see the introduction to Romero, *Home Fronts*.

6. This so-called science and its theory that the various groups of men represent separate species has long been discredited as bad sci-

ence; race is not recognized as a legitimate scientific category be-cause no test—by skin tone, blood type, phenotypical features, or genetic inheritance—has ever managed to delineate more difference *between* groups than within them. For further discussion of the con-cept of race in science, culture, and law, see Montagu, *The Concept of Race*; Gosset, *Race*; Gould, *The Mismeasure of Man*; Nelson, *National Manhood*, chapter 3; Fredrickson, *Racism*; Mills, *The Racial Contract*.

7. Later, when Heyward speaks approvingly of Uncas, Cora will comment, "Now Major Heyward speaks as Major Heyward should . . . who, that looks at this creature of nature, remembers the shades of his skin!" (1: 530).

8. In his history of *Sentimental Democracy*, Andrew Burstein traces the deep imbrication of U.S. nationhood with explicitly sentimental ideals:

> Nationalism describes the connectedness of these people, their shared loyalty to national principles, and the persistence of a common cultural idiom. Contained within this definition of national consciousness is the moral standard whose tradi-tional features include compassion, generosity and benevo-lence. Whether or not these qualities are real and applied, at least they are consistently articulated elements of America's national goals and values. . . . [Early American texts] reveal how zealous expressions of sympathy and affectionate ties joined with clear assertions of the reasoning intellect to pro-mote national union. (xvii)

9. Soon Child would be advocating openly for intermarriage. In her 1834 *Appeal in Favor of That Class of Americans Called Africans*, she argues against the laws forbidding racial intermarriage, arguing that without such laws, racism would eventually break down as the human heart would create bridges across these legally enforced racial "gulfs."

10. For a good sample of this so-called science, see Nott and Glid-don, *Types of Mankind*; Nott, "Diversity of the Human Race."

11. For an excellent, informative discussion of Cooper's multicul-turalist interests, see Simpson, *The Politics of American English*. In "Per-forming 'Wilderness' in *The Last of the Mohicans*," David Mazel pro-vides a fascinating reading of the novel's emphasis on the nation's white destiny in the scene where Alice is rescued a second time:

Near the novel's end, the captive Alice Munro is rescued from a cave at the Huron encampment: borne but also born out of the symbolic womb of the wilderness. This is the same womb from which her foil, the young Native American woman, in a gruesome reminder of the historical exclusions that gave birth to "nature's nation," will be carried dead on a bier: also borne, but stillborn. Alice's rescue may be viewed as the securing for an entire posterity, as another fictionalized origin, a (re)birth of a white race and an American civilization that will be reared on the grave of Alice's unfortunate counterpart. (113)

12. For a discussion of Ellen Wade's democratic resonance and "post-patriarchal" possibilities, see Baym (708–709).

13. For a discussion of a competing feminine ideal to the passivity prescribed by the cult of True Womanhood, see Cogan, *All-American Girl*. For a discussion of True Womanhood and suggestions for further reading, see note 5.

14. As Baym notes, "Much has been written about this episode, for by concentrating on Natty's rejection of Judith and ignoring his rejection by Mabel [Dunham in *The Pathfinder*] it has been possible to construct a myth of the Leatherstocking which is much more congenial to the 20th century critics' obsession with homoerotic purity than are the actual materials of the saga as Cooper wrote it. But Cooper's own audience, reading the books as they appeared, would recall *The Pathfinder* (published just the year before) and contrast his passion in the one case with his reluctance in the other" (706).

15. Person, "Cooper's Queen of the Woods," 254.

16. Ibid.

17. Ibid.

18. Here Hazel Carby's discussion of the ideological function of such an ideal as true womanhood, as opposed to the measurable lived realities of particular women's lives, is helpful. As she observes about the racial politics of this dominant and dominating ideology, it "attempted to bring coherence and order to the contradictory material circumstances of the lives of women" (24). Carby deftly elucidates how "true womanhood" depended structurally on its "dark other"—in her discussion, enslaved women—and was not a stand-alone ideal. Its idealization of sexual purity depended on the sexual debasement of women who could not aspire to its ideal, and thus it enforces not just racist ideals but racist practices. It is certainly inter-

esting to consider whether Cooper was trying to raise questions about the racist baggage of true womanhood as he played with his dark/fair lady pairings.

19. Relationships between women were perhaps the central experience of a young girl's life, regardless of the particular womanly norm she favored, as Carroll Smith-Rosenberg has famously argued in *Disorderly Conduct*.

20. Before Adam Smith wrote *The Wealth of Nations* (1776), with its famous invocation of the "invisible hand" of capitalism, he wrote *A Theory of Moral Sentiments* (1759). The most recent generation of scholars has begun to take more seriously the influence of the so-called Scottish Enlightenment School and its theory of moral sentiments, a group of philosophers that included Smith, Francis Hutcheson, Thomas Reid, and David Hume, on political and economic thought in the eighteenth and nineteenth centuries, and, more simply, in *men's* investments in sympathy and sentimentalism. See, for instance, Rothschild, *Economic Sentiments*; Burstein, *Sentimental Democracy*; Burgett, *Sentimental Bodies*; Stern, *Plight of Feeling*; Barnes, *States of Sympathy*; Hendler, *Public Sentiments*; Crain, *American Sympathy*.

21. For more information on William Apess, see O'Connell, *On Our Own Ground*; Lepore, *The Name of War*; Richter, *Facing East from Indian Country*.

22. Jane Tompkins argues:

> The two key events in understanding American attitudes toward race relations during this period are the founding of the American Colonization Society in 1816 and [President] Monroe's policy of Indian removal formulated in late 1824. The colonization effort, as Lawrence Friedman points out, attempted to maintain America's image of itself as a white man's nation by physically transporting blacks to another continent. The Indian removal policy had much the same result; it effectively prevented the mixing of Indian and white populations by removing the Indians to lands west of the Mississippi. (110)

23. In an analysis of Cooper's *Deerslayer*, Leland Person has noted that Harry "represents the worst case of frontier violence, symbolically assimilated as marketplace manhood run amok." "The Historical Paradoxes of Manhood," 81.

24. See Nelson, *National Manhood*, especially chapters 4 and 5.

25. I would argue that such foreclosures feel as present for white men today, given the popular and important sentimental success of such male friendship movies as *Rambo: First Blood*, and *Dances with Wolves*, along with Michael Mann's wildly popular remake of *The Last of the Mohicans*. For instance, Rambo's lament throughout the movie is his inability to sustain friendships with men now that he is back in the United States, and indeed the tragedy of his pursuit is heightened by the fact that it is commanded by the same man who commanded him in Vietnam. Similarly, escaping from the fratricidal Civil War, Lieutenant John Dunbar redeems his torn sense of self in forging friendships and, like Natty, a passionate identification with the Sioux whom he encounters on the frontier. The movie's most moving moment for most viewers comes when Wind-in-his-hair, who proclaimed himself Dunbar's enemy at first meeting, bids him farewell, insisting that he will always be Dunbar's friend. Mann's version of *Last of the Mohicans*, by recreating Natty more along the lines of the later *Deerslayer*, succeeds with modern audiences in the same way, forwarding "Nathaniel" both as a person who befriends Indians but also who identifies as one. I had resisted, like a typical literary critic, seeing this movie, but finally I did, swayed by countless male students who earnestly insisted that I must. To persuade me of the movie's worthiness, they told me that the movie made them *cry*. They were proud, not ashamed, of this response. It is possible that men respond so passionately to these movies because the norms for physical, economic, and social competition make forging meaningful relationships with other men as difficult and frustrating today as male readers were beginning to find it in the antebellum period.

26. For a history of this practice, see Deloria, *Playing Indian*. Deloria describes playing Indian as a "persistent tradition in American life" and finds its practice "clustered around two paradigmatic moments—the revolution, which rested on the creation of national identity, and modernity, which has used Indian play to encounter the authentic amidst the anxiety of urban industrial and postindustrial life" (7). On Maine's white Indians, see 41–43.

27. Cathy Davidson and Jessamyn Hatcher describe the "logic" of the separate spheres in their introduction to *No More Separate Spheres!*:

According to this separate spheres metaphor, there is a public sphere inhabited by men and a private sphere that is the domain of women. Scholars have searched for and found evidence of gender relations organized along these lines at various moments in the history of Western culture, but like to argue that the separate spheres ideology took on renewed power and urgency in nineteenth-century America. They insist that not only was nineteenth-century American society organized around the model of the separate spheres, but also that the female sphere of sentiment, home, and hearth suddenly became a source of great national value, pride, and inspiration. (7)

Davidson and Hatcher provide an excellent overview history of this concept, showing how scholars have *long* been arguing that it unnecessarily limits the way we understand nineteenth-century U.S. culture, which may have *preached* but did not clearly practice the rigid gender divisions seemingly required by the separate spheres model. My analysis of Cooper has highlighted another instance of such blinkering: if we believe only *women* wrote and read sympathetic novels, that only *women* practiced sympathy, it becomes impossible to see how men also deployed sympathy and to study the range of its possibilities in antebellum culture. Indeed, as I argue in an essay ("Representative/Democracy") included in Davidson and Hatch's volume, if one considers the developing range of sentimental practices attached to male sociality in the nineteenth century (such as secret fraternal ritualism or even U.S. patriotism), it becomes clear that sympathy was an enormously vital and widely contested ideology with numerous manifestations. What seems interesting in historical retrospect, then, is that the practices of sympathy associated with *women* have been so loudly and widely derided, whereas the practices associated with its uses among men in the same period have been quietly overlooked. Understanding how one set of associations became hypervisible and the other off-limits is an important question.

WORKS CITED

Barnes, Elizabeth. *States of Sympathy: Seduction and Democracy in the Early American Novel.* New York: Columbia University Press, 1997.

Baym, Nina. "The Women of Cooper's Leatherstocking Tales," *American Quarterly* 23. 5 (1971): 696–709.

Burgett, Bruce. *Sentimental Bodies: Sex, Gender and Citizenship in the Early Republic.* Princeton, NJ: Princeton University Press, 1998.

Burstein, Andrew. *Sentimental Democracy: The Evolution of America's Romantic Self-Image.* New York: Hill and Wang, 1999.

Carby, Hazel. *Reconstructing Womanhood: The Emergence of the Afro-American Woman Novelist.* New York: Oxford University Press, 1987.

Carnes, Mark. *Secret Ritual and Manhood in Victorian America.* New Haven: Yale University Press, 1989.

Chase, Richard. *The American Novel and Its Tradition.* Baltimore: Johns Hopkins University Press, 1957.

Child, Lydia Maria. *Appeal in Favor of That Class of Americans Called Africans.* 1834. Ed. Carolyn Karcher. Amherst: University of Massachusetts Press, 1996.

———. *Hobomok.* 1823. Ed. Carolyn Karcher. New Brunswick, NJ: Rutgers University Press, 1986.

Cogan, Frances B. *All-American Girl: The Idea of Real Womanhood in Mid-Nineteenth-Century America.* Athens: University of Georgia Press, 1989.

Cooper, James Fenimore. *The Leatherstocking Tales.* 2 vols. New York: Library of America, 1985.

Cott, Nancy F. *Bonds of Womanhood: "Woman's Sphere" in New England, 1780–1835.* New Haven: Yale University Press, 1977.

Crain, Caleb. *American Sympathy: Men, Friendship, and Literature in the New Nation.* New Haven: Yale University Press, 2001.

Crèvecoeur, J. Hector St. John de. *Letters from an American Farmer.* Ed. Albert Stone. New York: Penguin, 1981.

Davidson, Cathy, and Jessamyn Hatcher, eds. *No More Separate Spheres! A Next Wave American Studies Reader.* Durham, NC: Duke University Press, 2002.

Deloria, Philip. *Playing Indian.* New Haven: Yale University Press, 1998.

Fiedler, Leslie. *Love and Death in the American Novel.* 1966. Normal, IL: Dalkey Archive Press, 1997.

Fredrickson, George M. *Racism: A Short History.* Princeton, NJ: Princeton University Press, 2002.

Gossett, Thomas. *Race: The History of an Idea in America*. New York: Schocken, 1963.

Gould, Stephen J. *The Mismeasure of Man*. New York: Norton, 1981.

Hendler, Glenn. *Public Sentiments: Structures of Feeling in Nineteenth-Century American Literature*. Chapel Hill: University of North Carolina Press, 2001.

Jennings, Francis. *Invasion of America: Indians, Colonialism and the Cant of Conquest*. New York: Norton, 1976.

Kaplan, Amy. *The Anarchy of Empire in the Making of U.S. Culture*. Cambridge, MA: Harvard University Press, 2002.

Kerber, Linda. *Women of the Republic: Intellect and Ideology in Revolutionary America*. Chapel Hill: University of North Carolina Press, 1980.

Kolodny, Annette. *The Land Before Her: Fantasy and Experience of the American Frontiers, 1630–1860*. Chapel Hill: University of North Carolina Press, 1984.

Lawrence, D. H. *Studies in Classic American Literature*. 1923. New York: Penguin, 1983.

Lepore, Jill. *The Name of War: King Philip's War and the Origins of American Identity*. New York: Vintage, 1998.

Lewis, R. W. B. *The American Adam: Innocence, Tragedy, and Tradition in the Nineteenth-Century*. Chicago: University of Chicago Press, 1955.

Lowell, James Russell. *A Fable for Critics* (1848). In *Fenimore Cooper: The Critical Heritage*, ed. George Dekker and John P. McWilliams. London: Routledge & Kegan Paul, 1973.

Mazel, David. "Performing Wilderness in *The Last of the Mohicans*." In *Reading under the Sign of Nature: New Essays in Ecocriticism*, ed. John Tallmadge and Henry Harrington, 101–114. Salt Lake City: University of Utah Press, 2000.

Mills, Charles W. *The Racial Contract*. Ithaca, NY: Cornell University Press, 1997.

Montagu, Ashley, ed. *The Concept of Race*. London: Collier Books, 1964.

Nelson, Dana D. *National Manhood: Capitalist Citizenship and the Imagined Fraternity of White Men*. Durham, NC: Duke University Press, 1998.

———. "Representative/Democracy: Presidents, Democratic Management and the Unfinished Business of Male Sentimentalism." In Davidson and Hatcher, 325–344.

Norton, Mary Beth. *Liberty's Daughters: The Revolutionary Experience of American Women, 1750–1800.* Boston: Little, Brown, 1980.

Nott, Josiah. "Diversity of the Human Race." *De Bow's Review* 10 (1851): 113–132.

Nott, Josiah, and George Gliddon. *Types of Mankind, or Ethnological Researches Based upon the Ancient Monuments, Paintings, Sculptures and Crania of Races. . . .* Philadelphia: Lippincott, Grambo, 1854. Rpt. Miami: Mneomosyne, 1969.

O'Connell, Barry, ed. *On Our Own Ground: The Complete Writings of William Apess, a Pequot.* Amherst: University of Massachusetts Press, 1992.

Person, Leland S. "Cooper's Queen of the Woods: Judith Hutter in *The Deerslayer.*" *Studies in the Novel* 21.3 (fall 1989): 253–267.

———. "The Historical Paradoxes of Manhood in Cooper's *The Deerslayer.*" *Novel: A Forum on Fiction* 32.1 (fall 1998): 76–98.

Porte, Joel. *The Romance in America: Studies in Cooper, Poe, Hawthorne, Melville and James.* Middletown, CT: Wesleyan University Press, 1969.

Richter, Daniel K. *Facing East from Indian Country: A Native History of Early America.* Cambridge, MA: Harvard University Press, 2001.

Ringe, Donald. *James Fenimore Cooper.* New York: Twayne Publishers, 1962.

Romero, Lora. *Home Fronts: Domesticity and Its Critics.* Durham, NC: Duke University Press, 1997.

Rothschild, Emma. *Economic Sentiments: Adam Smith, Condorcet, and the Enlightenment.* Cambridge, MA: Harvard University Press, 2001.

Ryan, Mary. *Empire of the Mother: American Writing about Domesticity, 1830–1860.* New York: Haworth, 1982.

Simpson, David. *The Politics of American English, 1776–1850.* New York: Oxford University Press, 1986.

Smith-Rosenberg, Carroll. *Disorderly Conduct: Visions of Gender in Victorian America.* New York: Knopf, 1986.

Stansell, Christine. *City of Women: Sex and Class in New York, 1789–1860.* New York: Knopf, 1986.

Stauffer, John. *The Black Hearts of Men: Radical Abolitionists and the*

Transformation of Race. Cambridge, MA: Harvard University Press, 2002.

Stern, Julia. *Plight of Feeling: Sympathy and Dissent in the Early American Novel*. Chicago: University of Chicago Press, 1997.

Thoreau, Henry David. *Walden*. 1854. Ed. Stephen Fender. New York: Oxford University Press, 1997.

Tompkins, Jane. *Sensational Designs: The Cultural Work of American Fiction, 1790–1860*. New York: Oxford University Press, 1985.

Tyler, Royall. *The Contrast*. In *The Heath Anthology of American Literature*. 2nd ed. Vol. 1. Lexington, MA: D. C. Heath, 1994.

Welter, Barbara. *Dimity Convictions: The American Woman in the Nineteenth-Century*. Athens: University of Ohio Press, 1976.

Wexler, Laura. "Tender Violence: Literary Eavesdropping, Domestic Fiction and Educational Reform." *Yale Journal of Criticism* 5 (fall 1991): 151–187.

Race Traitor

Cooper, His Critics, and Nineteenth-Century Literary Politics

Barbara Alice Mann

James Fenimore Cooper did not set out to become the target of the racist movement with his Leatherstocking Tales. Indeed, when he first set pen to paper, he could have anticipated only a warm welcome from the American literary elite, which initially saw him as one of its own. The story of his slide into the bad graces of his political enemies has already been told, but there remains one large, and largely unexplored, patch of ground that modern critics have gingerly skirted. It is none other than the staging point of attack on Cooper by his Antebellum critics: his honorary position as a "race traitor."

In the rush to condemn Cooper as the racist of the drama, modern critics of the Leatherstocking Tales betray their ignorance of what true racists acted and sounded like between 1823 and 1841. Instead of grounding their criticism in historical and cultural knowledge, especially of Native America, they indulge in what I call Cry-Baby Criticism. This is a western method that richly deserves to be named and decried as applied to received Cooper criticism, however uncomfortable the naming, decrying, and applying may feel to western literary critics, the primary practitioners of it. Of the many unsavory traits of Cry-Baby

Criticism, its Eurocentricity, emphatically forbidding the use of any Other discourse style—say, Native American sacred clowning—is the most disturbing to me. "Trickster discourse" may be all the rage with western critics as long as it remains safely theoretical, but heaven help it should it show up in practice, for the linearity approved by Aristotle tied to the hrmphful discourse of his grim-faced cohort, the Puritan Father, rule. Thus, Native American discourse, which *requires* pointed satire, not to mention sarcastic jabs at the issues, often couched in scatological terms, is scorned, with firm editorial steps taken to civilize and christianize any unreconstructed savages lurking about the halls of academia. Alas, being a fast runner, I am neither civilized nor christianized, so I herewith advise Miss Lydia Crenshaw (the Iron Maiden) to fetch her smelling salts, for she reads on at her own peril.

In the case of Cooper, the sad result of Cry-Baby Criticism is to gut Other discourse, substituting instead the western-style of quick offense at fancied faux pas and mashing perception as smooth, and bland, as last night's potatoes. It seriously distorts Cooper's literary messages by responding to his texts as though they had been written ten minutes ago, in blatant and intentional transgression of modern sensibilities. Cry-Baby Criticism wags shaming fingers at a bit of minstrelsy here or condemns a slur term there, without the slightest regard for historical context. Then, still no wiser as to context, Cry-Baby Criticism concludes that Cooper was a racist and, therefore, beyond the pale of appreciative consideration. The worst Cooperian effect of Cry-Baby Criticism is to obscure the real point of contention between Cooper and his contemporary critics, to wit, just who *were* the real racists of the story, thereby seriously deforming any discussion of the Leatherstocking Tales.

To rectify this distortion, I adopt (and recommend to others) the Seven-Span Skin, the traditional requirement of any Iroquoian Speaker entering a public forum. A skin as thick as seven thumbs together, the Seven-Span Skin makes me "proof against anger, offensive actions and criticism,"[1] allowing me to survive the casual racism inherent in *every* Antebellum discourse while freeing me to zero in on Cooper's actual issues. Seven-Span Criticism clears the underbrush of easy affront, so that truths larger than any individual or ahistorical sensibility may emerge.

The first truth I see is that, although most Cooper critics are aware of the unconscionable attacks to which his enemies subjected his reputation, as well as the flurry of libel lawsuits he filed to vindicate his name, they fail to apply this knowledge beyond the level of mere personalities. Instead, like George Dekker and John P. McWilliams, they choose to believe that Cooper "oversimplified" by charging journals and newspapers with "political hostility."[2] Indeed, it is not Cooper but the critics who are "oversimplifying" when they contend that personal rather than political considerations accounted for Cooper's righteous ire. Cooper was absolutely the victim of a large-scale, organized political assault that deliberately sought out and destroyed dissenters, especially when their dissent challenged the primary rationale behind the European seizure of North America: the myth of racial supremacy. Critics attacked Cooper specifically because he challenged the hegemony of racism by depicting people of color in sympathetic ways that upended the racist dogma of the day. What is missed today is the depth and complexity of the racial formulas permeating the Antebellum atmosphere. Cooper toyed with these, to the mounting animosity of those with the most to gain from their rigid application.

Removed in time and mentality from that dire period, critics focus on Cooper's obvious "Indians" to the exclusion of his more delicate portraits of racial struggle in mixed bloods, including, most importantly of all, Natty Bumppo—Hawkeye himself. For the reading public of 1823–1841, the trail leading to Natty's Native identity was actually quite broad, providing a portrait of a mixed-blood man desperately "passing for white." Natty's bobs, weaves, and feints—all still too frighteningly familiar to any mixed bloods in the crowd—were unmistakable to the defenders of racial purity in Cooper's time.

Cooper was, therefore, outraging racist dogma as it hardened from the more liberal colonial stance on mixed bloods into the ferocious codes of Antebellum America. Far from adding to the storehouse of racial stereotypes, Cooper was critiquing racism. *This* was the high crime that put him on the hit list of literary and political critics alike. To make out as much, however, modern critics need first to appreciate that the thing looking frighteningly liberal between 1823 and 1845 was, specifically, Cooper's depiction of Natty Bumppo. In Hawkeye, Cooper was challenging the contemporary "science" of race.

There is a reason that Natty was not construed as the "hero" of the Leatherstocking Tales until the twentieth century, and it only superficially attaches to his low socioeconomic status. The true reason is the same reason that the mulatta Cora Munro was avidly painted platinum blonde in the 1936 film version of *The Last of the Mohicans* and that both Natty and Cora were earnestly presented as "white" in the 1997 *Mohicans* film. Mixed blood in love is still too politically hot to handle. Moreover, so accustomed are critics to Natty's man-without-a-cross mantra that they take it at face value, never asking the obvious question: Was Natty *really* a man without a racial cross? I say, not a chance. Seen against the backdrop of Lenape ("Delaware") colonial history, of which Cooper was intimately aware through his source, John Heckewelder, Natty could only have been a mixed blood.[3]

Modern critics tend to assume, ahistorically, that the one-drop rule of racial identity was always in force in North America, legally disallowing any wiggle room to people of racially mixed ancestry. In fact, between 1700 and 1850, there were *three* rules of racial identity, each competing with the others: (1) generational passing, (2) the rule of recognition, and (3) the rule of descent. Generational passing, the British standard under colonialism, allowed third-generation cross-bloods to pass as "white," regardless of how Native or African they might look.[4] By 1825, racist theory was gaining ground in America, positing two new, conflicting rules of race, those of recognition and descent. The rule of recognition was the eye test of identity—whoever "looked white" might pass—whereas the rule of descent, the infamous one-drop rule, forbade passing at all times, regardless of generation or appearance.[5] After 1825, only the rules of recognition and descent remained to vie for social control. From 1850 on, the one-drop rule alone applied. In Natty's lifetime, however, the generational rule and the rule of recognition were in force. Under the rule of recognition, and quite possibly (depending on his parents) under the rule of generation, too, Natty was legally "white." It was only in later, one-drop America that he would not have been categorized as "white." Cooper was aware of these three rules, and even made characters in *The Pioneers* (1823) allude to them in their speculations regarding Oliver Edwards, who clearly passed the eye test, although Dickon Jones brought up the third-generational rule, whereas Elizabeth inclined to the one-drop theory (*Pi* 204–205). Over the next eighteen years, Natty's cross-less tagline developed in tandem with the racial rules as they slid from liberality to one-drop dogma. Natty did not start out fixated on his heritage or pressed to reveal it in every other speech. It is a statistical fact, however, that, as the Tales progressed, the number of racial disclosures increased significantly as their tone turned desperate. In the first tale of the series, *The Pioneers*, the preponderance of references—eighteen—were to Natty as *Native*, as opposed to four indicating Natty was European. By the time Cooper arrived at *The Deerslayer* in 1841, however, both he and Natty were practically frantic over the issue of race. I counted Natty alluding to his supposedly European identity seventy-two times, often several times on the same page and, sometimes, even within the same speech. Skin color in these speeches is always the linchpin of Natty's "white" credentials.

Today, this same point of color is still offered as proof of Natty's European identity, but it is a seriously uninformed point. Throughout the eastern woodlands, Natives generally had light skin *at contact*. In fact, the "whiteness" of Natives of the Northeast was common knowledge, often mentioned in first-contact chronicles.[6] It wasn't until 1795 that the rubric of Europeans as the world's only light-skinned people became a touchstone of racist fantasy, pushed by Johann Friedrich Blumenbach's influential "science" of race.[7] Thereafter, the going notion was that Europeans had, somehow, gotten into the Native mix, with the three main explanations featuring the French, the Welsh, and wayward Yankees as the intermingling culprits. Cooper was one of the folks who knew all about "white Indians," giving all three types of "white" Indians walk-on roles in the Leatherstocking

Tales (for "a nation of Welshers," see *Pr* 190; for French "metifs" or half-breeds, see *Pr* 107; for "them Yankee Indians," see *Pi* 452). Then, of course, there is Natty.

As racism grew in intensity in the new United States, Euro-Americans began to wax a bit hysterical over the number of mixed bloods in their midst, especially any lurking about undetected. Intensifying the frenzy was something Euro-Americans knew, though seldom acknowledged: that amalgamation between themselves and the light-skinned woodlanders resulted quickly and easily in passable offspring with the first "cross." Unwilling to admit that they simply could not tell when someone was passing for white, nervous racists devised eye tests of identity by which a clever European observer could ferret out anyone's "true" racial identity at a glance. Based on the checklist originally supplied by Blumenbach, who had never seen most of the people he presumed to describe, the litmus test turned European tastes in beauty into benchmarks of racial identification.[8]

Natty rather resoundingly flunked this litmus test of identity, but not because Cooper was ignorant of its content. In *The Wept of Wish-ton-Wish* (1829), he allowed a Puritan (anachronistically) to list Blumenbach's biological markers—"familiar to men who have made the physical peculiarities of the two races their study"—by way of supporting his contention that the Narragansett adoptee, Whittal Ring, was actually European, not Native.[9] Given this knowledge of Blumenbach, Cooper deliberately engineered Natty's "ugliness." Hawkeye's most offending features were his "enormous mouth," "gray eyes," "lank, sandy [reddish] hair," and skin that took too well to the sun, all sure signs of Native descent under the European eye test of identity (*Pi* 21, 22–23). Worst of all, however, was Natty's sun-welcoming skin. Critics may cling to Natty's suntan as overlaying "the original color of a Pale Face," as though this conclusively demonstrates his European descent, but color mattered little at the time, given the high incidence of "white Indians," as Cooper had his sage of *The Wept of Wish-ton-Wish* caution (*Pr* 208).[10] Furthermore, in Cooper's age, "burning" did not indicate what modern readers think of as a sunburn but, instead, the darkening effect of melanin exposed to the sun. Thus, Cooper's continual references to Natty's darkening under the sun—"his sun-burned and hard features"; his "weather burned features"; his face "burnt by the sun to a hue scarcely less red than that of" Chingachgook—were highly suspicious traits as far as racists were concerned (*Pa* 37, 160, 207; *D* 201).

Natty's height and body structure likewise suggest Native origin. Northeastern Natives were (and still are) thin, tall, and broad-shouldered, whereas Europeans were by comparison bulky and short. Natty's height, "about six feet in his moccasins," did not mark him as a European but as a Northeastern Native (*D* 20). He was also extraordinarily thin, "so meager as to make him seem above even the six feet that he actually stood in his stockings" (*Pi* 22; for other references to his slight build, see *D* 20 and *LM* 29). In middle age, he had bulked up a bit, but not enough to overcome his suspicious lankiness, "rather too angular for the proportion that the eye most approves" (*Pa* 160). Gray eyes; wide mouth; tall, slender, angular build; straight hair; sunnable skin: these were simply not the attributes that the racist eye most approved. These were Native traits.

Importantly, Natty was not the only racially confused character created by Cooper. It is worth noting that Cooper more than once played with the theme of individuals deluding themselves and others on the score of their racial identity. Whittal Ring was a sort of reverse Natty, stoutly maintaining that he was racially Narragansett, even as he stood in the midst of Puritan relations, all claiming him as friend and brother.[11] Meantime, the adoptee Narra-mattah flatly refused to believe Conanchet when he told her that she belonged to that "hungry and craving" race, the Europeans. She refused to allow the color of her skin to second his news, despite the purported meaning of her name as "the driven snow."[12] Cooper's commentary here went well beyond the observation that human beings acquire their attitudes and values from the environment of their youth rather than from their biology at birth. Cooper was also directly quizzing habits of denial in situations where the racial "truth" was simply too painful—or too dangerous—to bear.

When pressed on the matter of identity, Natty defined himself behaviorally rather than biologically. He emphasized over and over that it was his behavior, as opposed to himself, that was European: "My gifts are white," he insisted, "I am of a christian [*sic*] stock" (D 122). Such claims, repeated over and over in the Tales, are deceptive, for Christians come in all colors, whereas European behavioral standards are learned, not acquired genetically. Significantly, Natty's habit was to scrutinize behavioral options for their Native or European bent and then take the purportedly European tack. Sorting out "white" behavior was a yeoman effort requiring far more thought than any of Cooper's Euro-American characters ever put on the matter.

Natty was unable to alter his education, however, remaining "as illiterate as a Mohawk," having "never passed a day within reach of a spelling book" or "read a book in [his] life" (Pa 296; Pr 184; Pi 293). There were inescapable repercussions attached to illiteracy, for, to Europeans, illiteracy in a professed Christian was one sure sign of a questionable heritage. Even the redoubtable Esther Bush could make out her Bible, while a simpleton like Hetty Hutter was taught to read specifically so that she might peruse hers. Even (real-life) Native converts, such as Hendrick Aupaumut, David Cusick, and Samson Occom, could make shift to write a little. Aware of all this, Natty was ashamed of his illiteracy, admitting it reluctantly. In *The Deerslayer*, simple Hetty put words to Natty's predicament: "Only think of that; a white man, and not know how to read his bible, even! He never could have had a mother, sister!" (D 312). Nevertheless, as Cooper had carefully made clear earlier in the same novel, Natty had *both* a mother *and* a sister (D 43). In that day, when it was the pious colonial woman's duty to impart at least functional literacy to her male relatives the better to inculcate Christian values, the implication was that Natty's mother and sister—and, by logical extension, Natty himself—were not European.

The scattered tidbits on Natty's personal history, as provided in the Tales, are even more suggestive than his personal appearance and habits. Intriguingly, the most succinct biography of Natty, from the lips of Oliver Edwards in *The Pioneers*, is utterly unreliable. According to Oliver, Natty "was reared in the family of my grandfather [Major Effingham]; served him for many years during their campaigns at the west, where he became attached to the woods; and he was left here as a kind of locum tenens on the lands that old Mohegan (whose life my grandfather once saved) induced the Delawares to grant to him, when they admitted him as an honorary member of their tribe" (*Pi* 441). The coherence of this account is deceptive for, in substance, it conflicts in almost every detail with what Natty has to say of himself throughout the five Tales, other references in *The Pioneers* inclusive. On the other hand, Natty's self-information is internally consistent. The distinctions between Oliver's account and Natty's accounts are highly suggestive of concealment, not the least because Oliver himself was most probably a third-generation mixed blood, as Louisa Grant and Elizabeth Temple twice surmised during "naughty" girl-talk (*Pi* 214, 304).

According to Natty, he stayed with his parents, "when they was living," until he was orphaned, at which time he took up residence with the Lenape (*D* 541). Geographically, Natty said that he had been born "nigh York," but it was not, as so often supposed, the York of England, as related references make clear (*Pi* 206). Natty gave *his* York as the one abutting the Catskills, a range he remembered seeing "to the left," following the "river up from York" (*Pi* 292). There are no Catskill Mountains up the river from York, England. Moreover, Natty stated that, although his life had "been passed in the woods," his "eyes were first opened on the shores of the Eastern sea" (*Pr* 23, 250). His "Eastern sea" had to have been the Atlantic Ocean, which is the "Western sea," if one's starting point were England. Clearly, Natty was from *New* York. He had been born along the mid-Atlantic coast, from which his family soon moved inland. Living later with the Catskills in sight pushed him two hundred miles inland and to the northwest: Natty was in the heart of Iroquoia when he looked up the York to the Catskills.

Between 1661 and 1740, the people retreating from the mid-Atlantic coast inland to the sanctuary of Iroquoia were the Lenapes. A child wound up residing with the Lenape refugees in Iroquoia in exactly one of two ways: She or he was adopted in after having been taken captive in a mourning war, or she or he was a born Lenape. Had Natty been taken captive during a raid, he would surely have mentioned this stunning fact at some point in his many reminiscences. He made no such mention. The only other explanation for his life among the Lenape was access by birth; one of his parents had to have been Native.

Thus, Natty was *not* a grown man at the time the Lenape took him in, as Oliver indicated, but still a child. Natty and Chingachgook were approximately the same age, for, past seventy in 1793, Chingachgook had himself been born circa 1720 (*Pi* 410). Chingachgook was Natty's " 'arliest and latest fri'nd," meaning that they had been bonded friends (a legal status in woodlands culture) since first meeting in boyhood (*D* 153). These facts of Native law are pregnant with implications concerning Natty's identity.

First, since Chingachgook and Natty met as children, it was long before Chingachgook was a sitting member of the council, which admitted only mature adults. As a child, Chingachgook was in no position to "induce" the sachems to grant another child land, let alone to instruct them to adopt Natty, something that no male, grown or otherwise, was ever empowered to do. Thus, even in early adulthood, Chingachgook would not have had a seat on the council. He would have been among "the young men," a term usually mis/translated as "warriors" in western sources.[13] Second, the Clan Mothers alone decided who was to be adopted.[14] Under all woodlands governments, the young men were under the direction of their civil sachems and Clan Mothers, *not* the other way around. (Cooper knew that, for he depicted that "young man," Magua, as submitting to the judgment of the Tamenund.) In any case, even as a Young Man (as opposed to a child), Chingachgook was in no position to "induce" the council to grant Natty land, for the land and its disposition belonged exclusively to the women.[15] Thus, Oliver's account of Natty's "locum tenens" was completely specious and, moreover, obviously so to anyone even slightly ethnoliterate in Cooper's day.

Again contrary to Oliver's biography, Natty never spoke of having lived with or been reared by Major Effingham, although he was deeply attached to the old man and had campaigned with him as an adult. Instead, Natty stated that he had been born of "honest" (i.e., married) parents with whom he lived till they died (*Pi* 206). At that point, he went to the Lenape. Beyond this,

Hawkeye made stray, noncommittal references to his father, but of his mother, the reader heard only once, and that once, but obliquely, for the pertinent description focused on Natty's emotional impressions, not on facts. The revelation came at the wrenching moment in *The Deerslayer* when he stepped into Muskrat Palace and was unexpectedly flooded with memories of his mother—*and a sister* (D 43). One wonders about this sister, never acknowledged yet so achingly recalled. How came she to be so absent from Natty's life?

In any discussion of Natty's mother, the dearth of European women on the so-called frontier must be considered. As late as 1757, the year of *The Pathfinder*, Mabel Dunham was "the only marriageable white female on this frontier," and she resided in a populous fort (Pa 150). When Natty was born circa 1720, there were even fewer "marriageable white females" lurking about in the backwoods. Who, therefore, was his mother? It was Britain's practice in its colonies to encourage intermarriage with Native women, who could be abandoned when the officer returned to England to marry again, this time, a proper Englishwoman. The Englishwoman was recognized as the only wife; her children inherited.[16] This policy, to which Cooper had referred openly (in terms of Oliver) in *The Pioneers*, had the effect of littering the colonial landscape with "halfbreeds," a source of "scouts" as well as scandal. How did Natty's mother and father meet? Who *was* his mother? Who, indeed, was his *father*? The only way to reconcile Oliver's account of Natty's origins with Natty's accounts of himself is to posit Major Effingham as Natty's father, an intriguing possibility that I do not have the space to explore here.

The sole point on which the accounts of Natty and Oliver agree was that Natty had served with the major as an adult, a racially neutral claim. Even so, Natty could not always have been with the major, for Natty had "seen the inimy in the 'seventy-six business,'" that is, the Revolutionary War in which the major and his son, Edward, sided with England (Pi 374). As Tories, both Effinghams would have *been* "the inimy" that Natty had "seen" in the War! On all other points, Natty's and Oliver's accounts were at wide variance, with Oliver's version failing to square with *any* other account of Natty given *anywhere* else in *any* Leatherstocking Tale. The reasons for Oliver's fudging are obvious: The implications of the facts as Natty related them indicated racial mixture and, if pursued, threw not a little suspicion on Oliver Young Eagle Edwards, as well. There is an etiquette to passing that still eludes most Euro-Americans: People who are passing do not out Others who are also passing, and certainly not when those Others are blood relations.

Contrary to Oliver's fiction, Natty's tenure with the Lenape can be confidently deduced. The Leatherstocking Tales clearly indicate that Natty was a child when he was orphaned and went to the Lenape. In *The Deerslayer*, set "between the years 1740 and 1745," Natty was twentyish, implying that he had been born around 1720 (D 16). Using the mean year of 1743 for *The Deerslayer* and 1722 for the year of his birth, Natty took up residence with the Lenape in 1733, when he was ten years old. Elsewhere in *The Deerslayer*, Natty claimed to have been living with the Lenape for the past "ten years," again dating his residence with them from 1733 on (D 22). Other references yield similar dates. By 1803, the year of *The Prairie*, Natty had been on his parentless trail for "seventy and five years," living in the "very bosom of natur' " for seventy (Pr 23, 250). This would place the year of his first residence with the Lenape at 1733. *The Last of the Mohicans* was set in 1757, when Natty was still in vigorous middle age, and *The Pathfinder*, also set in the 1750s, depicted Natty as "well advanced towards forty" (Pa 36, 141). Again, both facts place his birth at around 1720. In *The Pioneers*, spanning the year 1793, Natty claimed to be "threescore and ten," which he quickly amended to seventy-one (Pi 370, 374). This adjusted his birth slightly forward to the year 1722. Toward the close of *The Prairie*, set in 1803, he gave his exact age as eighty-seven, pushing his birth back to the year 1716 (Pr 9, 314). This date seems anomalous, as it would have made Natty twenty-seven in 1743, the mean year of *The Deerslayer*, an age in emphatic conflict with Cooper's statement that Natty was "several years" the junior of Hurry Harry (D 21). Thus, Natty was most probably born in 1720, although perhaps as early as 1716.

The foregoing is awash with racial meaning for anyone even a little aware of the Moravian tenure in North America, as Cooper was from his source, Heckewelder. The Moravians first arrived in

North America in 1735, a date that coincided neatly with the second year of Natty's residence among the Lenape. It is historically true that, prior to setting up shop among the Lenape, they stopped off in the colony of Georgia for about ten years, not contacting the Lenapes until 1740 and not formally proselytizing them until 1743.[17] Cooper would have had no reason to know these minutiae of church history, however. Short of performing exhaustive research on the Moravian missions, he would simply have used the common knowledge of their arrival in 1735. Assuming (as most still do to this day) that they immediately missionized the Lenapes, he would have used that date to construct Natty's personal history.

In any case, the salient point in the Natty-Moravian link is not the dating but the fact that the Moravians in America *did not minister to settler congregations*. In 1748, their missionaries deliberately abandoned settler evangelism, thereafter proselytizing *only* Natives. Reaching the souls of "heathens" was the whole purpose of their "Scattered Seed" missions, of which the American mission, headquartered in Bethlehem, was one. Any European among them was, like Heckewelder, Moravian before ever reaching American soil. Only in the later years of the mission might a European be born Moravian in America, but that was in a period well after Natty's contact with the missionaries. According to *The Deerslayer*, set in 1743, being "not good enough for the Moravians" (yet too good for other preaching "vagabonds"), Natty had left the Moravian congregation (*D* 119). First and foremost, then, this crucial fact ruled out Natty as a settler child at the same time that it classed him as a Native child.

Second, it made Natty quite exotic. The Moravians were Antebellum objects of horror and titillation, and, even in the twenty-first century, a quick glance at their beliefs and practices makes it easy to see why. The Moravian theology of Count Nicholas Ludwig Zinzendorf that was practiced in North America was frankly sexual and not a little fixated on gore. To begin with, Moravianism defined sex as sacred, not shameful. Moreover, Zinzendorfian theology posited all souls as female, upending nineteenth-century sex roles by casting male believers as spiritually female. Scandal heightened as it then put these fe/male souls, termed "playmates," into the bed of a firmly male Creator. In the intensively sexist and homophobic atmosphere of Antebellum America, these were jaw-dropping propositions.[18]

Sexualization of worship also occurred through the unique Zinzendorfian "wounds theology," which dwelt on the wounds of Jesus in graphic detail, including that inflicted on his penis by circumcision. By far the most important wound was the gash in his side, which was presented as a womb with vagina for birthing converts. The wounds litany presented the female soul as licking and tasting these wounds, "succulent" and "juicy," to gain strength. Moravians were also startlingly frank about human sexual functions generally, having rejected the traditional Christian contempt for human genitalia. These theologies, taught to the youngest children, sent clerics of other Christian denominations into nervous collapse.[19] The unique content of Moravian theology was fairly common, if shushed, knowledge in Cooper's day.

It was also common knowledge that Moravians transgressed the racial barrier. Not only did they form genuinely loyal friendships with Native Americans, but they also freely intermarried with them. A central Moravian missionary, Frederick Post, *twice* married Lenape women, and not necessarily serially.[20] The first man killed "in a most cruel manner" during the 1782 genocide against the Ohio Lenapes was Shebosh, the son of the lay minister John Bull and a mixed-blood Moravian-Lenape convert.[21] Another Lenape, Jacob, was Mr. Bull's son-in-law.[22] Much of the scorn heaped on Moravians by Euro-Americans sprang from this Moravian failure to observe the color line in contracting marriages. Thus, to allude simultaneously to *both* forbidden race *and* deviant sex, one had but to insert a Moravian into the discussion.

This was, for instance, the tactic that Charles Brockden Brown, who knew Cooper, chose for plotting *Wieland* (1798). By dropping the name of Count Zinzendorf, Brown was alerting his readers that gothic, illicit, and interracial sex formed the submerged text of his novel.[23] In denying the heroine's mother membership in a local church at the same time that he made her pray "after the manner of the disciples of Zinzendorf" (she licks it, she tastes it, succulent and juicy), Brown was hinting ever so delicately that Mrs. Wieland was a sexually perverted mixed blood, unwelcome in mainstream Protestant society.[24] This context throws considerable light on Brown's plot, helping to explain why Mr. Wieland was fated to burn in fact as well as in hell (for marrying out of his race); why the Wieland siblings could not marry, at least not long, at least not happily; why the ventriloquist Carwin attacked the Wieland children so relentlessly; and why the Wieland sister was emotionally unstable even as the Wieland brother was a closet maniac. Racist "science" posited mixed bloods as embodying the worst of both worlds, the very stuff of insanity and instability. This was something all Antebellum readers were simply to have taken for granted, hence Duncan Middleton's odd testimonial that, "unlike most of those who live a border life," Natty "united the better, instead of the worse qualities of the two people" (*Pr* 114).

In historical context, then, Natty's Moravian connection perks up with more meaning than just the spiritual devotion that modern critics attach to it. First and foremost, it ruled out Natty as a settler child. Second, it strongly indicated that he was a mixed blood. Third, it classed any European love interest Natty might have nursed as twisted sexuality, obviously answering the supposed riddle of Natty's bachelorhood, for—as he informed Chingachgook—he would consider only a European mate (*D* 238).

None of Natty's kinky cachet was lost on Cooper's contemporaries. Indeed, it was Cooper's frank, compassionate, and (for his age) liberal-minded discourse on mixed race that marked him as an "Indian lover" and a "race traitor," setting him up for ferocious attack by the racist right. To accomplish this end, discourse was managed through conservative venues such as the *North American Review*, which promoted Lewis Cass and Henry Rowe Schoolcraft over John Heckewelder and, soon enough, Fenimore Cooper.

In promulgating their triumphalist tale of European destiny manifesting in America, nineteenth-century hawks carefully silenced, banished, and otherwise uprooted all rival versions of history. As a result, alternative myths, which were readily available in the eighteenth and early nineteenth centuries, were buried under the rubble of an Antebellum neglect so profound that modern students are often quite unaware that dissent over the mistreatment of Native Americans ever existed. Nevertheless, dissent did exist, a whole chorus of it, passionately voiced, and Cooper belonged to the choir. Pivotal to recovering the full story on Cooper is the realization that he was acting in company with a host of like-minded cohorts when he put forward Native claims and quizzed racial privilege. Cooper was "savaged" as part of the general political raid on *all* dissenters.

Viewed in this light, Cooper's main achievement was his survival. In fact, he might be styled the sole survivor of a political massacre, in which all of his compatriots perished. Cooper is still read, whereas (just to name his most important dissenting contemporaries) John Heckewelder, John Hunter, Mary Jemison, and, yes, Washington Irving are slighted by critics—or worse, *unknown* to them. This skews modern assessments by leaving Cooper looking like a lone figure lost somewhere in outer darkness, acting obscurely for idiosyncratic reasons, when, in fact, he was walking in the middle of a wide, radical road cleared for him by others. It was only after all his compatriots had perished in the literary raid that Cooper seemed so sadly solitary. When Cooper is reset naturally, as one of a cadre of leftover Enlightenment thinkers stranded in a most unenlightened age, his struggles with the political and literary racists snap into something like perspective.

The attack was two-pronged, through literature and scholarship. On the literary prong stood such figures as Robert Montgomery Bird, Henry Wadsworth Longfellow, "Judge" James Hall, and Herman Melville. On the scholarly prong sat General Lewis Cass and his protégé, Henry Rowe Schoolcraft, along with lesser minions. All but Hall were socially well-connected. One of the wildest inaccuracies about "Indian haters" is the myth of their culturally marginal social status, as seeded by Hall and embedded in American thought by Melville in his "Metaphysics of Indian-hating," a whitewash of ethnic cleansing that continues, incredibly, to be classed as satire. Still afloat, this pernicious fable posits all acts of genocide as the unofficial misdeeds of cranky backwoodsmen who, apparently, are not to be held responsible for their crimes by reason of their lower-class origins.[25]

Far from obscure social outcasts, "Indian haters" occupied the

highest positions in society and government. That Cooper neme-
sis, General Lewis Cass, the great "Indian Fighter" and reputed
"Indian Scholar," was territorial governor of Michigan, a U.S.
senator, a U.S. ambassador to France, and President Andrew Jackson's secretary of war. Although Cass failed in his ultimate goal
of capturing the presidency, his career could only be considered
distinguished.[26] Politically, Cass was an archconservative, an
anti-abolitionist, an anti-Mexican, and—for all Schoolcraft's
attempts to paint him as a "Friend of the Indian"—a virulent
"Indian hater."

Henry Rowe Schoolcraft, who became the federal government's "Indian Scholar," was also the Michigan superintendent
of Indian Affairs, a member of the Michigan Territorial Congress, and the self-proclaimed "discoverer" of the source of the
Mississippi. Henry Wadsworth Longfellow, the most popular
American poet of the nineteenth century, who based his "Indian"
poems on Schoolcraft's work, was an international scholar and
linguist as well as the director of Harvard's Modern Language
Program. Because these men (and there were many more) occupied exalted stations in academia and government, they were not
aimlessly theorizing with their "Indian hating." They were in positions to force public action on their convictions. Their public
actions included defaming and debunking anyone who, like
Heckewelder and Cooper, stood in their political way.

When W. H. Gardiner offered his famous 1822 advice in the
North American Review that Cooper turn his talents to the "howl-
ing wilderness," he was doing no more than putting forward a
commonplace of his time.[27] Indeed, it was the extant popularity
of Native themes by 1822 that led Gardiner, in that same article,
to link Cooper with Washington Irving, the "graceful and hu-
mourous author of Knickerbocker," who had himself depicted a
pre-Natty mixed blood ("Dirty Dirk" Schuiler) in 1809.[28]

Irving's "Indian" discourse (which fingered the *Puritans* as the
savages of history) was hardly unique between 1809 and 1830. For
about twenty years after "Diedrich Knickerbocker" knocked the
stuffing out of "the cant of conquest," many bestsellers were
overtly sympathetic to the plight of Native Americans.[29] In this
window period before proto-eugenics seized the soul of Euro-

America, John Heckewelder published his *History, Manners, and Customs of the Indian Nations* (1818), followed swiftly by his *Narrative of the Mission of the United Brethren* (1820). Three years after Heckewelder's *Narrative* appeared, the public met with James E. Seaver's *Narrative of the Life of Mrs. Mary Jemison*, James Hunter's stunning *Memoirs of a Captivity among the Indians of North America*, and last, but hardly least, James Fenimore Cooper's *The Pioneers.*

All of the latter appeared in 1823; *all* were sympathetic to Native causes, and *all* were vastly popular with the reading public. Indeed, Heckewelder became a household name. Taken as a whole, these five works touched off what Schoolcraft historian Mentor L. Williams dubbed "the 'cult of Indian writing' that developed in America."[30] So far, so good—but not for long. In late 1825, Hunter was pulled up for ferocious personal attack; in 1826 and again in 1828, Heckewelder was mugged by the same cartel. The years 1826 and 1828 also saw the first vicious assaults on Cooper. By 1830, the political mood had soured considerably. The Enlightenment perspective typified by Hunter, Heckewelder, Jemison, Irving, and Cooper was no longer politically correct.

Clues to what could have effected such a radical change in perceptions between 1825 and 1830 are illustrated by the career of Schoolcraft. The range of dates for Mentor Williams's "Indian writing" craze, 1825 to 1855, is eloquent for anyone with more than a passing knowledge of the subject, for it is carefully selected to *include* Henry Rowe Schoolcraft, Lewis Cass, Judge James Hall, Robert Montgomery Bird, and Henry Wadsworth Longfellow but to *exclude* Irving, Heckewelder, Jemison, Hunter, and early Cooper.[31] Far from the historically neutral summary it seems, then, Williams's list is symptomatic of the partisan warfare that erupted between the socially marginalized "Indian-loving" camp of Heckewelder, Hunter, Cooper et al., and the socially ascendant "Indian-hating" coterie of Cass, Schoolcraft, Bird, et al. It was certainly no accident that polemical attacks linked the names of Hunter, Heckewelder, and Cooper, for they were foremost among writers nurturing a pro-Native public opinion. If unchecked or unsubverted, the sympathy they created for Native causes would have precluded land-grab schemes like Removal and forestalled further westward expansion. Clearly, the Native-friendly movement had to be stamped out.

If the social contest was heated, it was also unequal. Among the "Indian lovers," Cooper alone derived from anything resembling the same social class as his attackers; only he was able to mount a defense as a gentleman. Although Irving could have joined the lists, he moved on, not only to more likely literary fields, but also to other continents; by 1815, he was in Europe, not returning to America till 1832, by which time the battle was lost. (Neither would Irving's nor Cooper's presence in America in the 1820s to 1830s have made the slightest difference in this outcome, for the battle raged far beyond their political reach, over Slavery and the seizure of Native land.) No one else in Cooper's camp was even remotely genteel. Heckewelder's status as a clergyman was canceled out by his identity as a German Moravian who had lived forty-nine years as an adopted Lenape. Illiterate, the Seneca adoptee Mary Jemison was beneath contempt in racist America for having married not one, but two Native men and borne eight surviving Euro-Native children between them. If Hunter and Heckewelder were literate—though Hunter only barely—the fact that English was but their second or third language, behind *Native* tongues, counted heavily against them as evidence of low social standing.

Just as important as class standing was longevity. Of the main targets, Cooper alone lived long enough even to attempt a self-defense. One by one, his cohorts died before him. Jemison might have survived ten years after her *Narrative* appeared, but could not have defended her reputation in any case, given her interracial sexual activity. Her male counterparts died shortly after the publication of their works, Heckewelder in 1823 and Hunter in 1827. It was, therefore, Cooper alone who bore the brunt of racist attacks on the "Indian-loving" camp, and Cooper himself lived only until 1851.

By contrast, their primary critics, Cass and Schoolcraft along with Longfellow, all enjoyed long lives at the most refined end of the social scale. General Cass lived until 1866, tirelessly spewing out his racist venom to the end, seizing Michigan from the Natives in the 1830s; helping draft Removal law; then, as Andrew

Jackson's secretary of war, engineering Removal into a reality; and finally, running for president himself, twice, in 1848 and 1856, on specifically racist platforms.[32] Cass's personal friend and protégé Schoolcraft survived till 1864. Longfellow lived until 1882. Between their longevity and their high positions as institutional codifiers of Official Indian History, this trio and its literary toadies managed to bury every outlaw version of Native history *except* Cooper's.

The relationship between Cass and Schoolcraft was a pure exchange of back-scratching favors, with each using his position to puff the reputation (and fill the pockets) of the other. Schoolcraft's career was strategically advanced by the already famous General Cass in 1820, with his "highly laudatory recommendation" expressing the expectation that Schoolcraft was destined for professional eminence.[33] Cass thereafter nurtured and shepherded Schoolcraft's ascent into the political stratosphere, culminating with his appointment to the position of official "Indian" ethnographer. Schoolcraft ended on the payroll of the Department of the Interior, where the publication of his works, especially *Historical and Statistical Information Respecting the History, Condition and Prospects of the Indian Tribes of the United States* (1851–1857), was lavishly underwritten by congressional appropriations. Investigators have since tabulated the full tax-payer subsidy for all seven volumes of the *Historical and Statistical Information* at $600,000, a staggering sum at the time.[34] By contrast, Hunter died in poverty, Heckewelder lived but modestly, and Cooper's finances were a constant grind.

Schoolcraft returned the mighty favors Cass had done him with some fairly substantial favors of his own. Turning his writing talents and public visibility to account for his old mentor, he prepared a swaggering political biography of Cass, one noisy enough to kick off Cass's 1848 presidential bid. This tribute to the general's "character" sensationalized his qualifications for office by drawing heavily on his "Indian-hating" credentials that "put no faith in the sincerity of the Indians." Against such shifty-eyed foes, Cass was presented as a stalwart patriot, rushing to "the rescue of the frontiers," in arms as well as by pen, for he drafted the Removal Code as early as 1834.[35] To reinforce Cass's image as a no-nonsense "Indian fighter," Schoolcraft listed among his credentials Cass's role in "unmasking" John D. Hunter and in exposing "the true character" of John Heckewelder.[36]

The greatest travesty of the Cass-Schoolcraft Mutual Aid Society was the lingering aura of respectability with which it surrounded Schoolcraft's oeuvre. Cass set Schoolcraft up as the worthy rival and preferred alternative to Heckewelder and, in turn, Cooper. In fact, Schoolcraft was a third-rate scholar, a racist fraud, really, who set Native ethnography back to zero by mixing and matching stories from widely disparate Native nations with a breathtaking indifference to authenticity, as his contemporary, Francis Parkman, pointed out *at the time*.[37] Importantly, Schoolcraft did not succeed because more able ethnographers were unavailable. In addition to Heckewelder, there were William Rawle, Peter Duponceau, Caspar Wistar, and several more writing in English, as well as easily obtained French sources, from *Les Relations de Jésuites* to Joseph François Lafitau, Gabriel Sagard, and Pierre de Charlevoix.

Literature paced the political fight. If Cooper popularized Heckewelder's largely accurate ethnographies, Henry Wadsworth Longfellow compounded Schoolcraft's errors by taking his cockamamie "Algic Researches" mainstream in "The Song of Hiawatha."[38] Before condemning the supposed ethnological inaccuracy of Cooper's Natives, it behooves critics to check on what Cooper's literary peers were doing. Using Heckewelder as a source situated Cooper in a position far superior to that of any who used Schoolcraft as a source, while his Natty Bumppo was a brilliantly nuanced character, as opposed to the racially motivated serial killer, Nathan Slaughter, of *Nick of the Woods*, a work specifically offered up by Robert Montgomery Bird as a corrective to Cooper and Heckewelder.

Because of his political reputation as an "Indian fighter," it fell to Lewis Cass to fire the opening shots of the campaign against Hunter, Heckewelder, and Cooper. Late in 1825, Cass prepared a rabid review of Hunter's ethnography and memoir. The review did not actually appear until January 1826, however, and the delay in publication seems to have been to afford Cass time to work in a stray scattering of invective aimed at Heckewelder, plus a gratuitous slap at Cooper. This approach was typical of Cass's style: He liked to link present with future targets in a sort of preview of coming events. Cass's cruel attack on John Hunter was published, as was all his "Indian-hating" invective, in the conservative *North American Review*. Adopted by the Kansas as an infant and leaving Osage life for "civilization at nineteen," Hunter composed his *Memoirs*, raising racist ire by providing an unvarnished look at European invasion, hypocrisy, and racism. Cass purported, on very shaky arguments, to show that Hunter was a damnable liar, an imposter forging a captivity tale, but Hunter's true crime was palpable in Cass's charge that "he elevate[d] the Indian character far above its true standard, and he depresse[d] that of the frontier settlers as far below it."[39] In 1848, Cass was still preening himself on the hatchet job he had done on the long-dead teenager, "one of those *bad and artificial abortions of circumstance and education*" (italics in the original) who showed "all the traits and moral obliquities and prejudices of an Indian."[40]

Although Hunter had assuredly enraged "Indian haters," it was Heckewelder, an eyewitness to genocide, who had pushed the most sensitive buttons with his frank admission that he was "ashamed of being a *white man*" (italics in original).[41] Heckewelder was a far more formidable target than young Hunter, so greater caution was required in approaching him. However ideological, Cass was astute enough to realize that Heckewelder had powerful friends in the philosophical societies who would not easily brook the same character assassination he had used on a friendless boy. Neither would simply denigrating Heckewelder as an "Indian lover" suffice to derail his reputation among scholars. It would be necessary to offer some alternative form of supposed scholarship that could be counted on to demonize Natives under the guise of describing them, hence Cass's promotion of Schoolcraft. The hidden agenda behind the 1828 review was to build the career of his political ally, Henry Rowe Schoolcraft, on the ruins he anticipated making of the reputations of Heckewelder and Cooper.

There was more than ideological ire involved in the attacks on Heckewelder and Cooper. Cass had nursed grudges of long standing against both men, although he had not bothered to mention as much to either before sharpening his tongue against them. Heckewelder had undercut his position with Congress, and Cooper had spurned Cass personally if inadvertently. Cass's resentment of the missionary had been brewing since 1818, with the first publication of the *History*. In it, Heckewelder had exhibited scant patience with armchair ethnographers like Cass and Schoolcraft. Not in the habit of pulling his punches, Heckewelder frankly and accurately charged that work like theirs was "full of the most ridiculous mistakes."[42] He had the audacity to show up several self-appointed experts, cautioning them that, in some of their conversations, the Natives had been toying with their credulity, telling tall tales, "while they laugh at the same time at their being able to deceive a people who think themselves so superior to them in wisdom and knowledge."[43] The thought that Native Americans might be *making fun of them* was profoundly unsettling to nineteenth-century ethnographers.

Worse, in a more pointed affront, Heckewelder submitted his complete works to the U.S. Senate, including the *Narrative*, which exposed the truth of the Goschochking ("Gnadenhütten") genocide, by way of setting the Native record straight.[44] (On 8 March 1782, the Pennsylvania militia, acting on general orders to seize Ohio, brutally murdered 126 women, children, and elders of the Lenapes and Mahicans. Those killed were at peace and had been allies of the United States throughout the Revolution. Washington and others hastily covered up the facts, destroying reports to keep the massacre under wraps.)[45] Both Heckewelder's *History* and his *Narrative* were preferred to Cass's racist screed, *Inquiries respecting the History, Traditions, Languages, Manners, Customs, Religion, & Character of the Indians, Living within the United States* (1821). Thereafter, Cass lay in wait, watching for his chance to revenge himself upon Heckewelder. It came in 1826, when he was asked to prepare the review of Hunter, in which he castigated Heckewelder's intellect, language skills, and ethnography, singing the praises of Schoolcraft in alternate breaths.[46] Cass's attack depended almost entirely on his upper-class credentials and racist fondness for stereotype over ethnography, for, in reality, the tin ear for language belonged to Cass, who spoke no native tongue.[47] (His linguistic discussions all derived from Schoolcraft.) Moreover, far from the significant cultural ambassador he impersonated, Cass is yet recalled in the oral tradition of Michigan-Ohio Natives as "The Butcher."

Significantly, like Hunter, Heckewelder was conclusively dead at the time of the attacks, thus unable to defend himself. Even in 1826, however, Cass's discourse was so transparently bigoted that it sparked a spirited defense of Heckewelder by luminaries and linguists of the philosophical societies. The pluckiest "Vindication," penned by William Rawle in 1826, refuted Cass point for point, taking both him and the *North American Review* to task for their ungentlemanly conduct in mauling the deceased Heckewelder.[48] Against such imposing opposition, Cass was unable to finish off Heckewelder until 1828, when the mood of the country had turned conclusively racist. Under the guise of making amends for his 1826 transgressions, Cass opened in 1828 by assailing *Rawle's* competence as a scholar, an act of pure effrontery on Cass's part, for scholarly organizations, including Rawle's Historical Society of Pennsylvania, had taken great pains over the preceding fifty years to accumulate the best information available on Native culture.[49] Cass then redirected his gimlet glare in the direction of Heckewelder, reiterating the theme of his 1826 attack and concluding that Heckewelder was a senile, Injun-lovin' dupe.[50]

Destroying Heckewelder was only one of three objects in Cass's 1828 "Review." His second purpose was to introduce and exalt Schoolcraft as the appropriate scholarly alternative to Heckewelder.[51] The third purpose in the 1828 "Review" might have been his last, but it was certainly not his least, being no less than to demolish the reputation of James Fenimore Cooper. Cass sought to sink him beneath the "just and philosophical reflections" of Schoolcraft by locating him squarely on the poop deck of Heckewelder's foundering ship. Interestingly, Cass did not zero in on Cooper until after Cooper had spurned his advances.

The connection between Cooper and Cass began in 1822. With an eye to his political career, Cass had noted Cooper's budding popularity and hoped that the lionized author would single him out as the source for his new project on Native America, thereby conferring a celebrity that Cass could then use to promote his own political pretensions.[52] Knowing that Cooper had already taken W. H. Gardiner's advice on Native themes, looking up his rival Heckewelder as a source, and piquing himself on his "Indian" knowledge, Cass caused his own pitiful pamphlet, the *Inquiries*, to be put into Cooper's hands as the superior source. At first, as Cooper confessed to his bookseller, Charles Wiley, he felt as bewildered by the choice as "an ass between two locks of hay," adding that Cass "condemns all that his rival praises, and praises all that his rival condemns."[53] Soon enough, however, Cooper—who made a point of meeting and interviewing as many Native Americans as possible—set Cass aside in favor of Heckewelder. It was only *after* Cooper had turned Cass down that the general launched his personalized attacks on Hunter, Heckewelder, and Cooper.

Piqued that, by choosing Heckewelder, Cooper had effectively chosen *not* to endorse his aspirations to the White House, Cass spitefully pretended to find the "effect" of Heckewelder's "enfeebled faculties" transferred wholesale from the elder to the younger author. He sniffed that, if Cooper tried real-life experience over "the shadowy representations he has studied," he would then realize how far he "wandered from nature" (meaning the conclusions of racist science) "in following the path marked out by Mr. Heckewelder."[54] Thus did insult substitute for analysis.

Cooper himself identified Cass's onslaught as the origin of his difficulties with contemporary critics over the Leatherstocking Tales. In 1850, when he composed his well-known preface to the combined edition of the Leatherstocking Tales, Cooper was still angry enough with Cass's spiteful reviews to revisit the debate. Writing of himself in the third person, Cooper began with a glowing defense of Heckewelder: "One of his critics [Cass], on the appearance of the first work in which Indian character was portrayed, objected that its 'characters were Indians of the school of Heckewelder, rather than of the school of nature.' These words quite probably contain the substance of the true answer to the objection. Heckewelder was an ardent, benevolent missionary, bent on the good of the redman, and seeing in him one who had the soul, reason, and characteristics of a fellow being." Having thus deftly described the difference he saw between the views of Heckewelder and those of Cass, Cooper next turned sarcastically on Cass, suggesting that his knowledge of Native culture was severely limited, hindered by its confinement to the corrupt element that cooperated with governmental land grabs at kangaroo treaty councils. He concluded with a nifty slap at the general's presidential aspirations: "As just would it be to draw conclusions of the general state of American society from the scenes of the capitol, as to suppose that the negotiating of one of these treaties is a fair picture of Indian life."[55] Because he died in 1851, not long after composing this preface, Cooper may be said to have stood by his informed choice of sources to the end of his days. In so doing, he exhibited more awareness of the origin, character, and hidden agenda of the "Indian-hating" attacks on him than modern scholars generally appreciate.

The temptation for modern critics is to avert their gaze from these Antebellum attacks, dismissing them as so much racist froth (as indeed they were) and therefore irrelevant to modern Cooper criticism (as indeed they are not). Because the naked racism at the root of Cooper criticism has never been openly confronted, its inertia continues quietly informing opinions to this day. As Edwin Stockton Jr. wrote unnoticed in 1964, the legacy of racism in Cooper criticism constitutes "one of the greatest paradoxes in literary history."[56] I agree. How can it be that modern critics, who would never knowingly bow to a racist proposition in the present, still honor the ignoble attacks of the past, penned by a man, Lewis Cass, whose whole renown rested on his credentials of genocide?

NOTES

1. Arthur C. Parker, *The Constitution of the Five Nations, or the Iroquois Book of the Great Law* (Albany: The University of the State of New York, 1916), 38. For my fuller discussion of Cry-Baby Criticism, see Barbara Alice Mann, *Iroquoian Women: The Gantowisas* (New York: Peter Lang, 2000), 8–9.

2. George Dekker and John P. McWilliams, "Introduction," *Fenimore Cooper: The Critical Heritage* (London: Routledge & Kegan Paul, 1975), 17.

3. Cooper freely acknowledged Heckewelder as his source. See James Fenimore Cooper, letter to Mr. Charles Wiley, Bookseller, reproduced in James Fenimore Cooper, *The Pioneers* (1823; New York: Rinehart & Co., 1959), xxv; James Fenimore Cooper "Preface to the Leatherstocking Tales" (1850), reproduced in *The Deerslayer, Or The First Warpath* (1841; New York: Bantam, 1982), x; James Fenimore Cooper, *Pages and Pictures from the Writings of James Fenimore Cooper*, ed. Susan Fenimore Cooper (1861; Secaucus, NJ: Castle Books, 1980), 149. For an extended discussion of Cooper and Heckewelder, see Barbara A. Mann, *Forbidden Ground: Racial Politics and Hidden Identity in James Fenimore Cooper's Leatherstocking Tales*, PhD diss., University of Toledo, 1997. Further citations to the Leatherstocking Tales are to the State University of New York edition and appear in the text, preceded by the following abbreviations: *The Pioneers (Pi); The Last of the Mohicans (LM); The Prairie (Pr); The Pathfinder (Pa)*; and *The Deerslayer (D)*.

4. Fawn Brodie, *Thomas Jefferson: An Intimate History* (New York: Norton, 1974), 433–434.

5. Neil Gotanda, "A Critique of 'Our Constitution Is Color-Blind,'" in *Critical Race Theory: The Key Writings That Formed the Movement*, ed. Kimberlé Crenshaw, Neil Gotanda, Gary Peller, and Kendall Thomas (New York: New Press, 1995), 258.

6. Reuben Gold Thwaites, ed. and trans., *Les Relations de Jésuites, or The Jesuit Relations: Travels and Explorations of the Jesuit Missionaries in New France, 1610–1791*, 73 vols. (New York: Pageant Book Company, 1959), 5: 23; Joseph François Lafitau, *Customs of the American Indians Compared with the Customs of Primitive Times*, ed. and trans. William N. Fenton and Elizabeth L. Moore, 2 vols. (1724; Toronto: Champlain Society, 1974), 1: 89; Pierre de Charlevoix, *Journal of a Voyage to North America*, 2 vols. (1761; Ann Arbor, MI: University Microfilms, 1966), 2: 90.

7. Johann Friedrich Blumenbach, *On the Natural Varieties of Mankind (De Generis Humani Varietate Nativa)* (1795, 1865; New York: Bergman, 1969).

8. Ibid., 246–257.

9. James Fenimore Cooper, *The Wept of Wish-ton-Wish: A Tale* (1829; New York: The Co-operative Publication Society, 1900), 264.

10. Ibid.

11. Ibid., 265–271.

12. Ibid., 351 (name), 351 (denial, quote), 348–352.

13. For linguistic and lexical explanation of the term "young men," see Barbara Alice Mann, *George Washington's War on Native America* (Westport, CT: Praeger, 2005), 219–220, n. 642. For a typical Native sachem's reference to "the young men," see Richard White, *The Middle Ground: Indians, Empires, and Republics in the Great Lakes Region, 1650–1815* (Cambridge, UK: Cambridge University Press, 1991), 501–502.

14. Mann, *Iroquoian Women*, 175–178.

15. Ibid., 214–215.

16. Alexander Wood Renton and George Grenville Phillimore, eds., *Burge's Commentaries on Colonial and Foreign Laws* (1908; Buffalo, NY: William S. Hein, 1981), 3: 46–48, 242.

17. Craig Atwood, *Community of the Cross: Moravian Piety in Colonial Bethlehem* (University Park: Pennsylvania State University Press, 2004), 115. Paul A. W. Wallace gave the date as 1734 in *Thirty Thousand Miles with John Heckewelder* (Pittsburgh: University of Pittsburgh Press, 1958), 24. Although most sources cite the winter of 1742–1743 as the inception date of the Delaware-Mahican mission, Edwin Stockton correctly notes that the first two missionaries actually staked out the grounds in 1740. See Edwin L. Stockton Jr., "The Influence of the Moravians upon the Leather-Stocking Tales," *Transactions of the Moravian Historical Society* 20 (1964): 27. By the time Cooper was writing, the Moravians were heavily invested in missionizing the Cherokees, helping to stir up intranational woes among them around the Moravian "half-breed" faction of Major Ridge.

18. Atwood, *Community of the Cross*, 91–95, 190–193. It is important for modern readers to understand that, just because hysterical contemporary enemies portrayed the Moravians as hedonistic, wife-swapping, salivating sex addicts does not mean that this was a just representation of their theology. The X-rated portrayals conjured up by rival clerics measured their own repression, not Moravian "hedonism."

19. Atwood, *Community of the Cross*, 233–236 (wounds theology litany); 88–90, 185–187 (the genitalia of Jesus); 178–179 (taught to infants); 185 (rejected contempt of the body); 68–70, 175–184 (gender roles).

20. White, *The Middle Ground*, 250–251.

21. John Heckewelder, *Narrative of the Mission of the United*

Brethren among the Delaware and Mohegan Indians from Its Commencement, in the Year 1740, to the Close of the Year 1808 (1818; New York: Arno Press, 1971), 313.

22. Wallace, *Thirty Thousand Miles with John Heckewelder*, 191.

23. Charles Brockden Brown, *Wieland, or The Transformation: An American Tale*, bicentennial ed. (1798; Kent, Ohio: Kent State University Press, 1977), 12.

24. Ibid.

25. James Hall, "The Indian Hater," 1829, in *Stories of the Early American West*, ed. Peter Bischoff, Arbeiten zur Amerikanistik (Essen: Verlag Die Blaue Eule, 1989), 3: 63–73; Herman Melville, *The Confidence-Man: His Masquerade*, ed. Hershel Parker (1857; New York: Norton, 1971), 124–131.

26. Frank B. Woodford, *Lewis Cass: The Last Jeffersonian* (New Brunswick, NJ: Rutgers University Press, 1950), 29–31, 53, 80, 90, 170, 171, 193–194, 228, 269, 313.

27. W. H. Gardiner, "Article XII," *North American Review* 15 (July 1822): 254.

28. Ibid., 282; Washington Irving ["Diedrich Knickerbocker"], *A History of New York, from the Beginning of the World to the End of the Dutch Dynasty*, ed. Stanley Williams and Tremaine McDowell (1809; New York: Harcourt, Brace, 1927), 308–309.

29. The phrase belongs to Francis Jennings, *The Invasion of America: Indians, Colonialism, and the Cant of Conquest* (New York: Norton, 1976).

30. Mentor L. Williams, preface to *Schoolcraft's Indian Legends, from Algic Researches, The Myth of Hiawatha, Oneóta, The Red Race in America, and Historical and Statistical Information Respecting . . . the Indian Tribes of the United States*, by Henry Rowe Schoolcraft, various dates, ed. Mentor L. Williams (East Lansing: Michigan State University Press, 1956), vi.

31. Ibid.

32. Cass's biography, written by Schoolcraft in consultation with the general specifically to promote Cass's presidential bids, is both frightening and enlightening concerning his racism as well as Schoolcraft's. See Henry Rowe Schoolcraft, *Outlines of the Life of Gen. Lewis Cass* (Albany, NY: J. Munsell, Printer, 1848).

33. Chase S. Osborn and Stellanova Osborn, *Schoolcraft→ Longfellow→ Hiawatha* (Lancaster, PA: Jacques Cattell Press, 1942), 365.

34. Ibid., 418, 420.

35. Schoolcraft, *Outlines*, especially, 8, 9, 19, 18, 31.

36. Ibid., 28–29, 52, 54.

37. For Parkman's evaluations, see Mason Wade, *Francis Parkman: Heroic Historian* (New York: Viking, 1942), 208; Francis Parkman, "Indian Superstitions," *North American Review* 102.212 (July 1866): top footnote, 11; n. 17. For Schoolcraft's interchanging of Native characters, see Paul A. W. Wallace, "The Return of Hiawatha," *Quarterly Journal of the New York State Historical Association* 29.4 (1948): 396. The main vehicle of Schoolcraft's inept wizardry was Henry Rowe Schoolcraft, "Manabozho, or the Great Incarnation of the North, an Algic Legend," in *Schoolcraft's Indian Legends*, 65–83. For Schoolcraft's racist perspective, see him on Native spirituality: Henry Rowe Schoolcraft, *Narrative Journal of Travels through the Northwestern Regions of the United States Extending from Detroit through the Great Chain of American Lakes to the Sources of the Mississippi River in the Year 1820*, ed. Mentor L. Williams (1855; East Lansing: Michigan State College Press, 1953), 68–69; on the "Character of the Red Man of America": Henry Rowe Schoolcraft, *The American Indians, Their History, Condition and Prospects, from Original Notes and Manuscripts* (Buffalo, NY: Derby, 1851), 69–70; on Native languages (specifically, the "Leech Lake Chippewa" dialect): Henry Rowe Schoolcraft, *Schoolcraft's Expedition to Lake Itasca: The Discovery of the Source of the Mississippi*, ed. Philip P. Mason (1834; East Lansing: Michigan State University Press, 1958), 62.

38. Paul A. W. Wallace, "The Return of Hiawatha," *Quarterly Journal of the New York State Historical Association* 29.4 (1948): 396–397.

39. Lewis Cass, "The Indians of North America," *North American Review* 22 (January 1826): 94.

40. Schoolcraft, *Outlines*, 28–29, 54.

41. John Heckewelder, *History, Manners, and Customs of the Indian Nations Who Once Inhabited Pennsylvania and the Neighboring States*, The First American Frontier Series (1820, 1876; New York: Arno Press and *New York Times*, 1971), 76.

42. Ibid. 318.

43. Ibid., 322.

44. Lewis Cass, "Review," *North American Review* 26 (April 1828): 372.

45. For a complete historical account of this episode, see Mann, *George Washington's War on Native America*, 149–170.

46. Cass, "The Indians of North America," 64–86 (on Heckewelder), 60 (paean to Schoolcraft).

47. Stockton, "The Influence of the Moravians," 110.

48. William Rawle, "A Vindication of the Rev. Mr. Heckewelder's History of the Indian Nations," *Memoirs of the Historical Society of Pennsylvania* 1, part 2 (1826): 258–275 (rebuke to Cass and *Review*).

49. Cass, "Review," 371, 372.

50. Ibid., 366, 371, 373.

51. Ibid., 365.

52. Stockton, "The Influence of the Moravians," 47.

53. Cooper, letter to Mr. Charles Wiley, Bookseller, xxv.

54. Cass, "Review," 373, 374.

55. James Fenimore Cooper, "Preface to the Leatherstocking Tales" (1850), reproduced in *The Deerslayer, or The First Warpath* (1841; Albany: State University of New York Press, 1987), 8.

56. Stockton, "The Influence of the Moravians," 51.

ILLUSTRATED
CHRONOLOGY

Cooper's Life*

1785–1786: William Cooper (father) first visits Lake Otsego in upstate New York and founds Cooperstown on the shore of Lake Otsego.

1788: William Cooper builds Manor House in the center of Cooperstown.

*With thanks to Hugh C. MacDougall's "Where Was James?," a day-to-day chronological list of Cooper's movements from his birth in 1789 until his death in 1851; Alan Taylor's *William Cooper's Town*; and Wayne Franklin's essay in this volume.

Map of Lake Otsego. Courtesy of the Biological Field Station of the State University College at Oneonta. The Village of Cooperstown is located at the southwest end of the lake.

Historical Events

1783: The Treaty of Paris between the United States and Great Britain officially ends the Revolutionary War.

1787: Thomas Jefferson, *Notes on the State of Virginia*; Royall Tyler, *The Contrast*; *The Federalist Papers* (1787–1788). The U.S. Constitution is completed and signed by delegates to the Constitutional Convention in Philadelphia. Congress passes the Northwest Ordinance, which includes an early version of the Bill of Rights. It also prohibits slavery in U.S. territories northwest of the Ohio River.

1789: William Hill Brown, *The Power of Sympathy*; Olaudah Equiano, *The Interesting Narrative of the Life of Olaudah Equiano*. George Washington is elected the first president; John Adams becomes the first vice president. The first Congress meets in New York City. Paris citizens storm the Bastille and release seven prisoners.

1790: Judith Sargent Murray, *On the Equality of the Sexes*. Benjamin Franklin dies in Philadelphia at age eighty-four. The District of Columbia is established as the seat of the U.S. government. First U.S. census establishes the population at nearly 4 million.

North Eastern Part of the United States. *Engraved by W. H. Bartlett.* Bartlett's Classic Illustrations of America *(Mineola, NY: Dover Publications, 2000).* Originally published in *American Scenery: or, Land, Lake and River Illustrations of Transatlantic Nature *(London: George Virtue, 1840). *Cooperstown is located in the center of the map, which also shows the Erie Canal from Albany to Buffalo.*

George Washington and slaves on his farm at Mt. Vernon. *Painted by Junius Brutus Stearns; lithograph by Regnier. Library of Congress, Prints and Photographs Division, LC-USZ62-3912.*

1789: James Cooper born on September 15 in Burlington, NJ, the youngest of seven children. Cooper had four older brothers (Richard, Isaac, William, and Samuel) and two older sisters (Hannah and Ann).

1790: Cooper accompanies parents to Cooperstown.

1794: William Cooper elected to Congress.

1796: William Cooper defeated in bid for reelection to Congress.

1798: William Cooper wins reelection to Congress.

1799: Otsego Hall built. William Cooper owns one slave. (New York's gradual emancipation law frees all slaves by July 4, 1827.)

1800: Cooper's oldest sister, Hannah, killed when thrown from a horse (September 10).

1801: Cooper attends school in Albany.

1803: Cooper enrolls at Yale College in New Haven, CT.

1805–1807: Cooper expelled from Yale for setting off a gunpowder charge; spends a year as a seaman on the merchant vessel *Stirling*, visiting England and Spain.

1791: Benjamin Franklin, *The Autobiography* (Part 1); Susanna Rowson, *Charlotte: A Tale of Truth*. Haitian Revolution begins with revolt of slaves under the leadership of Toussaint l'Ouverture. The Bill of Rights takes effect.

1792: Jeremy Belknap, *The Foresters: An American Tale*. George Washington is reelected president and John Adams vice president.

1793: Gilbert Imlay, *The Emigrants*. Fugitive Slave Law is passed, allowing slave owners to "seize or arrest" fugitive slaves in free states and territories.

1794: Timothy Dwight, *Greenfield Hill: A Poem in Seven Parts*. Eli Whitney receives a patent for the cotton gin.

1796: Joel Barlow, "The Hasty Pudding." John Adams defeats Thomas Jefferson in presidential election; Jefferson is elected vice president.

1797: Hannah Foster, *The Coquette*; Ann Eliza Bleecker, *The History of Maria Kettle*. Albany becomes the capital of New York State, replacing New York City.

1798: Charles Brockden Brown, *Wieland*. Mississippi Territory is created. Congress passes the Sedition Act.

Albany, New York. Engraved by W. H. Bartlett. Bartlett's Classic Illustrations of America *(Mineola, NY: Dover Publications, 2000). Originally published in* American Scenery: or, Land, Lake and River Illustrations of Transatlantic Nature *(London: George Virtue, 1840).*

1808–1810: Cooper becomes midshipman in U.S. Navy, but most of his service is limited to Lake Ontario. He is also assigned to be a recruiting officer in New York City.

1809: William Cooper dies in December.

1811: Cooper marries Susan Augusta Delancey (January 1), leaving the Navy and moving to Mamaroneck on Long Island Sound in Westchester County. Cooper pays $50 to his brother Richard to buy a seven-year-old mulatto boy as a slave. Daughter Elizabeth Cooper born (September 27).

1799: Charles Brockden Brown, *Edgar Huntly*. George Washington dies at Mount Vernon.

1800: U.S. population is 5,308,483. Charles Brockden Brown, *Arthur Mervyn*. Thomas Jefferson is elected president. Library of Congress is established. First major slave rebellion, led by Gabriel Prosser in Richmond, VA, is foiled by state militia.

1801: Tabitha Tenney, *Female Quixotism*.

1803: Importation of slaves to the United States officially ends. The United States purchases the Louisiana Territory from France. Ohio is admitted to the union as the seventeenth state.

Map Showing Political Boundaries in the Era of the Louisiana Purchase.
Library of Congress.

William Clark. *Original watercolor by Charles Willson Peale (1903). Library of Congress, Prints and Photographs Division, LC-USZ62-10609.*

Meriwether Lewis. *Original watercolor by Charles Willson Peale (1903). Library of Congress, Prints and Photographs Division, LC-USZ62-20214.*

1813: Cooper and family settle at Fenimore Farm in Cooperstown. Cooper's oldest brother, Richard, dies (March 5). Susan Fenimore Cooper born (April 17), and the Coopers' older daughter, Elizabeth, dies a month later.

1817: Ann Charlotte Fenimore Cooper born (May 14). Cooper's mother, Elizabeth Fenimore Cooper, dies (September 15); Cooper returns to Westchester County, living in Scarsdale and Mamaroneck.

1818: Cooper's brother Isaac dies (January 1).

1819: Cooper's brothers Samuel (February 15) and William (October 19) die, leaving Cooper to settle large debts accumulated by the Cooper estate. Cooper sells various land holdings in New York State. Desperate for money, he invests in a whaling ship, a venture that is reasonably profitable.

1820: Cooper runs DeWitt Clinton's successful gubernatorial campaign in Westchester County. Elizabeth Delancey, Cooper's mother-in-law, dies unexpectedly. Cooper publishes *Precaution*, his first novel (an English novel of manners with debts to Jane Austen and others).

1804: John Vanderlyn, *Death of Jane McCrea* (painting). Explorers Meriwether Lewis and William Clark leave St. Louis on their expedition into the Louisiana Purchase territory.

1805: Michigan Territory is created. Lewis and Clark reach the Pacific Coast.

1807: Joel Barlow, *The Columbiad*. Robert Fulton launches first steamboat, the *Clermont*.

1808: James Madison is elected president. Importation of slaves is outlawed by Congress.

1809: Washington Irving, *A History of New York*. Illinois Territory is created.

1810: U.S. population is 7,239,880.

1812: Rebecca Rush, *Kelroy*. Louisiana is admitted to the union as the eighteenth state. United States declares war on Great Britain, beginning the War of 1812. Missouri Territory is created.

1813: British blockade U.S. ports and burn Buffalo, NY.

The Taking of the City of Washington (August 24, 1814). *War of 1812.*
Library of Congress, Prints and Photographs Division, LC-USZ62-1939.

1821: Birth of son Fenimore Cooper (October 23). Cooper sells Otsego Hall in Cooperstown at auction. Cooper publishes *The Spy: A Tale of the Neutral Ground*, a novel of the Revolutionary War set in Westchester County, where Cooper was living. The novel includes George Washington as a prominent character, although Cooper's creation of Harvey Birch (the spy) represents his most notable achievement. The book was a great success, selling 1,000 copies in its first month, 6,000 copies in its first year.

1814: British forces invade Washington, DC, and set fire to the Capitol and the White House. Francis Scott Key writes "The Star-Spangled Banner." War of 1812 officially ends.

1815: Hugh Henry Brackenridge, *Modern Chivalry.*

1816: James Monroe is elected president. Indiana enters the union as the nineteenth state. American Colonization Society is founded to resettle freed American slaves in Africa.

1822: Cooper moves the family to New York City, where he becomes a member of a prominent literary club, The Bread and Cheese, whose members include William Cullen Bryant and Fitz-Greene Halleck.

1823: Cooper publishes *The Pioneers; or, The Sources of the Susquehanna*, the first novel in the Leatherstocking Tales featuring Natty Bumppo and the Mohican chief, Chingachgook. *The Pioneers* sells 3,500 copies in its first day. The Coopers' son, Fenimore, dies (August 5). Fenimore House, Cooper's unfinished mansion in Cooperstown, burns to the ground (July 23–24).

James Fenimore Cooper, *1822, by John Wesley Jarvis. Courtesy Fenimore Art Museum, Cooperstown, New York.*

View on the Susquehanna above Owego. *Engraved by W. H. Bartlett. Bartlett's Classic Illustrations of America (Mineola, NY: Dover Publications, 2000). Originally published in* American Scenery: or, Land, Lake and River Illustrations of Transatlantic Nature *(London: George Virtue, 1840). The Susquehanna River has its source in Lake Otsego and flows south through New York and Pennsylvania, eventually emptying into Chesapeake Bay in northern Maryland. Owego, New York, is downstream from Cooperstown about 100 miles.*

The Turkey Shoot *(1857), from* The Pioneers, *by Tompkins Matteson. Courtesy Fenimore Art Museum, Cooperstown, New York.*

John Paul Jones. *Library of Congress, Prints and Photographs Division, LC-USZ62-10884.*

The Pilot: Tom Coffin on the wreck of the Ariel

Tom Coffin on the Wreck of the *Ariel*. The Pilot. *Drawing by F. O. C. Darley. Engraving by J. Wrightson.* Pages and Pictures from the Writings of James Fenimore Cooper by Susan Fenimore Cooper *(1865; Secaucus, NJ: Castle Books, 1980).*

1824: Cooper publishes *The Pilot: A Tale of the Sea*, set in England and the first of his many sea novels. The novel includes John Paul Jones as a mysterious stranger. Birth of Paul Fenimore Cooper.

1825: Cooper publishes *Lionel Lincoln; or, The Leaguer of Boston*, a Revolutionary War novel featuring the battles of Lexington, Concord, and Bunker Hill, but the novel's lack of success causes Cooper to abandon his plan to write a novel about each of the thirteen colonies.

Daniel Boone. *Library of Congress, Prints and Photographs Division, LC-USZ62-16240.*

1817: William Cullen Bryant, "Thanatopsis." Erie Canal construction begins. Mississippi enters the union as the twentieth state. New York passes law ending all slavery in the state on July 4, 1827. First Seminole War (1817–1818) begins as the U.S. Army under General Andrew Jackson invades northern Florida.

1818: Illinois enters the union as the twenty-first state.

1819: Alabama enters the union as the twenty-second state. Panic of 1819 leads to the first major American economic depression.

1820: U.S. population is 9,638,453. New York City population is 124,000. Washington Irving, *The Sketchbook*. Maine enters the union as the twenty-third state. Missouri Compromise prohibits slavery in the Louisiana Purchase territory north of the line 36°30′. Daniel Boone dies in Missouri at the age of eighty-five. U.S. Navy Capt. Nathaniel B. Palmer discovers the continent of Antarctica.

1821: Missouri enters the union as the twenty-fourth state. Spain cedes Florida to the United States. Santa Fe trail is opened. Sir Walter Scott publishes *Ivanhoe*.

The Battle of Lexington. *April 1775. Library of Congress, Prints and Photographs Division, LC-USZ62-8623.*

1826: Cooper adds Fenimore as his middle name and publishes *The Last of the Mohicans: A Narrative of 1757*, centered on the French and Indian War battle at Fort William Henry on Lake George. In June the Coopers leave for Europe, where they live until 1833. With the help of Governor DeWitt Clinton, Cooper is appointed U.S. consul for Lyons.

1827: Living in Paris (on the "third story of the old Hotel de Jumièges, in the Fauborg St. Germain," according to his daughter), Cooper completes *The Prairie*, a novel set in the Louisiana Purchase territory and the novel in which Natty Bumppo dies.

1822: Catharine Maria Sedgwick, *A New-England Tale*. Florida becomes a U.S. territory. Slave uprising led by Denmark Vesey is foiled in Charleston, SC. National Road (Cumberland, MD, to present-day Wheeling, WV) is completed.

1823: Clement Moore, "A Visit from St. Nicholas," published in the Troy (NY) *Sentinel*. Mississippi enacts legislation prohibiting teaching of reading and writing to blacks. President James Monroe outlines his doctrine warning European countries not to establish colonies in North and South America.

1824: Lydia Maria Child, *Hobomok: A Tale of Early Times*. John Quincy Adams is chosen the winner of the presidential election over Andrew Jackson and Henry Clay.

Montcalm Trying to Stop the Massacre of Civilians Leaving Fort William Henry. *An incident of which Cooper makes considerable use in* The Last of the Mohicans. *Library of Congress, Prints and Photographs Division, LC-USZ62-120704.*

Landscape Scene from The Last of the Mohicans *(1827), by Thomas Cole. Courtesy Fenimore Art Museum, Cooperstown, New York.*

Scene among the Highlands on Lake George. *Engraved by W. H. Bartlett.*
Bartlett's Classic Illustrations of America *(Mineola, NY: Dover Publications,*
2000). Originally published in American Scenery: or, Land, Lake and River
Illustrations of Transatlantic Nature *(London: George Virtue, 1840). Lake*
George in upper New York State and the area surrounding it provide the setting for
The Last of the Mohicans.

Appearance of the Trapper to the Emigrants. The Prairie. *Drawing by*
J. Hamilton. Engraving by G. H. Cushman. Pages and Pictures from the
Writings of James Fenimore Cooper *by Susan Fenimore Cooper (1865;*
Secaucus, NJ: Castle Books, 1980).

1828: Cooper publishes *The Red Rover*, another sea novel (set in and around Newport, RI), and *Notions of the Americans: Picked Up by a Travelling Bachelor*, a fictionalized travel narrative about America. Cooper travels to England and Switzerland before settling in Italy (Florence, Rome, Venice) for nearly two years.

1829: Cooper publishes *The Wept of Wish-ton-Wish*, a frontier novel set during Puritan times (King Philip's War) in what is now Connecticut. Like Sedgwick's *Hope Leslie*, the novel features a captured Puritan girl (Ruth Heathcote), who marries a Narragansett Indian.

1825: Erie Canal (363 miles from Albany to Buffalo) is completed.

1826: Thomas Jefferson and John Adams both die on July 4, the fiftieth anniversary of the Declaration of Independence. American Temperance Society is founded.

1827: Catharine Maria Sedgwick, *Hope Leslie*. Delegates of the Cherokee Nation meet to write their constitution, modeled after the U.S. Constitution.

Lockport, Erie Canal. *Engraved by W. H. Bartlett.* Bartlett's Classic Illustrations of America *(Mineola, NY: Dover Publications, 2000). Originally published in* American Scenery: or, Land, Lake and River Illustrations of Transatlantic Nature *(London: George Virtue, 1840). Under the leadership of New York Governor DeWitt Clinton, whom Cooper strongly supported, construction of the Erie Canal began in 1817. The canal connecting Albany and Buffalo was completed in 1825.*

1830: Cooper visits Germany before returning to Paris, where he and his family live for their remaining three years in Europe. Cooper publishes *The Water-Witch; or, The Skimmer of the Seas*, a novel set in early eighteenth-century New York.

1831: Cooper publishes *The Bravo*, his first European novel (set in eighteenth-century Venice), as well as *Letter of J. Fenimore Cooper, to Gen. Lafayette.*

1832: Cooper publishes *The Heidenmauer; or, The Benedictines, A Legend of the Rhine.*

1833: The Coopers return to the United States and to New York City, where they live for three years while Otsego Hall, which Cooper purchased upon his return from Europe, is renovated. He publishes *The Headsman; or, The Abbaye des Vignerons*, another European novel (set in Switzerland) and *A Letter to His Countrymen*.

Otsego Hall (1890), by unknown artist. Courtesy Fenimore Art Museum, Cooperstown, New York.

1828: Noah Webster, *American Dictionary of the English Language.* Andrew Jackson is elected president.

1829: William Apess, *A Son of the Forest*; David Walker, *An Appeal to the Colored Citizens of the World.* Gold is discovered at Dahlonega, on the western boundary of the Cherokee Nation in Georgia.

1830: U.S. population is 12,866,020. Congress passes Indian Removal Act, giving the U.S. government the authority to remove American Indians from their tribal lands. Town of Chicago is planned at site of Fort Dearborn. Church of Jesus Christ of Latter-Day Saints is organized by Joseph Smith in Fayette, NY.

1831: James Kirke Paulding, *The Dutchman's Fireside* and *The Lion of the West.* William Lloyd Garrison starts publishing *The Liberator.* Nat Turner leads seventy slaves on two-day rebellion in Southampton, VA, killing seventy whites. Supreme Court rules against the Cherokees in *Cherokee Nation v. Georgia.* British naturalist Charles Darwin sets out on a voyage to the Pacific Ocean aboard the HMS *Beagle.*

President's Levee, or All Creation Going to the White House. *Andrew Jackson's first inaugural reception in 1829. Library of Congress, Prints and Photographs Division, LC-USZ62-1805.*

HORRID MASSACRE IN VIRGINIA·

Horrid Massacre in Virginia. *Nat Turner's rebellion (1831). Library of Congress, Prints and Photographs Division, LC-USZ62-38902.*

1835: Cooper publishes *The Monikins,* a satiric allegorical novel featuring two Antarctic countries, Leaphigh (England) and Leaplow (America), of educated monkeys.

1836: Cooper publishes *Sketches of Switzerland* (2 volumes), the first of five European travel narratives. The Coopers settle into the renovated Otsego Hall in Cooperstown.

1837: Cooper publishes *Gleanings in Europe* and *Gleanings in Europe: England.*

King Andrew the First. *Caricature of Andrew Jackson. Library of Congress, Prints and Photographs Division, LC-USZ62-1562.*

1832: James Hall, *Legends of the West;* Frances Trollope, *Domestic Manners of the Americans.* Andrew Jackson is reelected president. Black Hawk War begins in northern Illinois. Seminole chiefs sign a treaty ceding their lands in Florida to the United States. First major outbreak of Asiatic cholera in United States (June); especially virulent in New York, where it kills thousands.

1833: Black Hawk, *Life of Black Hawk;* Lydia Maria Child, *An Appeal in Favor of That Class of Americans Called Africans.* American Anti-Slavery Society is founded in Philadelphia. Canada abolishes slavery.

1834: George Bancroft, *History of the United States from the Discovery of the American Continent.* The U.S. Senate votes to censure President Jackson for the removal of federal deposits from the Bank of the United States. Cyrus McCormick patents a horse-drawn reaper. Parliament orders abolition of slavery in the British colonies.

1838: Cooper publishes *The American Democrat* (a pithy analysis of contemporary political issues), as well as *Gleanings in Europe: Italy, Chronicles of Cooperstown,* and the two-part fictionalized account of his family's return to America, *Homeward Bound* (a sea romance) and the controversial *Home as Found,* a novel of manners set mostly in Cooperstown (still Templeton, as in *The Pioneers*) and including an account of the dispute Cooper was having with the townspeople over use of the Three Mile Point picnic grounds. The incident sparked the first of many lawsuits that Cooper would file against newspapers that, he believed, had libeled him.

1835: Alexis de Tocqueville, *Democracy in America* (vol. 1); William Gilmore Simms, *The Yemassee;* Lydia Maria Child, *History of the Condition of Women.* Cherokee sign treaty at New Echota ceding all lands east of Mississippi. Second Seminole War (1835–1842) begins. Pro-slavery mob attacks abolitionists in Boston, parading William Lloyd Garrison through the streets with noose around his neck.

Cooperstown from Three Mile Point *(ca. 1855), by Louis R. Mignot and Julius Gollmann. Courtesy Fenimore Art Museum, Cooperstown, New York. When the Cooper family returned from Europe in 1833, they attempted to deny the people of Cooperstown the right to use picnic grounds at Three Mile Point that they believed they had every right to use. The move caused considerable controversy.*

A Water Party. *J. D. Harding.* Godey's Lady's Book 27 *(October 1843).*

Hunting Indians in Florida with Blood Hounds. *Zachary Taylor in the Second Seminole War. Library of Congress, Prints and Photographs Division,* LC-USZ62-89725.

Blue and Black Eyes. *Engraved by T. B. Welch.* Godey's Lady's Book 40 (*June 1850*).

Osceola, a Seminole. *Artwork by George Catlin, ca. 1837. Courtesy U.S. National Archives, photo no. 530983.*

1836: Ralph Waldo Emerson, *Nature*; Thomas McKenney and James Hall, first of three volumes of *History of the Indian Tribes of North America*. Martin Van Buren is elected president. Arkansas enters the union as the twenty-fifth state. The Territory of Wisconsin is established by Congress. Inventor Samuel Colt patents his revolver. Texas declares independence from Mexico. The Alamo in San Antonio, TX, falls to Mexican forces.

1837: Nathaniel Hawthorne, *Twice-Told Tales*; Robert Montgomery Bird, *Nick of the Woods*. Michigan enters the union as the twenty-sixth state. Financial Panic of 1837 results in 618 bank failures. Queen Victoria ascends the British throne.

1838: Edgar Allan Poe, *The Narrative of Arthur Gordon Pym*, "Ligeia"; Sarah Grimké, *Letters on the Equality of the Sexes*. Samuel Morse demonstrates his telegraph in Morristown, NJ. The Iowa Territory is organized. Frederick Douglass escapes from slavery in Baltimore. Trail of Tears (winter 1838–1839), forced removal of some 10,000 Cherokee from Georgia to Oklahoma Indian Territory. Underground Railroad is established to help escaping slaves. Seminole Chief Osceola dies in prison at Fort Moultrie, SC.

Chief of the Little Osages. *Artwork by Charles B.J. de Saint-Memin, ca. 1807. Courtesy U.S. National Archives, photo no. 532931.*

1839: Edgar Allan Poe, "The Fall of the House of Usher," "William Wilson"; Theodore Dwight Weld, *American Slavery as It Is*; Caroline Kirkland, *A New Home—Who'll Follow? Amistad* mutiny. Abner Doubleday establishes the first set of rules for baseball in Cooperstown, NY.

1840: U.S. population is 17,069,453. Richard Henry Dana, *Two Years Before the Mast*; Alexis de Tocqueville, *Democracy in America* (vol. 2). William Henry Harrison is elected president.

The Death of the Indian. The Deerslayer. *Drawing by J. Hamilton. Engraving by B. J. Newman.* Pages and Pictures from the Writings of James Fenimore Cooper *by Susan Fenimore Cooper (1865; Secaucus, NJ: Castle Books, 1980). The* Deerslayer, *whose subtitle is* The First Warpath, *depicts Natty Bumppo killing his first man, an Indian, in a dispute over possession of a canoe. The elaborately staged scene represents a rite of passage in Natty's achievement of manhood, as the dying Indian bestows the nickname "Hawkeye" on Natty.*

1839: Cooper publishes *The History of the Navy of the United States of America.*

1840: Cooper returns to the frontier novel and to Natty Bumppo in *The Pathfinder; or, The Inland Sea*, which makes use of Cooper's own earlier experiences on Lake Ontario. He also publishes *Mercedes of Castille*, a novel about Christopher Columbus.

1841: Cooper publishes *The Deerslayer; or, The First Warpath*, the fifth and final Leatherstocking novel, set at Lake Otsego (called Lake Glimmerglass) in 1740.

1842: Cooper publishes *The Two Admirals* and *Wing-and-Wing* (a Mediterranean Sea novel).

1843: Cooper publishes *Wyandotté; or, The Hutted Knoll*, a frontier novel set in the vicinity of Cooperstown during the Revolutionary War period, *Ned Myers*, an as-told-to sea narrative that Cooper "edited" for an old shipmate (Ned Myers), and *The Battle of Lake Erie.*

1844: Cooper publishes two more sea novels, *Afloat and Ashore; or, The Adventures of Miles Wallingford* and the sequel, *Miles Wallingford.*

1841: Ralph Waldo Emerson, *Essays*; Thomas Bangs Thorpe, "The Big Bear of Arkansas"; Edgar Allan Poe, "The Murders in the Rue Morgue."President Harrison dies of pneumonia after serving only one month as president; John Tyler becomes president. Supreme Court decides the *Amistad* case, freeing the fifty-three mutineers and paving the way for their return to Africa. P. T. Barnum opens Barnum's American Museum in New York.

1842: Col. John C. Fremont begins four-year exploring expedition to Rocky Mountains. Charles Dickens tours America to great fanfare. The New York Philharmonic gives its first concert.

1843: Edgar Allan Poe, "The Black Cat," "The Tell-Tale Heart."

1844: Ralph Waldo Emerson, *Essays: Second Series*; Margaret Fuller, *Summer on the Lakes*; Edgar Allan Poe, "The Purloined Letter." James K. Polk is elected president. Samuel F. B. Morse opens America's first telegraph line between Washington and Baltimore with the message, "What hath God wrought!" Baptist Church splits into northern and southern conventions over the slavery issue.

1845: Cooper publishes *Satanstoe* and *The Chainbearer*, the first and second of three novels featuring Corny Littlepage and detailing the antirent wars in Albany County, New York (1839–1845) that erupted when tenant farmers protested the efforts of the Van Rensselaer heirs to collect back rent on land they had leased from Stephen Van Rensselaer.

1846: Cooper publishes *The Redskins*, the third novel of the Littlepage trilogy, and *Lives of Distinguished Naval Officers*.

1847: Cooper publishes *The Crater; or, Vulcan's Peak*, a tale of shipwreck set on a Pacific island.

1848: Cooper publishes *Jack Tier; or, The Florida Reef*, a sea romance.

1849: Cooper publishes *The Oak Openings; or, The Bee-Hunter*, his last frontier novel (set in Michigan during the early 1800s), and *The Sea Lions; or, The Lost Sealers*, his last sea novel (set in Antarctica).

1850: Cooper publishes *The Ways of the Hour*, a murder mystery that also features debates about New York's Married Women's Property Act of 1848.

1845: Frederick Douglass, *A Narrative of the Life of Frederick Douglass*; Margaret Fuller, *Woman in the Nineteenth Century*; George Lippard, *The Quaker City; or, The Monks of Monk Hall*. Florida enters the union as the twenty-seventh state. United States annexes the Republic of Texas, which enters the union as the twenty-eighth state. Irish potato famine forces massive Irish emigration to United States. The term "manifest destiny" appears in an article by John O'Sullivan in *The United States Magazine and Democratic Review*. Henry David Thoreau begins living at Walden Pond near Concord, MA.

1846: Herman Melville, *Typee*; Nathaniel Hawthorne, *Mosses from an Old Manse*. Iowa enters the union as the twenty-ninth state. United States annexes California. Congress charters the Smithsonian Institution.

1847: George Copway (Ojibwa), *The Life, History, and Travels of Kah-ge-ga-gah-bowh*; Henry Wadsworth Longfellow, *Evangeline*; Herman Melville, *Omoo*. Frederick Douglass begins publication of an abolitionist newspaper, *The North Star*. Mormon leader Brigham Young and his followers arrive in the valley of the Great Salt Lake. Hiram Powers's sculpture, *The Greek Slave*, begins its year-long tour of the United States.

James Fenimore Cooper. *By Matthew Brady. Library of Congress, Prints and Photographs Division (Brady Collection).*

Cooper Statue in Cooperstown. Photograph by Lee Person.

1848: Karl Marx, *The Communist Manifesto*. Zachary Taylor is elected president. James W. Marshall discovers a gold nugget at Sutter's Mill in northern California, sparking the Gold Rush of 1849. Mexican War ends; Treaty of Guadalupe Hidalgo cedes much of southwest territory to United States. Wisconsin enters the union as the thirtieth state. First women's rights convention is held at Seneca Falls, NY. Free Soil Party, formed in Buffalo, NY, nominates Martin Van Buren for president. The Oregon Territory is established. Cornerstone for Washington Monument is laid. Married Women's Property Act passes in New York.

1849: Herman Melville, *Mardi* and *Redburn*; Henry David Thoreau, *A Week on the Concord and Merrimack Rivers* and "Civil Disobedience"; Asher B. Durand, *Kindred Spirits*. Maryland slave Harriet Tubman escapes to the North and begins a career as a "conductor" on the Underground Railroad.

1850: U.S. population is 23,191,876. Nathaniel Hawthorne, *The Scarlet Letter*; Herman Melville, *White-Jacket*; Susan Warner, *The Wide, Wide World*. Zachary Taylor, the twelfth president of the United States, dies after serving only sixteen months in office; Millard Fillmore becomes president.

The Buffalo Hunt. *Library of Congress, Prints and Photographs Division, LC-USZ62-10355. Free Soil Party Presidential candidate Martin Van Buren sends Democratic candidate Lewis Cass and Whig candidate Zachary Taylor flying. Taylor would go on to win the 1848 presidential election.*

Effects of the Fugitive-Slave-Law. *Library of Congress, Prints and Photographs Division, LC-USZ62-1286.*

1851: Cooper dies on September 14 (the eve of his sixty-second birthday) at Otsego Hall in Cooperstown.

1850: New York City tailors launch strike; 300 marchers are attacked by police, two are killed. Fugitive Slave Act (Compromise of 1850) requires free states to return escaped slaves to slaveholders and allows territories of Utah and New Mexico to decide whether to be free or slave.

1851: Herman Melville, *Moby-Dick*; Nathaniel Hawthorne, *The House of the Seven Gables*. Fugitive slave Thomas Sims is arrested in Boston and returned to his Georgia owner. The Dakota Sioux sign a treaty ceding most of their territory in Minnesota, about 28 million acres, to the U.S. government. *New York Times* begins publication.

Bibliographical Essay

Cooper and America

Jeffrey Walker

James Fenimore Cooper's place in American literature and culture has been among the more debated issues in American literary history. When Mark Twain penned his grossly exaggerated lampoon recounting "Fenimore Cooper's Literary Offenses" in the July 1895 issue of the *North American Review*, accusing Cooper of literary incompetence by attacking—with tongue firmly planted in cheek—his use of imprecise language, his development of improbable characters, and his creation of impossible plots in the Leatherstocking novels, he forever condemned Cooper as a second-rate hack in the minds of many Americans. Some readers have not stopped laughing long enough over Twain's essay to recognize that it was not serious literary criticism, but primarily a tour de force in the history of American humor, and the damage done has not yet been completely reversed. But in the past thirty-five years, scholars have taken advantage of an abundance of rich material found in Cooper's letters (published and unpublished) and have unearthed new documents—biographical, bibliographical, and historical—that they have used as the basis of the historical introductions to "The Writings of James Fenimore Cooper" (the "Cooper Edition") texts of his works, as well in other scholarship, to establish a more accurate portrait of Cooper. These discoveries have helped

bring to near conclusion a full-scale biography and have produced new critical studies of Cooper and his oeuvre, an achievement that now begins to cement his role not only as a major
writer in our national literature, but also as a perceptive reader of
gender, class, and race in America.

Editions

One of the most important events in Cooper scholarship occurred in 1976, when James Franklin Beard, after completing his
monumental six-volume edition of *The Letters and Journals of
James Fenimore Cooper* (1960–1968), initiated a critical scholarly edition of all Cooper's works by holding an organizational meeting
of prospective editors and editorial board members and by publishing a year later, with James P. Elliott, a detailed manual, *The
Cooper Edition: Editorial Principles and Procedures*, that set forth the
principles for responsibly editing Cooper's works of fiction and
nonfiction. In 1980, the first volumes, *The Pioneers* and *Gleanings
in Europe: Switzerland*, were published by the State University of
New York Press. That same press issued fifteen more titles: *The
Pathfinder* (1981), *Wyandotté* (1982), *Gleanings in Europe: England*
(1982), *Gleanings in Europe: Italy* (1981), *The Last of the Mohicans*
(1983), *Gleanings in Europe: France* (1983), *The Prairie* (1985), *Lionel
Lincoln* (1984), *The Pilot* (1986), *Gleanings in Europe: The Rhine*
(1986), *The Deerslayer* (1987), *The Two Admirals* (1990), *Satanstoe*
(1990), *The Red Rover* (1991), and *Notions of the Americans* (1991).
After printing seventeen of Cooper's books, however, SUNY
Press lost interest in the project, and it was not revived until AMS
Press agreed in 2002 to publish the rest of the series and issued its
first title, *The Spy*, that year, and its second, the two volumes of
Afloat and Ashore, in 2004. At present, several more (*The Bravo,
Ned Myers, The Wept of Wish-ton-Wish, The Water-Witch, The Heidenmauer, Home as Found, Homeward Bound*) are at various stages
of scholarly preparation. All of these editions conform to the re-
quirements of the Center for Editions of American Authors or
the Center for Scholarly Editions of the Modern Language Association, and, as critical, eclectic, and unmodernized texts, they

provide scholars with accurate texts on which to base their criticism. For the general reader, the Library of America has published the SUNY texts of the Leatherstocking Tales in two volumes—*The Leatherstocking Tales I: The Pioneers, The Last of the Mohicans, The Prairie* (1985) and *The Leatherstocking Tales II: The Pathfinder, The Deerslayer* (1985)—and *Sea Tales: The Pilot, The Red Rover* (1991) in one volume. Oxford University Press and Penguin have published paperback copies of all of the Leatherstocking Tales, photographically reproducing the SUNY editions as texts.

Until authoritative editions of all of Cooper's works are available in the Cooper Edition series, readers must continue to rely on texts of varying and uncertain quality. Two incomplete collections of the fiction published before Cooper's death in 1851 contain authorial corrections. Works revised between 1831 and 1834 appeared in Richard Bentley's "Standard Novels" edition, and eleven of the twelve volumes of the Author's Revised Edition (*The Ways of the Hour* was not revised) were issued by George Palmer Putnam (1849–1851). Works not contained in either the Bentley or Putnam editions can be found in one or more of those published after Cooper's death; none of them, of course, holds any authority. W. A. Townsend's F. O. C. Darley–illustrated edition (1859–1861), descended from the Putnam and other earlier editions, contains all the novels. Numerous other minor works known or attributed to Cooper exist only in their first editions or in reprinted versions difficult to access. Cooper's nonfiction *Early Critical Essays* (1822) *by James Fenimore Cooper* was reissued in facsimile by Scholars Facsimiles & Reprints (1955) and contains book reviews he wrote for *The Literary and Scientific Repository, and Critical Review*. Robert E. Spiller's *James Fenimore Cooper: Representative Selections* (1936) contains Cooper's nonfiction prose.

The Cooper Edition, therefore, has become a critical watershed for subsequent scholarship because it has determined that Cooper was not the careless, slipshod artist Twain and others had declared. Cooper's texts were remarkably corrupt because compositors had difficulty reading his script, because he had not read proof against printer's copy, and because frequent resettings had left a heavy toll of corruptions. The Cooper Edition, however, has disclosed that Cooper was a far better craftsman than scholars have admitted. The 1987 publication of *The Deerslayer* underscores the importance of the Cooper Edition to contemporary Cooper scholarship by illustrating that Cooper was also a far more sensitive reader than Americans have recognized. Using the extant manuscript of the novel as copy-text, Lance Schachterle, Kent Ljungquist, and James Kilby, the editors of the text, discovered that Cooper himself had missed a compositor's crucial misreading of the manuscript (at page 545.20–21) where Judith Hutter's own "consciousness of undue erring" was transcribed as "consciousness of undeserving," an error that significantly altered authorial intention and one that persisted through all 211 editions of the book previous to the Cooper Edition's text. Cooper clearly intended to show Judith accepting at last the onus of her misconduct and thus exonerating Deerslayer when he refused her proposal of marriage. Such errors have led scholars to misinterpret the texts of many authors and to misrepresent authorial intention. By establishing authoritative texts, the Cooper Edition has moved the critical study of Cooper's writings into the contemporary scholarly world and set the table for far more accurate and sensitive assessments of his canon, his person, and his literary skill.

Biographies

The earliest biographical treatment of Cooper surfaced in William Cullen Bryant's "Discourse on the Life, Genius, and Writings of J. Fenimore Cooper." Delivered at the Public Memorial Meeting at Metropolitan Hall, New York City, on 25 February 1852, and printed in George Palmer Putnam's *Memorial of James Fenimore Cooper* (1852), it remained for thirty years the closest approach to formal biography. Cooper's daughter, Susan, constructed a series of unscholarly "Family Memories" for her father in her *Pages and Pictures from the Writings of James Fenimore Cooper* (1861), and though valuable for their anecdotes and the fact that they were written by his daughter, a novelist herself, they did not deal with Cooper's life as a writer. Because the immediate family wanted to avoid a diminution of their patriarch's literary reputation and because Cooper himself had asked that no biography be authorized, they refused to allow more traditional biographical studies of him, and nothing else surfaced until 1882, when Thomas Lounsbury penned the *Cooper* entry for the American Men of Letters series. Lounsbury's assessment lacked any real firsthand knowledge or critical understanding of Cooper's writing, producing somewhat accidentally a rather distorted scholarly view, one full of the same kinds of mistakes caused by carelessness or unsubstantiated scholarship that Cooper's compositors and editors produced in the editions of his work. It did little to advance the art of biography in nineteenth-century America.

It was not until W. B. Shubrick Clymer inherited holographs of Cooper's letters to his grandfather Admiral Shubrick and used them as the basis of his *James Fenimore Cooper* (1900) that the life of Cooper began to take shape. Similarly, when Mary E. Phillips used other Cooper letters she borrowed from his grandnephew George Pomeroy Keese as the basis of her own *James Fenimore Cooper* (1913), she utilized letters as a biographical tool for providing a more intimate portrait of Cooper the man. More than a century earlier, in his life of Johnson, Boswell quoted Plutarch when he argued that it is not "always in the most distinguished achievements that men's virtues or vices may be best discerned, but very often in the action of small note, a short saying, or a jest, [that] shall distinguish a person's real character more than the greatest sieges, or the most important battles."[1] This approach helped later biographers to enter a new phase with the publication of the *Correspondence of James Fenimore-Cooper* (1922), edited by his grandson and namesake. By injecting into a memoir the details, however minor, of a life in letters, biographers could use informal incidents recounted in Cooper's adventures and information culled from the writer's correspondence to breathe life into the novelist and the biography.

Even though the family recoiled against using their patriarch's letters as a basis for an accurate portrait of his life—publishing details of a private life was still considered somewhat unpalatable at the turn of the century—the existence of the correspondence generated several new biographical treatments in the first half of the twentieth century. Robert Spiller's chapter on Cooper in *The American in England* (1926) portrayed Cooper as a representative American, a man whose writing helped forge a new American identity. His later seminal study, *Fenimore Cooper: Critic of His Times* (1931), though not strictly biographical, nevertheless helped locate Cooper in his time and place, retracing his travels and his opinions of the times. Henry Boynton's *James Fenimore Cooper* (1931) employs a similar approach, studying Cooper as man rather than as man of letters. Most of the subsequent biographical treatments of Cooper's life were more semibiographical, but each contributed a piece to the ever growing puzzle of what makes a life. Because the family was tight-lipped about revealing much of Cooper's development as father and husband, as writer and social critic, and as public citizen, and because most of the minutiae of that life had not been recorded systematically or in detail throughout his life, the art of writing a Cooper biography continued to be an adventure in constructing a life out of anecdote or a series of improbable stories, a practice Plutarch might have applauded but that historians do not.

Of the remaining attempts at a biography published in the prior century, Ethel R. Outland's *The "Effingham" Libels on Cooper* (1929) and Dorothy Waples's *The Whig Myth of James Fenimore Cooper* (1938) both address Cooper's political problems in a semibiographical form. And Marcel Clavel's *Fenimore Cooper: Sa Vie et Son Oeuvre, La Jeunesse, 1789–1826* (1938), encyclopedic in scope, spends most of its time considering Cooper's career in his first six novels (until 1826). Like many of his European colleagues, Clavel treats Cooper in much more detail than many of Cooper's countrymen do. Donald Ringe's *James Fenimore Cooper* (1962), which he republished in an "updated edition" in 1988 to survey the developments in Cooper scholarship since the first edition of his book, provides readers with a solid critical introduction to the works, supplemented by biographical materials. Along with Robert Emmet Long's *James Fenimore Cooper* (1990), and like many of the biographical treatments, Ringe engages in a long look at Cooper in his own world. Stephen Railton's *Fenimore Cooper: A Study of His Life and Imagination* (1978) is the first Freudian treatment of Cooper's inner and outer life and its relationship to his writings. Despite all of these attempts at writing a readable and comprehensive biography of Cooper, however, none has succeeded. Part of the blame can be laid at the feet of his contemporaries, who failed to collect his letters or to interview his friends at his death as a means of recording the facts of his life. But blame must also be attributed to Cooper himself, whose own insistence that the family not allow access to his papers was probably more important than any other factor in keeping the world in the dark regarding him.

With the publication of Cooper's *Letters and Journals* and the scholarly editing of his works, both of which required locating, and then retrieving, the details of his life, newly discovered information has contributed to the preparation of the first comprehensive critical biography. Such a biography is now forthcoming from Yale University Press. Wayne Franklin's projected two-volume biography will explore the life of Cooper in more detail and in more depth than any before it, utilizing not only extant scholarship but newly discovered materials about Cooper, his family, and the world in which he lived. Franklin's biography is the first to draw thoroughly on Cooper's papers, and it employs Beard's edition of *Letters and Journals* to its fullest advantage. Franklin also had the benefit of using additional manuscript materials dealing with financial records and correspondence, as well as the collective findings of the Cooper Edition. Both contain information never before published that will make them unparalleled in the history of Cooper studies. The first volume, *James Fenimore Cooper: The Early Years*, covering the period of his life through his departure for Europe in 1826, will be published in 2007. The second volume is currently underway. When Franklin's *Biography* is printed, it will unleash probably the greatest outpouring of Cooper scholarship since 1980. With a comprehensive and definitive biography of Cooper on hand, one that conflates and collates the important details of his life in readable prose, scholars should never again run the risk of misreading Cooper's truths, "avoid uttering" them, and "even when prudence demand[s] silence," fail to admit with "a consciousness of undue erring" their own mistakes.[2] Wayne Franklin's opus promises to be the most important publishing event in Cooper scholarship in decades, and it will finally provide an accurate assessment of his accomplishments as a major American writer and citizen.

Criticism: Cooper and America

To understand Cooper and his relationship to American literary culture, readers first need to recognize the kinship Cooper established with his audience in the nineteenth century. One way to gauge that reception is to dip into reviews by his contemporary readers. In *Fenimore Cooper: The Critical Heritage* (1973), George Dekker and John P. McWilliams provide a collection of representative nineteenth-century reader responses to Cooper's work. Later criticism can be found in Warren Walker's *Leatherstocking and the Critics* (1965) and Wayne Fields's *James Fenimore Cooper: A Collection of Critical Essays* (1979). Both are valuable collections and symptomatic of the diverse critical reaction to Cooper through the twentieth century. Still, no collection of criticism has really adequately addressed the reason for Cooper's position as the most popular and acclaimed novelist in nineteenth-century America and, therefore, provided a raison d'être for establishing his place alongside Melville, Hawthorne, and Whitman. Constructing a solid place for him in the canon of American literature has been difficult, partly because most Americans have never been able to forget the reputation that Cooper earned as the writer of "boys' books," a reputation established with the help of the Twain school of realists and one bad enough to discourage most readers. Although the quality of Cooper scholarship has been high and has rightly tended to center on his relationship with America and the contributions he made with his romances of forest and sea, of colonial and revolutionary history, and of politics and society, it has not convinced many modern readers of Cooper's genius or of his relevance to contemporary American society.

Most Cooper reviewers have tended to define where he stands in the line of authors who contributed to an American literary tradition. His roles as social commentator, literary artist, and historian characterize most early criticism. Much of the debate in the past quarter century, however—since the Cooper Edition established and published twenty responsibly edited texts—has centered on issues of race and gender, as new historicist interpretations of his canon have taken the field.

Warren Walker fashions the traditional argument in *James Fenimore Cooper: An Introduction and Interpretation* (1962) that the author's use of folk culture popularized his fiction. By tracing how Cooper "drew heavily from folk sources for his material" and delineated "so clearly the features of the frontiersman, the retreating red man, the Yankee, the squatter, or the American Negro" by revealing their "manners, their habits, and their customs" (27), he argues that Cooper's fiction served as a pot into which he stirred all the elements of what it meant to be an American in the years of the early republic. Thomas Philbrick's seminal study *James Fenimore Cooper and the Development of American Sea Fiction* (1961) concentrated on Cooper's mastery of the folklore of the sea, and George Dekker in *The American Historical Romance* (1987) treated Cooper's adaptation of Scott's "narrative device of the 'wavering hero' to American circumstances and his own unwavering temperament" (vii). Both studies helped cement Cooper's role as a major shaper of American romance and suggested that he learned a lot from his British predecessors. That he learned from Homer and Milton serves as the foundation of Joel Porte's *The Romance in America* (1969), and John P. McWilliams goes one step further in *The American Epic: Transforming a Genre, 1770–1860* (1989) when he addresses the many attempts to fashion a new kind of American epic literature, one that had to be "something other than a Homeric, Virgilian, or Miltonic poem" (2) by creating new epic forms: prose history (Irving, Prescott, and Parkman), fictional romance (Cooper and Melville), and free verse (Whitman). "Only after *The Last of the Mohicans* was published," McWilliams reveals, "did the likelihood of America's epic appearing in the form of a prose romance about the Indian explicitly emerge" (144).

Just as Cooper's debt to Austen, Defoe, and Swift produced a scattering of articles that all argue his knowledge of the novel as a social document, so, too, have other scholars established the impact of Cooper's work on later American novelists and their stories. Alexander Cowie's *The Rise of the American Novel* (1948), Ernest E. Leisy's *The American Historical Novel* (1950), and Henry Nash Smith's classic *Virgin Land: The American West as Symbol and Myth* (1950) place Cooper and his fiction in the western tradition and set the stage for an increased interest in Cooper's relationship with his times. That increased interest led to a plethora of studies that dealt with Cooper's sociopolitical principles, his view of his fellow Americans, and his influence on the development of an American cultural myth. John P. McWilliams's *Political Justice in a Republic: James Fenimore Cooper's America* (1972) unravels the implications of those political principles in Cooper's fiction and nonfiction by showing how his "neutral ground" was a metaphor for the kinds of struggles his Americans endured in their quest for power. Kay Seymour House's *Cooper's Americans* (1965), however, provides us with a broad spectrum of Cooper's characters, those representing classes and a second group who are "still unformed, open to experience, and capable of surprise." For House, "All of these open characters [sailors, aborigines, and African Americans, in particular] are men," each of whom "leaves his defining community and risks the experiences offered by the sea or the wilderness where, in Cooper's fictional world as in America itself, a man could escape his native culture" (14). House's assessment of Cooper's women gives them a social significance, and this argument has been used by later scholars as a springboard for a discussion of Cooper's characters, female or male. Other critics, such as Edwin Fussell in *Frontier: American Literature and the American West* (1965) and Leslie Fiedler in *The Return of the Vanishing American* (1968), speak to class and the disenfranchised on the frontier, just as James Tuttleton treats Cooper's gentry and the record of "transformations in the wilderness—clearing the forest, building the houses, schools, jails, and churches—that produce civilization, and the transformations in the people—the acculturation to the New World— that produced Americans out of diverse European nationalities" (32) in a chapter from *The Novel of Manners in America* (1972). Donald Darnell handles these issues in far more detail in *James Fenimore Cooper: Novelist of Manners* (1993) by addressing Cooper's attitudes toward class and social distinctions, birth, breeding, ladies, and gentlemen—all the criteria Cooper used in his fiction to define his idea of manners and the way American manners could be improved. By examining fifteen novels, from *Precaution* to *The Ways of the Hour*, Darnell shows—even in those that do not deal primarily with manners—how Cooper integrated manners, and a discussion of them, as the basis for initiating character development and dramatic incident.

Negotiating with Cooper's idea of progress and the past takes scholarship in another direction. His affinity with the Hudson River Valley artists is the subject of two seminal articles. James Franklin Beard first introduced the idea of a connection in "Cooper and His Artistic Contemporaries" in 1954, and Donald Ringe connected the dots in "James Fenimore Cooper and Thomas Cole: An Analogous Technique" in 1958. Ringe later developed his ideas in greater detail in *The Pictorial Mode: Space and Time in the Art of Bryant, Irving, and Cooper* (1971). This study of affinities reinforces Cooper's historiographical beliefs and his use of the pictorial technique to illustrate them. H. Daniel Peck's *A World by Itself: The Pastoral Moment in Cooper's Fiction* (1977) locates the power of Cooper's work in his use of space and considers his fiction as an "imaginative world with structures, tensions, and resonances of its own" (17). Peck returns to D. H. Lawrence's interpretation of Cooper's forest world in *Studies in Classic American Literature* (1923) as a lyrical expression of wish fulfillment and offers it as a "silent model for moral instruction" (11). Blake Nevius reinforces the Hudson River connection in *Cooper's Landscapes: An Essay on the Picturesque Vision* (1976) by placing Cooper's landscapes in the context of the British and Italian tradition of landscape painting and the literature of landscape gardening. This comparison helps Nevius show how Cooper's seven-year visit to Europe influenced his use of landscape in his fiction, yet he also argues that even before his European stay, Cooper's "way of looking at landscape was conditioned to some degree by both ideal and topographical landscape art and poetry, by contemporary books of travel, and to a less important degree by the prose romance" (103). It is only with *The Last of the Mohicans*, Nevius concludes, that he "begins to explore the range and possibilities of the picturesque (or what he called then the 'romantic') vision" (104).

The romantic vision has been described in other forms by many Cooper scholars. Eric Sundquist in *Home as Found: Authority and Genealogy in Nineteenth-Century American Literature* (1979) offered a Freudian analysis of *Home as Found*, and Annette Kolodny in her chapters on Cooper in *The Lay of the Land: Metaphor as Experience and History in American Life and Letters* (1975) and Joel Porte in *The Romance in America: Studies in Cooper, Poe, Hawthorne, Melville, and James* (1969) offer additional psychological interpretations of theme and image in the Leatherstocking Tales. Richard Slotkin pulls from anthropological archetypes a number of examples in *Regeneration through Violence: The Mythology of the American Frontier, 1600–1860* (1973) to analyze the myth of the Leatherstocking Tales. All of these critics suggest that Cooper possessed a mythopoeic power unusual for his time. In *The American Adam: Innocence, Tragedy, and Tradition in the Nineteenth Century* (1955), R. W. B. Lewis identifies Cooper's one great gift, "possibly the one gift indispensable to the narrative artist who aspires to transmute American experience into story: the gift for seeing life dramatically as the measurement by conduct of institutions and the measurement by institutions of conduct" (100). "This is no doubt," he continues, "why it is always so hard to locate the source of Cooper's power: we look for it in the wrong places and, not finding it there, are inclined to deny its existence, wondering the while at the taste of our ancestors" (101).

Most of those critics interested in rehabilitating Cooper's reputation as artist try to help readers identify the places where they can find the source of his power. Most challenge readers to discover it for themselves. Wayne Franklin provides a provocative analysis of Cooper's four major border novels—*The Pioneers, The Wept of Wish-ton-Wish, Wyandotté* and *The Last of the Mohicans*— in *The New World of James Fenimore Cooper* (1982) and asks the reader to "understand Cooper on his own ground . . . before we seek to place him in a broader context" (7) in order to determine how he shaped the American literary imagination. Such a challenge tends to typify Cooper scholarship penned in the past quarter century, and it coincides in large measure, I would argue, with the publication of the first volumes in the Cooper Edition in 1980 and the ones that have appeared in print from SUNY and AMS since then. These twenty authoritative editions (with more to follow) have fueled a reawakening of interest in Cooper studies, and they have helped scholars bolster Cooper's critical reputation and return his texts to their rightful owner: James Fenimore Cooper himself.

Coinciding with the preparation for and the publication of the new editions, the State University College of New York at Oneonta began sponsoring a biennial conference on Cooper in 1978. Contributors and participants in the seminar have included American and international scholars, as well as a number of nonacademics. The papers from each of the fourteen seminars to date have been published as proceedings from the conference by SUCNY, Oneonta, in volumes entitled *James Fenimore Cooper: His Country and His Art*, and they contain many of the latest approaches to Cooper and his work. To devote an entire seminar to one apparently forgotten American writer, and to attract not only specialists but also lay readers, is a somewhat remarkable phenomenon, and it suggests that Cooper is undergoing a kind of grassroots revival. The *James Fenimore Cooper Society Newsletter*, a publication issued thrice yearly and containing short Cooper articles, reviews of books and Cooper-based films, and news of upcoming conferences, reinforces this impression. At the same time, to publish a collection of essays as W. M. Verhoeven did with *James Fenimore Cooper: New Historical and Literary Contexts* (1993) is yet another way to spark debate on an author's worth. Verhoeven's collection contains essays that employ a variety of critical approaches, from new critical to new historicist, and confront Cooper's fiction in terms of its historical context. One essay argues that women play an important role in the early novels as the vital link between property and manners; another makes a case for *The Spy* as the first American novel. One helps define middle-class ideology in Cooper, and yet another argues that *Lionel Lincoln* was the first American novel that celebrated the battles of Lexington, Concord, and Bunker Hill. Others consider Cooper's use of the Gothic and mock heroic, his attempt to establish a morally legitimate relationship between America and race, and his treatment of the intersection of myth and history. All of the essays in Verhoeven's collection are at odds enough with each other to kick up a fuss and trigger a set of quarrels we might call conversations.

As Verhoeven's collection indicates, the resurgence of Cooper as important American author has resulted in a number of new approaches to him and to his work that appeared in the last decades of the twentieth century. Richard Chase announced thirty years earlier in *The American Novel and Its Tradition* (1957), that "to read the tales in the order in which they were written is, as D. H. Lawrence says, to experience a *'decrescendo* of reality, and a *crescendo* of beauty' and to observe the creation of a myth" (56); Allan Axelrad responded to Lawrence's essay on Cooper and argues in "The Order of the Leatherstocking Tales: D. H. Lawrence, David Noble, and the Iron Trap of History" (1982) that readers should not follow Lawrence and read the Leatherstocking Tales in the order of their publication, but instead read in the "chronological order of Leatherstocking's life" (190). The debates that have surfaced over the Leatherstocking Tales have taken the lead in the Cooper renaissance and generated more articles and books on Cooper than any other novel or set of novels.

William P. Kelly's *Plotting America's Past: Fenimore Cooper and the Leatherstocking Tales* (1983) is an excellent example of how new critics depart from previous criticism and, in Kelly's case, see the five tales as Cooper's attempt to address his "culture's relation to the past and struggles to achieve a coherent sense of historical form" (vii–viii). Because the last two tales were published thirteen years after *The Prairie,* the third of the tales and putative final volume in the series, Kelly describes Cooper as gradually reshaping his historical vision. Unlike the first three tales, Cooper does not call for a "redirection of America's course in *The Pathfinder,* nor does he mourn the loss of past greatness, but he observes that from its inception, the nation has maintained a naïve conception of its possibilities" (158). By returning to the setting of *The Pioneers* in *The Deerslayer,* Kelly argues that Cooper inverts the design of the last novel, turning a "myth disguised as history [into] . . . history disguised as myth" (187). No longer appeased by his usual contrivances in plot, Cooper confronts the limits of history. Geoffrey Rans extends the discussion of history in his *Cooper's Leather-Stocking Series: A Secular Reading* (1991). He faults other scholars by suggesting, for example, that "[H. Daniel] Peck's book [*A World by Itself*] exacts a heavy penalty for his decision to eliminate the social, political, and historical from his treatment of Cooper" (199) and that "Kelly's attempts to make an Eden of the wilderness and his speculations on Natty as Jehovah (*Plotting America's Past*, 146) seem as farfetched as Porte's attempt to make Mabel a figurative Lilith / Eve (*The Romance*, 27)" (274). These differences are not as important in themselves as they are as indicators that Cooper's fiction is beginning to make some noise once again.

And the noise seems unwilling to abate when it comes to the approaches critics see as valuable in presenting Cooper to a new generation of readers. Robert Clark's edition of eight original pieces, *James Fenimore Cooper: New Critical Essays* (1985), includes discussions as diverse as those approaching Cooper's difficulties in creating readers for his fiction, establishing sources for historical romance, constructing the image of a Jacksonian Democrat, and addressing issues on race, gender, and environment. By encouraging a better understanding of Cooper's writing, Clark's stable of established Cooper scholars, representing critics from America, Germany, and England, do a commendable job of making Cooper relevant for a contemporary audience. Cooper's audience itself is the subject of James Wallace's *Early Cooper and His Audience* (1986), an especially original treatment of the audience Cooper decided he had to invent before he could meet success as a writer in America. Wallace treats Cooper's first three novels— *Precaution*, *The Spy*, and *The Pioneers*—as a bridge to explain Cooper's theory of fiction, his use of popular literary forms, and his attention to the kind of reception his work might earn from a young American audience. That Cooper was successful in creating and attracting an audience for his fiction, Wallace argues, was no mistake. Newspapers regularly announced works for sale of the same kind as *The Spy* and *The Pioneers*, and more important, later writers—Hawthorne, Melville, and Stowe—were "quite aware of what the reading public expected to find in a new novel, and each strove according to his or her own temperament to satisfy the prevailing taste" (183). And Cooper did establish the taste for the novel in the first half of the nineteenth century.

Warren Motley's *The American Abraham: James Fenimore Cooper and the Frontier Patriarch* (1987) offers an understanding of the frontier patriarchs in Cooper's novels, especially those in *The Wept of Wish-ton-Wish*, *The Crater*, *Satanstoe*, *The Pioneers*, and *The Prairie*. Motley combines his readings of these novels with an analysis of Cooper's own "evolving position in family and society" (2), using much of the biographical information he culls from Beard's edition of more than 1,200 Cooper letters; he concludes from his observations that even "writers known for their Adamic solitaries turn to the patriarch and the possibilities of the frontier when they want to ask questions of American society" (173–174). Cynthia Jordan also deals with patriarchal figures in *Second Stories: The Politics of Language, Form, and Gender in Early American Fictions* (1989), a study of Cooper and other early American writers. Jordan begins by telling the "first" stories of Franklin, Brackenridge, and Brown, stories that "represent their authors' attempts to tell that 'new story' to a newly constituted American audience" (1). She then argues that these stories are informed by a different ethos from the ones found in nineteenth-century fictions, and that the heroes of these early American tales are agents of patriarchal authority because their authors write in the language of fathers and father figures. Nineteenth-century writers (Cooper, Poe, Hawthorne, and Melville) reject the patriarchal language and tell the "second stories": women who represent the oppressed "other" in American society. By treating *The Last of the Mohicans* as a story like "every story [that] has its two sides" (113), Jordan uncovers tensions between patriarchal narratives and the portrait of gender and race in early American society. Mary Suzanne Schriber carries on the gender discussion in *Gender and the Writer's Imagination* (1987) when she argues that Cooper seemed to "understand on some level that the imposition of essentially aristocratic, European forms on the materials of American womanhood, desirable as they were for shaping first a woman's manners and then a man's, would put at risk a woman's identity as an American." Jordan further argues that Cooper's "novels of manners send malleable young heroines like Eve Effingham to Europe, where they learn to conduct the business of the drawing room and to inspire young men to genteel behavior without taking on the hauteur and artificiality, antithetical to the American spirit, that Cooper's contemporaries associate with European womanhood. A heroine such as Eve is Cooper's version of 'the American girl' " (10–11). Equally provocative is Margaret Reid's *Cultural Secrets as Narrative Form: Storytelling in Nineteenth-Century America* (2004), an assessment of how writers like Cooper, Hawthorne, and Owen Wister use their fiction to construct historical memory. By addressing the interplay between the familiar and the forgotten in tales of America's first century as a nation, Reid offers new insight into the making of a nation through storytelling and explains how these stories of self-definition have achieved near mythic stature in the national imagination. In her section on *The Spy*, for example, Reid argues that the novel's great contribution lies in "its dynamic representation of that narrative strategy entailed in cultural storytelling, a simultaneous dependence on memory and invention, paradoxically fortified by an insistence on uncertainty, a refusal to conflate them into one imaginative structure. In *The Spy*," she concludes, "[Hawthorne's] 'Actual and Imaginary' do not mingle harmlessly but struggle without resolution to promote their respective, and conflicting, stories of experience" (8).

Probably no Cooper story has achieved greater mythic importance than *The Last of the Mohicans*, and it continues to be the novel most frequently discussed, both in articles and in book form. H. Daniel Peck's *New Essays on "The Last of the Mohicans"* (1992), an entry in the Cambridge "New Essays" series, contains six new compositions penned by established Cooper scholars that address such issues as the critical reception of the novel since its publication in 1826, Cooper's use of language in the novel that mirrors its frontier setting, essays on the Fort William Henry massacre that tend to treat it as a synecdoche of American history, and others on race and gender. All of the essays posit new theories of interpretation, and they predate two books that treat only the novel. John McWilliams uses *"Last of the Mohicans": Civic Savagery and Savage Civility* (1994), part of Twayne's Masterworks Studies, as a vehicle to address a multitude of critical issues surrounding the novel. He talks about the literary traditions Cooper drew from to shape his story to his own purpose, and he provides us with a close reading of the text to illustrate the kinds of issues—race, gender, style, genre—that effected and affected readers' responses to the novel and revealed their attitudes toward Native Americans. McWilliams does an especially good job of explaining, patiently and clearly for the reader, how Cooper and his fiction are relevant to issues that cloud our century, and he does a good job of salesmanship. Although both the Peck and the McWilliams texts tend to be addressed to general readers whose knowledge may be more polished than most, both texts are readable studies that clearly underscore and articulate the complexities of the novel and generate a curiosity and a desire to read Cooper.

Just as Peck and McWilliams work hard to position Cooper as a vital cog in the history of nineteenth-century America, Martin Barker and Roger Sabin use another approach in *The Lasting of the Mohicans: History of an American Myth* (1995) to revive Cooper's career. They focus on the making and remaking of media versions of *The Last of the Mohicans*. For the most part, their efforts tend to show that each version of *Mohicans* provides a different and, in some cases, more vibrant image of the American myth. Each new media version tends to address meanings differently, and each raises questions about such issues in the Cooper myth as the relationships between men and between races. It is a useful and entertaining study, but it does not necessarily answer the question of how so many Americans who have heard of but not read the novel can use it as a template for their version of the American dream and the American frontier.

Although Cooper was nineteenth-century America's first accomplished novelist and the subject of more multimedia treatments of his work than any other writer of the period, he has not worn as well as masters of shorter fiction such as Poe, Hawthorne, and Melville. To read Cooper is to discover the valuable lessons he teaches us about our society and our environment, our nation and our identity. And because James Fenimore Cooper has undergone a renaissance of critical interest in the past twenty-five years—the nature and volume of scholarship primarily stemming from the publication of his letters and the authoritative editing of his texts—this rebirth will engage those readers trying to understand the ever changing development of American attitudes toward democracy, racial boundary making, and the environment, crucial issues in contemporary America. Such scholarship may not create a vogue for reading Cooper, but it will most certainly reawaken and encourage serious and renewed conversation in the twenty-first century about America's first successful and popular novelist.

NOTES

1. See James Boswell's *Life of Johnson* (London: Oxford University Press, 1953), 24.
2. Cooper's words in *The Deerslayer* (New York: State University of New York Press, 1987), 545, seem appropriate here.

SECONDARY BIBLIOGRAPHY

Adams, Charles Hansford. *"The Guardian of the Law": Authority and Identity in James Fenimore Cooper.* University Park: Pennsylvania State University Press, 1990.

Axelrad, Allan M. *History and Utopia: A Study of the World View of James Fenimore Cooper.* Norwood, PA: Norwood Editions, 1978.

———. "The Order of the Leatherstocking Tales: D. H. Lawrence, David Noble, and the Iron Trap of History." *American Literature* 54 (May 1982): 189–211.

Barker, Martin, and Roger Sabin. *The Lasting of the Mohicans: History of an American Myth.* Jackson: University Press of Mississippi, 1995.

Baym, Nina. "The Women of Cooper's Leatherstocking Tales." *American Quarterly* 23.5 (1971): 696–709.

Beard, James Franklin. "Cooper and His Artistic Contemporaries." *New York History* 35 (1954): 480–495.

———. "James Fenimore Cooper." In *Fifteen American Authors before 1900: Bibliographical Essays on Research and Criticism.* Rev. ed. Ed. Earl N. Harbert and Robert A. Rees, 80–127. Madison: University of Wisconsin Press, 1984.

Beard, James Franklin, and James P. Elliott Jr. *The Cooper Edition: Editorial Principles and Procedures.* Worcester, MA: Clark University Press, 1977.

Bewley, Marius. *The Eccentric Design: Form in the Classic American Novel.* New York: Columbia University Press, 1963.

Boynton, Henry W. *James Fenimore Cooper.* 1931. Reprint, New York: F. Ungar, 1966.

Brownell, W. C. *American Prose Masters.* New York: Scribners, 1909.

Chase, Richard. *The American Novel and Its Tradition.* Garden City, NY: Doubleday, 1957.

Clark, James, ed. *James Fenimore Cooper: New Critical Essays.* Totowa, NJ: Barnes and Noble, 1985.

Clavel, Marcel. *Fenimore Cooper: Sa Vie et Son Oeuvre, La Jeunesse, 1789–1826.* Aix-en Provence: Imprimerie universitaire de Provence, 1938.

Clymer, W. B. Shubrick. *James Fenimore Cooper.* Boston: Small, Maynard, 1900.

Cooper, James Fenimore. *The American Democrat.* Cooperstown, NY: H & E Phinney, 1838.

———. *Cooper's Novels.* 32 vols. New York: W. A. Townsend & Company, 1859–1861.

———. *Correspondence of James Fenimore-Cooper.* 2 vols. Ed. James Fenimore Cooper. New Haven: Yale University Press, 1922.

———. *Early Critical Essays, 1820–1822.* Ed. James Franklin Beard. Gainesville, FL: Scholars' Facsimiles & Reprints, 1955.

———. *The History of the Navy of the United States of America.* 2 vols. Philadelphia: Lea & Blanchard, 1839.

———. *The Leatherstocking Tales I: The Pioneers, The Last of the Mohicans, The Prairie.* Ed. Blake Nevius. New York: Library of America, 1985.

———. *The Leatherstocking Tales II: The Pathfinder, The Deerslayer.* Ed. Blake Nevius. New York: Library of America, 1985.

———. *The Letters and Journals of James Fenimore Cooper.* 6 vols. Ed. James Franklin Beard. Cambridge, MA: Belknap Press of Harvard University Press, 1960–1968.

———. *Sea Tales: The Pilot, The Red Rover.* Ed. Kay Seymour House and Thomas Philbrick. New York: Library of America, 1991.

———. *The Writings of James Fenimore Cooper.* James Franklin Beard, editor-in-chief. Albany: State University of New York Press, 1980–1989; Kay Seymour House, editor-in-chief, 1990–2002.

———. *The Writings of James Fenimore Cooper.* Lance Schachterle, editor-in-chief. New York: AMS Press, 2002–.

Cooper, Susan Fenimore. *Pages and Pictures from the Writings of James Fenimore Cooper.* New York: Townsend, 1861.

Cowie, Alexander. *The Rise of the American Novel.* New York: American Book Co., 1948.

Darnell, Donald G. *James Fenimore Cooper: Novelist of Manners.* Newark: University of Delaware Press, 1993.

Dekker, George. *The American Historical Romance.* Cambridge, UK: Cambridge University Press, 1987.

———. *James Fenimore Cooper the Novelist.* London: Routledge and Kegan Paul, 1967.

Dekker, George, and John P. McWilliams. *Fenimore Cooper: The Critical Heritage.* Boston: Routledge and Kegan Paul, 1973.

Fiedler, Leslie. *Love and Death in the American Novel.* New York: Criterion, 1960.

———. *The Return of the Vanishing American.* New York: Stein and Day, 1968.

Fields, Wayne. *James Fenimore Cooper: A Collection of Critical Essays.* Englewood Cliffs, NJ: Prentice-Hall, 1979.

Franklin, Wayne. "Fathering the Son: The Cultural Origins of James Fenimore Cooper." *Resources for American Literary Study* 21 (2001): 149–178.

———. *James Fenimore Cooper: A Literary Life.* New Haven: Yale University Press, 2007.

———. *The New World of James Fenimore Cooper.* Chicago: University of Chicago Press, 1982.

Fussell, Edwin. *Frontier: American Literature and the American West.* Princeton, NJ: Princeton University Press, 1965.

Grossman, James. *James Fenimore Cooper.* New York: W. Sloane, 1949.

Henderson, Harry B., III. *Versions of the Past: The Historical Imagination in American Fiction.* New York: Oxford University Press, 1974.

House, Kay Seymour. *Cooper's Americans.* Columbus: Ohio State University Press, 1965.

Jones, Howard Mumford. "James Fenimore Cooper and the Hudson River School." *Magazine of Art* 44 (October 1954): 243–251.

Jordan, Cynthia. *Second Stories: The Politics of Language, Form, and Gender in Early American Fictions.* Chapel Hill: University of North Carolina Press, 1989.

Kaul, A. N. *The American Vision: Actual and Ideal Society in Nineteenth-Century Fiction.* New Haven: Yale University Press, 1963.

Kelly, William P. *Plotting America's Past: Fenimore Cooper and the Leatherstocking Tales.* Carbondale: Southern Illinois University Press, 1983.

Kolodny, Annette. *The Lay of the Land: Metaphor as Experience and History in American Life and Letters*. Chapel Hill: University of North Carolina Press, 1975.

Lawrence, D. H. *Studies in Classic American Literature*. New York: Seltzer, 1923.

Leisy, Ernest E. *The American Historical Novel*. Norman: University of Oklahoma Press, 1950.

Levine, Robert S. *Conspiracy and Romance: Studies in Brockden Brown, Cooper, Hawthorne, and Melville*. New York: Cambridge University Press, 1989.

Lewis, R. W. B. *The American Adam: Innocence, Tragedy, and Tradition in the Nineteenth Century*. Chicago: University of Chicago Press, 1955.

Long, Robert Emmet. *James Fenimore Cooper*. New York: Continuum, 1990.

Lounsbury, Thomas. *James Fenimore Cooper*. Boston: Houghton, Mifflin, 1910.

MacDougall, Hugh C., ed. *James Fenimore Cooper: His Country and His Art*. Oneonta: State University College of New York, 1995–2003.

McWilliams, John P. *The American Epic: Transforming a Genre, 1770–1860*. Cambridge, UK: Cambridge University Press, 1989.

———. *"Last of the Mohicans": Civil Savagery and Savage Civility*. New York: Macmillan, 1994.

———. *Political Justice in a Republic: James Fenimore Cooper's America*. Berkeley: University of California Press, 1972.

Motley, Warren. *The American Abraham: James Fenimore Cooper and the Frontier Patriarch*. New York: Cambridge University Press, 1987.

Nevius, Blake. *Cooper's Landscapes: An Essay on the Picturesque Vision*. Berkeley: University of California Press, 1976.

Newman, Russell T. *The Gentleman in the Garden: The Influential Landscape in the Works of James Fenimore Cooper*. Lanham, MD: Lexington Books, 2003.

Outland, Ethel R. *The "Effingham" Libels on Cooper*. Madison: University of Wisconsin Studies in Language and Literature, 1929.

Overland, Orm. *The Making and Meaning of an American Classic: James Fenimore Cooper's "The Prairie."* New York: Humanities Press, 1973.

Parkman, Francis. "Review of the Works of James Fenimore Cooper." *North American Review* 74 (January 1852): 147–161.

Peck, H. Daniel. *New Essays on "The Last of the Mohicans."* New York: Cambridge University Press, 1992.

————. *A World by Itself: The Pastoral Movement in Cooper's Fiction.* New Haven: Yale University Press, 1977.

Philbrick, Thomas. *James Fenimore Cooper and the Development of American Sea Fiction.* Cambridge, MA: Harvard University Press, 1961.

Phillips, Mary E. *James Fenimore Cooper.* New York: John Lane, 1913.

Porte, Joel. *The Romance in America: Studies in Cooper, Poe, Hawthorne, Melville and James.* Middletown, CT: Wesleyan University Press, 1969.

Putnam, George Palmer. *Memorial of James Fenimore Cooper.* New York: Putnam, 1852.

Railton, Stephen. *Fenimore Cooper: A Study of His Life and Imagination.* Princeton, NJ: Princeton University Press, 1978.

Rans, Geoffrey. *Cooper's Leather-Stocking Novels: A Secular Reading.* Chapel Hill: University of North Carolina Press, 1991.

Reid, Margaret. *Cultural Secrets as Narrative Form: Storytelling in Nineteenth-Century America.* Columbus: Ohio State University Press, 2004.

Ringe, Donald A. *American Gothic: Imagination and Reason in Nineteenth-Century Fiction.* Lexington: University Press of Kentucky, 1982.

————. "James Fenimore Cooper and Thomas Cole: An Analogous Technique." *American Literature* 30 (March 1958): 26–36.

————. *James Fenimore Cooper.* Boston: Twayne, 1962.

————. *James Fenimore Cooper, Updated Edition.* Boston: Twayne, 1988.

————. *The Pictorial Mode: Space and Time in the Art of Bryant, Irving, and Cooper.* Lexington: University Press of Kentucky, 1971.

Romero, Lora. *Home Fronts: Domesticity and Its Critics in the Antebellum United States.* Durham, NC: Duke University Press, 1997.

Ross, John F. *The Social Criticism of Fenimore Cooper.* Berkeley: University of California Press, 1933.

Schachterle, Lance, and Kent Ljungquist. "Fenimore Cooper's Literary Defenses: Twain and the Text of *The Deerslayer*." In *Studies in the American Renaissance*, ed. Joel Myerson, 401–417. Charlottesville: University Press of Virginia, 1988.

Schriber, Mary Suzanne. *Gender and the Writer's Imagination.* Lexington: University Press of Kentucky, 1987.

Schulenberger, Arvid. *Cooper's Theories of Fiction: His Prefaces and Their Relation to His Novels.* Lawrence: University Press of Kansas, 1955.

Slotkin, Richard. *Regeneration through Violence: The Mythology of the*

American Frontier, 1600–1860. Middletown, CT: Wesleyan University Press, 1973.

Smith, Henry Nash. *Virgin Land: The American West as Symbol and Myth.* Cambridge, MA: Harvard University Press, 1950.

Spiller, Robert E. *The American in England.* New York: Henry Holt, 1926.

———. *Fenimore Cooper: Critic of His Times.* New York: Minton, Balch, 1931.

———. *James Fenimore Cooper: Representative Selections.* New York: American Book Company, 1936.

Spiller, Robert E., and Philip C. Blackburn. *A Descriptive Bibliography of the Writings of James Fenimore Cooper.* New York: Bowker, 1934.

Sundquist, Eric J. *Home as Found: Authority and Genealogy in Nineteenth-Century American Literature.* Baltimore: Johns Hopkins University Press, 1979.

Taylor, Alan. *William Cooper's Town: Power and Persuasion in the Frontier of the Early American Republic.* New York: Knopf, 1995.

Test, George A., ed. *James Fenimore Cooper: His Country and His Art.* Oneonta: State University College of New York, 1979–1991.

Tompkins, Jane. *Sensational Designs: The Cultural Work of American Fiction, 1790–1860.* New York: Oxford University Press, 1985.

Tuttleton, James. *The Novel of Manners in America.* Chapel Hill: University of North Carolina Press, 1972.

Twain, Mark. "Fenimore Cooper's Literary Offenses." *North American Review* 161 (July 1895): 1–12.

Valtiala, Nalle. *James Fenimore Cooper's Landscapes in the Leather-Stocking Series and Other Forest Tales.* Helsinki: Academia Scientiarum Fennica, 1998.

Verhoeven, W. M. *James Fenimore Cooper: New Historical and Literary Contexts.* Amsterdam: Rodopi, 1993.

Walker, Warren S. *James Fenimore Cooper: An Introduction and Interpretation.* New York: Holt, Rinehart & Winston, 1962.

———. *Leatherstocking and the Critics.* Chicago: Scott, Foresman, 1965.

Wallace, James D. *Early Cooper and His Audience.* New York: Columbia University Press, 1986.

———, ed. *James Fenimore Cooper: His Country and His Art.* Oneonta: State University College of New York, 1993–1995.

Waples, Dorothy. *The Whig Myth of James Fenimore Cooper.* New Haven: Yale University Press, 1938.

Winters, Yvor. *Maule's Curse.* Norfolk, CT: New Directions, 1938.

Contributors

WAYNE FRANKLIN is Professor of English at the University of Connecticut and is author or editor of many books on nineteenth-century American literature, including *Discoverers, Explorers, Settlers: The Diligent Writers of Early America; The New World of James Fenimore Cooper;* and *New Essays on "The Last of the Mohicans."* He is currently completing volume 1 of *James Fenimore Cooper: A Literary Life,* which will be published in 2006.

J. GERALD KENNEDY is William A. Read Professor of English at Louisiana State University and is the author or editor of numerous books on American literature, including *Poe, Death, and the Life of Writing; Imagining Paris: Exile, Writing, and American Identity; Romancing the Shadow: Poe and Race;* and the *Oxford Historical Guide to Edgar Allan Poe.*

BARBARA ALICE MANN lives, teaches, researches, and writes in Ohio, the homeland of her Seneca ancestors for the last 1,500 years. Lecturer in English at the University of Toledo, she is the author of *George Washington's War on Native America;* editor of and contributor to *Daughters of Mother Earth;* author of *Native Americans, Archaeologists, and the Mounds,* and *Iroquoian Women: The Gantowisas;* author of *Land of the Three Miamis;* editor of and contributor to *Native American Speakers of the Eastern Woodlands;* and coeditor of and contributor to *Encyclopedia of the Haudenosaunee (Iroquois Confederacy).*

JOHN P. MCWILLIAMS is College Professor of Humanities at Middlebury College. He has published *Political Justice in a Republic: James Fenimore Cooper's America*; *Hawthorne, Melville, and the American Character: A Looking-glass Business*; *The American Epic: Transforming a Genre, 1770–1860*; *"Last of the Mohicans": Civil Savagery and Savage Civility*; and *New England's Crises and Cultural Memory: Literature, Politics, History, Religion, 1620–1860*.

DANA D. NELSON is the Gertrude Conaway Vanderbilt Professor of English and American Studies at Vanderbilt University. Author of *National Manhood: Capitalist Citizenship and the Imagined Fraternity of White Men* and *The Word in Black and White: Reading "Race" in American Literature 1638–1867*, she is currently working on a study of democratic frontiers in the late colonies and early nation.

LELAND S. PERSON is Professor of English and Department Head at the University of Cincinnati. He has written *Aesthetic Headaches: Women and a Masculine Poetics in Poe, Melville, and Hawthorne* and *Henry James and the Suspense of Masculinity* and recently edited the Norton Critical Edition of Hawthorne's *The Scarlet Letter*. He has published many essays on nineteenth-century American literature, including a half dozen on Cooper in such journals as *Novel*, *American Quarterly*, *ESQ*, and *Studies in the Novel*.

JEFFREY WALKER is Associate Professor at Oklahoma State University. He is coeditor of Cooper's *The Spy: A Tale of the Neutral Ground* and editor of *Reading Cooper, Teaching Cooper* and *Leather-Stocking Redux: Or, Old Tales, New Essays*. He is working on an edition of the unpublished letters of James Fenimore Cooper and a study of undergraduate literary culture in eighteenth-century American colleges.

Index

Page numbers in italics indicate illustrations.